J.D. Jones
Wolverhampton

Tom Mann J. Keir Hardie
Ben Tillett

Melbourne Jan: 1908:

AUSTRALIA'S FIRST FABIANS

AUSTRALIA'S FIRST FABIANS

*Middle-class Radicals, Labour Activists
and the Early Labour Movement*

RACE MATHEWS

FOREWORD BY GOUGH WHITLAM

CAMBRIDGE
UNIVERSITY PRESS

Published by the Press Syndicate of the University of Cambridge
The Pitt Building, Trumpington Street, Cambridge CB2 1RP, UK
40 West 20th Street, New York, NY 10011-4211, USA
10 Stamford Road, Oakleigh, Melbourne, Victoria 3166, Australia

Printed in Hong Kong by Colorcraft

National Library of Australia cataloguing in publication data
Mathews, Race, 1935–
Australia's first Fabians.
Bibliography.
Includes index.
ISBN 0 521 44133 1.
ISBN 0 521 44678 3 (pbk.).
1. Australian Labor Party – History. 2. Socialists – Victoria – History
3. Socialists – Australia – History. [4.] Fabian socialism.
5. Labor movement – Australia – History. I. Title.
335.14092294

Library of Congress cataloguing in publication data
Mathews, Race.
Australia's first Fabians: middle-class radicals, labor activists, and the early labour
movement/Race Mathews; Foreword by Gough Whitlam.
Includes bibliographical references and index.
ISBN 0-521-44133-1 (hardback). – ISBN 0-521-44678-3 (paperback)
1. Australian Fabian Society – History. 2. Fabian Society of Victoria – History.
3. Victorian Fabian Society – History.
4. Melbourne Fabian Society – History. 5. South Australian Fabian Society – History.
6. Socialists – Australia – History. 7. Labor movement – Australia – History. I. Title.
HX473.M38 1993
335′.14′0994 – dc 20   92-45211 CIP

A catalogue record for this book is available from the British Library

ISBN 0 521 44133 1 hardback
ISBN 0 521 44678 3 paperback

Contents

List of plates

Foreword

For Fabians everywhere, there is a most timely and encouraging message within Race Mathews' account of early Fabianism in the Antipodes. On its surface it may seem a study in failure, but, as Mathews points out, the seeds of Fabianism sown on the apparently unyielding ground of colonial society in the 1890s never died. For the whole of this century the seeds have been able to produce fresh crops of ideas and proposals profoundly relevant to the development of social democracy in Australia.

What is true for Australia is just as true for Western Europe, including Britain. In defiance of the triumphalists of the Cold War, I assert that Fabian thought and the Fabian approach remain crucial to any prospects for a reasonably cohesive, progressive and peaceful Europe after the collapse of communism. It is a measure of the intellectual aridity of Western leadership that its acknowledged chief should put forward as a justification for his re-election as President of the United States the boast: 'We won the Cold War' – and believe that thereby he has provided a meaningful policy for his country and the world. If this be their victory, they plainly have no idea what to do with it. Fabians may wryly note that it was precisely because Hannibal had no real idea of how to capitalise on his stupendous victory at Cannae that our patron was able to use his delaying tactics so effectively.

It is entirely relevant to any consideration of the present condition to emphasise that the Fabian Society and its antipodean offshoots were dedicated to developing an intellectual inspiration and practical alternative to Marxism at a time of recurring crises for industrial capitalism. Readers of this book in the 1990s will find a remarkable resonance in Mathews' description:

> The Society's debut [in Britain in 1884] coincided with a new mood of national introspection. Consciences and religious convictions were

under review as never before, along with more public questions, such as the sustainability of Britain's role in world affairs, and whether, as the conventional wisdom suggested, a cure for mass unemployment and impoverishment could emerge from the interaction of the 'invisible hand' of *laissez-faire* economics with philanthropic bodies such as Bosanquet's Charity Organisation Society. The great economic slump, which overtook Britain in the early 1870s and peaked around five years later deprived huge numbers of working-class breadwinners of their livelihoods, with the result that, as Charles Booth's poverty surveys revealed in the early 1880s, 30 per cent of the population of London – reputedly the richest city on earth – was living in destitution.

In the 1990s, more raucously and rancorously than at any time in the intervening century, those who worship at the altar of the 'market' preach their superstition to the established democracies, and even more ludicrously, even more insolently, to those struggling to emerge as democracies. It is as if Europe, North America and Australasia had forgotten the whole experience of the past century and were incapable of grasping its meaning and, specifically, the real meaning of the post-war years. For the truth is that none of the Western European democracies were prepared to consign their economies and social systems to unfettered capitalism on the pre-war model. The Marshall Plan itself was a massive repudiation of *laissez-faire* capitalism and its authors knew it. That is why President Truman and Secretary of State Marshall were mightily relieved when Stalin forced the Warsaw Pact countries to reject the proffered participation in the Plan. What Stalin rejected Congress accepted. The Plan in operation did more or less live up to General Marshall's promise at Harvard on 5 June 1947:

> Our policy is directed not against any country or doctrine but against hunger, poverty, desperation and chaos. Its purpose should be the revival of a working economy in the world so as to permit the emergence of political and social conditions in which free institutions can exist.

It was no accident that the working authors of the Marshall Plan – Dean Acheson, Clark Clifford, George Kennan and Charles Bohlen – had close personal relations with key members of the Attlee Labour Government. They knew from firsthand observations, and were able to convey urgently to Truman, the crucial importance of social democracy to the survival of Europe. In all probability, there would never have been a Marshall Plan except for the advocacy and example of the British Labour Government, itself the apogee of

Fabianism. When we reflect upon the seminal role of Fabians in power in 1947, and the huge achievements of social democratic governments throughout Europe ever since, not least in West Germany, culminating, I assert explicitly as a direct consequence of those successes, in the collapse of communism, we may treat the claims of the Cold Warriors and unreconstructed capitalists not so much with contempt as with ridicule.

More important is the confidence we may draw about the role of Fabianism for the future. Fabianism is not and never has been a body of fixed doctrine. It does not strive to develop a theory; it strives to develop a practical program towards the evolution of a social democratic society. And however unfashionable it may be to say so, the core of its principles is equality. Equally unfashionable, I suppose, is the key to the Fabian approach: a belief in the application of the intellect to human affairs, stubborn faith in human ability to solve the problems of human life through the application of human reason. It is an approach which insists on the importance of ideas in politics.

'In the event', Race Mathews writes about the most promising of the early Fabian ventures – in South Australia – 'the Society's hopes were disappointed'. To pitch one's faith so high, to assert the primacy of reason in an era of profound confusion and uncertainty, is to court inevitable disappointment. In another context, my account of the dismissal of my own government in 1975, I recalled that after the disaster of Cannae, the consul Varro was officially thanked for not 'having despaired of the Republic'. Nor did Fabius himself despair. Nor should Fabians now. Now more than ever, the Fabian approach is needed to fill the void in the political and intellectual leadership of the republic of ideas which the collapse of communism has so utterly exposed.

Race Mathews generously attributes to me the revival of the Fabian approach in Australia. With characteristic modesty, he fails to mention his own pivotal role in the development of the program I presented to the Australian people twenty years ago. Nor does he mention his immense efforts, at times almost singlehanded to keep the Fabian Society alive in Melbourne during the 1960s. Largely because of his perseverance, the Victorian Fabian Society remained a clear voice for reason, decency and common sense at a period notorious for the lack of those qualities elsewhere in the Labor Movement in Victoria and beyond. The historian who writes the sequel to *Australia's First Fabians* will have a far more successful and rewarding story to tell. Central to that account will be the contribution of Race Mathews.

GOUGH WHITLAM

Acknowledgements

This book began as a Master of Arts thesis for the Department of History at the University of Melbourne. I am deeply indebted to my supervisor, Ian Britain, for his unfailing support and guidance. His *Fabianism and Culture: A Study in British Socialism and the Arts 1844-1884* has provided me with a model of industry, scholarship and intelligence. I am also indebted to Andrew Reeves, whose drawing to my attention a copy of an 1895 Melbourne Fabian Society pamphlet in the La Trobe Library first suggested the project to me; to David Cragg who discovered the Fabian Society of Victoria minute book among the Merrifield Papers; and to Norman and Jeanne Mackenzie, whose use of 'group biography', in their study of the founder Fabians in Britain – *The First Fabians* – showed me how the Australian story might be told.

Valuable assistance has been provided by my examiners, John Rickard and Geoff Serle, by my editors, Phillipa McGuinness and Yvonne White, and by Alan McBriar, Hugh Anderson and Patricia Pugh. Peter Kellock's thesis on Harry Champion has been particularly useful to me, as has Graham Osborne's account of Tom Mann's sojourn in Australasia and Geoffrey Hewitt's history of the Victorian Socialist Party. My thanks are due to the staff of the Victorian Parliamentary Library, the La Trobe Library, the National Library of Australia, the British Library of Economic and Political Science and the University of Melbourne Archives – in particular Diane Reilly, Michael Mamouney, Frank Strahan and Cecily Close. The photographs are reproduced with the kind permission of the State Library of Victoria (plates 5, 6, 9 and 13); the National Library of Australia (plates 4, 7 and 12); the University of Melbourne Archives (plates 1 and 15); the Lothian family (plate 11) and the Shann family (plate 16). I acknowledge with deep gratitude my debt to the authors and publishers listed in the Bibliography. I am grateful finally – and most of all – to my late father, Ray Mathews, the late David Bennett and Gough Whitlam, who taught me to love politics and history.

Abbreviations

ACS	Australian Co-operative Society	RS	Rationalist Society
AFS	Australian Fabian Society	SAFS	South Australian Fabian Society
CCP	Charing Cross Parliament	SDF	Social Democratic Federation
FNL	Fellowship of the New Life	SDFV	Social Democratic Federation of Victoria
FRF	Free Religious Fellowship		
FSV	Fabian Society of Victoria	SDL	Social Democratic League
GSM	Guild of St Mathew	SDPV	Social Democratic Party of Victoria
HHS	Hampstead Historic Society		
IFL	Imperial Federation League	SQC	Social Questions Committee
ILP	Independent Labour Party	THC	Trades Hall Council (Melbourne)
LCL	Liberal Country League of South Australia		
		ULLP	United Labor and Liberal Party
LRU	Land Reform Union		
LFS	London Fabian Society	ULP	United Labor Party of South Australia
LSB	London School Board		
MDCC	May Day Convening Committee	UTLC	United Trades and Labour Council of South Australia
MFS	Melbourne Fabian Society	VFS	Victorian Fabian Society
NASL	National Anti-Sweating League	VLF	Victorian Labour Federation
		VSP	Victorian Socialist Party
PLC	Political Labour Council	WEWNC	War Emergency Workers' National Committee
PA	Progressive Association		
PPL	Progressive Political League	WEA	Workers' Education Association
RT	Round Table		

CHAPTER 1

The London connection and the Australian background

The First World War gave rise in Britain to an historic friendship between the best known Fabian socialist of the day, Sidney Webb, and the secretary of the Labour Party, Arthur Henderson. Webb and Henderson were brought together in the War Emergency Workers' National Committee, which Henderson chaired. Webb was the driving force behind the committee, and did most of its creative work. Joint action by Webb and Henderson later gave the Labour Party a new constitution, which Margaret Cole – honorary secretary of the London Fabian Society from 1939 until 1953, and its president from 1962 until 1980 – describes as 'a very "Fabian" compromise' between the party's socialist and trade unionist adherents. In the process, a climate was created which enabled substantial numbers of radical liberals to assume Labour Party affiliations, leaving behind Cobdenite liberalism and the Manchester school of radicalism (to be picked up half a century and more later by the Tories, at the instigation of Mrs Thatcher). Webb and Henderson were also co-authors of a new party program – *Labour and the New Social Order* – which represented, in Margaret Cole's view, 'as nearly as possible the purest milk of the Fabian word'.[1] The upshot was an enduring partnership between the Fabian Society and the Labour Party which outlived the vicissitudes of economic slump, party schism and war to emerge triumphant in Attlee's predominantly Fabian 1945 Labour government. The partnership remains in force, and was seen at work most recently in the major overhaul of party policy carried out under substantially Fabian auspices prior to the 1992 elections, at the instigation of the then leader, Neil Kinnock.

No comparable association of middle-class radicals with labour activists was achieved within the Australian Labor Party until the late 1960s, when Gough Whitlam played an antipodean Sidney Webb to the Arthur Henderson of Clyde Cameron and Mick Young in the rewriting of the party constitution and platform which preceded the 1972 elections. Earlier efforts date from 1891, with the establishment of Australia's first Fabian Society in South Australia by an expatriate London Fabian Society member, the Reverend Charles Latimer Marson. Marson was ahead of Webb and Henderson by a quarter of a century in recognising that any success that attempts to reconstruct the social order along socialist lines might achieve would be totally dependent on the labour movement and the Labour Party. Fabian bodies established in Victoria by three of Marson's erstwhile fellow London Fabians – Henry Hyde Champion, Ernest Besant-Scott and Tom Mann – failed because their relationship with the movement and the party was adversarial.

The Australian Labor Party and Australia's first Fabian Society were established within months of one another, in 1891. In all, Australia had four Fabian Societies (or organisations along Fabian lines) in the two decades from 1890 to 1910. In each case, the instigator was an expatriate London Fabian Society member. Marson – a fiery Anglican priest whose repeated clashes with church authorities in Britain prompted him to seek a colonial congregation – established his South Australian Fabian Society in 1891. The Melbourne Fabian Society was established in 1895 by the London journalists Champion and Besant-Scott, and Mann founded the Fabian-in-all-but-name Social Questions Committee (SQC) in Melbourne in 1905. The distinctively Fabian character of the SQC was retained for some time after its name was changed to the Victorian Socialist Party (VSP) in 1906. The Fabian Society of Victoria was founded in 1908 by the Reverend Frederick Sinclaire, a New Zealander who had recently arrived from Britain to take over the pulpit of the Melbourne Unitarian Church. Champion was a central figure in all three of Victoria's early Fabian organisations. He was not only a co-founder of the Melbourne Fabian Society – as he had been of the London Fabian Society before it – but gave Mann's Social Questions Committee its name, and was a co-sponsor of the inaugural meeting of Sinclaire's Fabian Society of Victoria.

The expatriates drew around them notable local supporters. Marson's South Australian Fabian Society attracted such leading local trade unionists as Tom Price, John McPherson, Robert Guthrie, David Charleston, William Archibald and George Buttery. Three of the unionist Fabians served terms as presidents of the United Trades and Labour Council of South Australia. Five became highly regarded members of parliament. The 1893 election of Charleston and Guthrie – in company with a third unionist, Andrew Kirkpatrick – to the Legislative Council marked the arrival of members of the Labor Party ('pledged to its platform, committed to its organisation, and promoted specifically as its representatives') in an Australian parliament.[2] In 1903, Price became the first Labor premier of an Australian colony or state – Anderson Dawson's seven-day tenure of office in Queensland in 1899 being by common consent too brief to count. The South Australian Fabian Society also included middle-class radicals such as Lucy Morice, who is best remembered for her contributions to kindergarten education and the women's movement. Lucy's husband James, another South Australian Fabian, became Clerk of the South Australian parliament.

Victoria's local Fabians were no less impressive. William H. Archer – polymath actuary, statistician, public servant, barrister, scholar, scientist, artist and leading Catholic layman of his day – was a Fabian. So too were the talented young writers Nettie Higgins and Vance Palmer, who later married. The Fabian convictions of the young historian and economist Edward Shann led him to become an *habitué* of London Fabian circles during a protracted stay in Britain, where he attended meetings of the Fabian-inspired National Committee for the Poor Law, dined at the House of Commons with Fabian luminaries such as Beatrice and Sidney Webb, and ultimately departed for Australia in 1910 'inspired by Fabian ideals and intense patriotism, and eager to participate in the building of a rational socialist society'.[3] J.G. Latham, rising young barrister and pillar of the cultural and intellectual community, was a further Fabian, who later became a notably conservative Commonwealth Attorney-General and Chief Justice of the High Court of Australia. Fabians among Latham's circle included Frederic Eggleston, the author and diplomat who was later an Australian representative at the inauguration of the United Nations in San Francisco; Walter Murdoch, who was later a much loved journalist, university teacher and philosopher; and Shann's brother Frank, who became a distinguished and long-serving headmaster of Trinity Boys' Grammar School in Melbourne.

The Victorian Fabians also included the Reverend Charles Strong, who gave up the pulpit of the fashionable Scots Church in Melbourne to become the founder and leader of the new Australian Church, and 'Melbourne's high priest of ethical religion'.[4] Other members were Thomas Palmer, who became the headmaster of

Wesley College; the early radio celebrity, John Howlett Ross; and Walter Hamilton, who was the Labor MP for Sandhurst and a leader of the colonial co-operative movement. Others again were the 'poet militant' public servant Bernard O'Dowd; the wealthy clothing manufacturer J.P. Jones, who was later a minister in several Labor cabinets; the leading feminist of the day Vida Goldstein; Elizabeth Lothian, who later had a long and distinguished career as senior classics mistress at Melbourne Church of England Girls' Grammar School; and Dr John Thompson, a general practitioner from Essendon who had been one of the University of Melbourne's most outstanding medical students and was later the Chief Medical Officer for Canberra.[5] A future prime minister – John Curtin – gravitated from a Marxist to a Fabian outlook within the Social Questions Committee and the Victorian Socialist Party, as did his closest associate and friend Frank Hyett, who founded the Australian Railways Union. Curtin and his future Cabinet colleague Norman Makin were the patrons of a resurrected South Australian Fabian Society with which the prominent London Fabian – and future Chancellor of the Exchequer – Hugh Dalton dined in Adelaide in 1938.[6]

South Australia and Victoria were fertile soil for the Fabian approach. This was in part because the more militant elements of progressive and labour movement opinion were less developed than in Queensland and New South Wales, and relations between the labour movement and the radical liberals, with whom the carriage of social reform had so far largely rested, were less soured. In Queensland, the revolutionary rhetoric of William Lane and the bloody-mindedness of the pastoralists and their urban allies gave rise to what Denis Murphy sees as 'the legend of the shearers, the noblest of bushworkers, defeated by the squatters, the princes of Australian capitalism, but rising undaunted to become the emerging political force in the colony'.[7] The aim of the colony's Labor Party was summarised in the pages of the Brisbane *Worker* in 1890 as 'to lay down a basis defining as clearly as possible the ultimate aim of the labour movement so that from the moment of its adoption, if it be adopted, labour in politics would take up a position which would place it at once beyond the narrow party lines with which the masses have hitherto been deluded, and would raise a distinct political issue which none but workers or true sympathisers with the workers would pretend to adopt'.[8] The upshot was an ideological climate inhospitable to reform among the colony's socialists. This was only incompletely exorcised by Lane's departure to found his ill-fated utopian colonies at Cosme and New Australia in Paraguay.[9]

The climate created in New South Wales by the Australian Socialist League's obdurate advocacy of a separate socialist party, the alienation of many within the League from the Labor Party's predominantly down-to-earth industrial reformers, and the New South Wales liberals' lack of interest in the union-supported protectionist policies and philosophy of their Victorian counterparts similarly left little room for organisation along Fabian lines. Prior to 1910, the solitary member recruited by the London Fabian Society from New South Wales or Queensland was W.E. Gundy, an associate of the prominent New South Wales feminist, Rose Scott, who was secretary of the Australasian Society for Social Ethics in the late 1890s, Officer in Charge of Correspondence Instruction at the Sydney Technical School from 1912 until 1936 and the author of the influential *Report on Technical Education by Correspondence in N.S.W. for the Department of Education, New Zealand* in 1935. Gundy joined the London Fabians in 1897 and had dropped out by 1901.

The work of early socialist agitators and militants within the Australian labour movement has been widely written about and celebrated. In the process, the movement's more moderate Fabian socialists – forebears of today's gradualist labour mainstream – have been substantially neglected. Whereas the inauguration of Fabian socialism by the London Society's 'little band of prophets'[10] in the 1880s is a familiar story, those members who carried organisation in the Fabian mould to Australia in the following two decades are mostly forgotten, or are remembered for their contributions in other fields. So too are the indigenous Fabians who embraced their example and became their associates and friends. The *Australian Dictionary of Biography* entry for Archer is a case in point. The entry overlooks Archer's socialist convictions and his having been the London Society's first Australian member.[11] The Fabian affiliations of Price, McPherson, Guthrie, Charleston and Archibald are similarly absent from their entries. History has largely stayed silent on the local bodies formed by Australia's first Fabians; the activities in which they involved themselves; the question of why they failed to take root; and the impact their existence nonetheless had on people, events and policies within the labour movement.

The socialist affiliations of the Fabian groups apart, their members mostly had common interests in such causes or movements as theosophy; rationalism; women's suffrage; co-operative enterprise in the tradition of Toad Lane and the Rochdale pioneers; the Single Tax economics of Henry George; and the 'organic unity' of the British Empire, as espoused by the Imperial Federation League and its successor the Round Table. The Australian groups shared characteristics with their London progenitors and adopted similar pursuits. Lectures were delivered, research projects undertaken and pamphlets published. Organisation – at the peak exemplified by the Social Questions Committee and the Victorian Socialist Party – equalled or improved upon the London model.

Even so, far from permeating the Australian Labor Party with socialist philosophy and policies as they intended – or reinforcing its industrial and electoral strengths with their research and propaganda skills – Australia's first Fabians inadvertently became significant contributors to an estrangement of much of the party mainstream from intellectual influences, an estrangement which lasted well into the second half of the century. Marson's success in enlisting trade unionist support for his South Australian Fabian Society was not repeated in Victoria. There, thanks to such factors as criticism of the 1890 Maritime Strike (which some have credited with contributing to its failure) and standing socialist candidates in opposition to the Political Labour Council at the 1908 state elections, a totally different situation was created. The belief took root that 'intellectuals' – Fabians among them – were people who both stabbed honest, loyal trade unionists in the back and subverted the electoral prospects of the political arm with which the union movement had equipped itself in order to pursue through parliament those goals it had not achieved by industrial means. Following the disappearance of the Fabian Society of Victoria in 1909, Australia's next Fabian Society – again in South Australia – did not emerge until nearly thirty years later, and it was not until the years immediately subsequent to the Second World War that the long build-up to the flowering of the Fabian approach under Gough Whitlam finally began, with the establishment in 1947 of a further Victorian Fabian Society, which became the Australian Fabian Society in 1984.[12]

The difficulties the Victorian Fabians encountered were exacerbated by their efforts' coinciding with a period which is seen by John Rickard as one 'in which class emerges as the major determinant of political loyalties in Australia'.[13] Even so, Champion and Mann carry major shares of the responsibility for the unhappy outcome.

Thanks in part to the affronts to the labour movement they caused or condoned, no advantage was taken of the opportunity prior to the hardening of class lines, when – as the South Australian experience indicates – middle-class radicals and labour activists might have learned how to work together to mutual advantage, and a partnership equalling or excelling that between the London Fabian Society and the British Labour Party might have been achieved. Champion and Mann were, in part, tragic figures who, with the best of intentions, did their cause more harm than good.

Despite the allegiance of notable Victorians to the Fabian cause, it never became the enduring force for enabling reason, education and ideas to play a part in the affairs of the Labor Party which was achieved in Britain. However their principal organisation – the Social Questions Committee, later the Victorian Socialist Party – was a significant influence in the party's adoption of its Socialist Objective. The SQC also provided a political nursery for key figures in the Labor governments which held office during and immediately after the Second World War: these included Curtin, and the first of the two John Cains – father and son – to hold office as premiers of Victoria. Members of the Curtin and Chifley cabinets, such as the Minister for Immigration and Information Arthur Calwell, consistently identified themselves as Fabians, and their colleagues included such notable former VSP members as Donald Cameron and E.J. Holloway.

The example of Curtin and his ministers, in its turn, fired the imagination of yet another generation of Labor leaders, including the young Gough Whitlam. Whitlam adopted the Fabian approach of sustained policy analysis and exposition from the day he entered parliament in 1952, and the seminal 1972 Whitlam policy speech was a drawing together of twenty years of systematic Fabian planning and research by networks instigated or appropriated on his behalf.[14] Two of the Whitlam government's Treasurers – Frank Crean and Jim Cairns – helped to establish the Victorian Fabian Society, while the third, Bill Hayden, lectured and wrote for the Society. Other members of the first Whitlam ministry who were also AFS members included the Deputy Prime Minister and Minister for Defence, Lance Barnard; the Senate Leader, Attorney-General and Minister for Customs and Excise, Lionel Murphy; the Education Minister, Kim Beazley; the Minister for Labour, Clyde Cameron; and the Minister for Urban and Regional Development, Tom Uren.[15]

The comment could have been made of the Whitlam government, as it was of the Attlee government following the King's Speech to the House of Commons in 1945: 'It's just like a Fabian Summer School – all the same faces'.[16] Whitlam's claim in 1988 that 'Among Australian Fabians, I am Maximus' is no less accurate for being, in part, self-parody.[17] The Fabian presence among Labor leaders has been carried on through Bill Hayden, Bob Hawke, Don Dunstan, John Bannon, Neville Wran, Bob Carr and the younger John Cain.

THE LONDON FABIANS

The London Fabian Society was established in 1884 with an initial membership of nine, which included Edward Pease, Frank Podmore, Frederick Keddell, Hubert Bland and Bland's wife, Edith Nesbit. It was shortly augmented by Bernard Shaw, Sydney Olivier, Graham Wallas, Annie Besant, Ramsay MacDonald, Stewart Headlam and Sidney Webb. Prominent Fabians, who joined the Society later included Webb's wife Beatrice (formerly Beatrice Potter), H.G. Wells, Keir Hardie, Ben Tillett and Tom Mann. Early lists of Society members also included names now more commonly associated with H.M. Hyndman's Social Democratic Federation, such as H.H. Champion and J.L. Joynes.[18] Shaw and Webb had met in 1880 as fellow committee members of the Zetetical Society, an offshoot of the London Dialectical Society where discussions took place 'on all matters affecting the interests of the human race; hence no topic theological or otherwise, discussed with decorum, is excluded from its programme'.[19] Webb, in Shaw's view, was 'the ablest man in England': 'Quite the wisest thing I ever did was to force my friendship on him and to keep it; for from that time I was not merely a futile Shaw but a committee of Webb and Shaw'.[20] His sentiment was reciprocated. 'It is a long time since we first met at the Zetetical Society', Webb wrote to him in the early 1930s:

> It led to nearly half a century of a friendship and companionship, which has been most fruitful to me. I look back on it with wonder at the advantage, and indeed, the beauty of that prolonged friendship. Apart from marriage, it has certainly been the biggest thing in my life; which without it would have been poor indeed.[21]

Webb and Olivier were fellow clerks at the Colonial Office at the time of the Society's inception. Olivier and Wallas had been friends at Oxford. Webb, Wallas and Olivier became known among their fellow Fabians as the Society's Three Musketeers, with Shaw as its D'Artagnan. Hardie was the first leader of the Labour Party. MacDonald succeeded him, after resigning from the Society in 1900, in protest against its refusal to take a stand against the Boer War.[22] He became the first Labour prime minister of Britain, and the party's best-known apostate.

Webb's courtship of Beatrice Potter touched off one of the more remarkable romances of twentieth century politics. Far from being the arid, asexual bureaucrats of conventional supposition – 'dessicated calculating machines' in the terms of Churchill's famous putdown of Beatrice's nephew, Stafford Cripps – the Webbs were passionately in love with one another throughout their long and exceptionally productive lifetimes. Shaw has provided an engaging picture of the couple at work together at an early stage of the marriage. Beatrice, he wrote, would periodically put down her pen and 'hurl herself on her husband in a shower of caresses'.[23] A tea-party in the company of the Webbs in 1903 prompted the observation from the young Raymond Asquith (son of the future Liberal prime minister, and a future casualty in the First World War) that Sidney was 'certainly most enviable in his wife – a woman of great beauty (although forty-four) and charm: she has a most lustrous eye, most graceful figure, and any quantity of intelligence'.[24]

Beatrice, Asquith continued, had told him that 'she had everything she desired – work, exercise and love'.[25] A 1901 entry in her diary reads:

> Nearly nine years of married life leads me to bless the institution and my good fortune in entering it with such a partner. We are still on our honeymoon and every year makes our relationship more tender and complete.[26]

Nearing the end of her life in 1943 – tormented by ill health and in failing spirits – she confided in a letter to Shaw's secretary, Blanche Patch, that she would be glad to die if it were not for the thought that Sidney, 'the Other One' and 'the beloved partner' as she had for years referred to him, or, more exuberantly, 'my boy', would be left alone:

> We have lived the life we liked and done the work we intended to do. What more can a mortal want but a peaceful and painless death?[27]

Cynthia Asquith – whose mother, Lady Elcho, had been prominent among the Edwardian smart society figures collectively known as 'the Souls', and a close friend of Beatrice – wrote that what had impressed her about the Webbs even more than their amazing industry was their mutual devotion: 'There can be no doubt', she concluded, 'that theirs was a deep and lasting love affair'.[28]

THE FABIANS' OBJECTIVES

The Fabian Basis – a statement of objectives adopted in 1887 – begins with the words:

> The Society consists of Socialists. It therefore aims at the reorganisation of Society by the emancipation of Land and Industrial Capital from individual and class ownership, and the vesting of them in the community for the general benefit. In this way only can the natural and acquired advantages of the country be equitably shared by the whole people.[29]

Socialism, in Sidney Webb's definition, was 'the conscious and deliberate substitution, in industrial as well as political matters, of the collective self-government of the community as a whole, organised on a democratic basis, for the individual control over other men's lives, which the unrestrained private ownership of land and industrial capital inevitably involves'.[30] Beatrice Webb believed that 'The job of the intelligent and self-respecting was to build an efficient, incorruptible and non-acquisitive society'.[31]

In the view of Margaret Cole, the basic Fabian aims were those 'of the abolition of poverty, through legislation and administration; of the communal control of production and social life; and of the conversion of the British public and of the British governing class, by a barrage of facts and informed propaganda'.[32] The Fabians were described by the historian George Macaulay Trevelyan as 'intelligence officers without an army who influenced the strategy and even the direction of great hosts moving under other banners'.[33] Shaw's hope for the Society was that its members would become 'the Jesuits of Socialism'.[34] The Society, he believed, should consist not of 'dreamers of the New Jerusalem and the Second Advent' but of 'unsentimental scientific pioneers of the next steps'.[35]

Webb endowed the Fabians with his memorable encapsulation of their guiding principle as 'the inevitability of gradualness'. 'Let me insist', he reminded the Labour Party in his presidential address to its 1923 Conference, 'on what our opponents habitually ignore, and indeed, what they seem intellectually incapable of understanding, namely the inevitable gradualness of our scheme of change':

> The very fact that Socialists have both principles and a programme appears to confuse nearly all their critics. If we state our principles, we are told, 'That is not practicable'. When we recite our programme the objection is 'That is not Socialism'. But why, because we are idealists, should we be supposed to be idiots? For the Labour Party, it must be plain, Socialism is rooted in political democracy; which, necessarily compels us to recognise that every step towards our goal is dependent upon gaining the assent and support of at least a numerical majority of the whole people. Thus, even if we aimed at revolutionizing everything at once, we would be compelled to make each particular change only at the time, and to the extent, and in the manner in which ten or fifteen million electors, in all sorts of conditions, of all sorts of temperaments, from Land's End to the Orkneys, could be brought to consent to it. How anyone can fear that the British electorate, whatever mistakes it may make or condone, can ever go too fast or too far, is incomprehensible to me. That, indeed, is the supremely valuable safeguard of any effective democracy.[36]

Shaw summarised the Society's method of working for socialism no less memorably, in the slogan 'Educate. Agitate. Organise'.[37] Shaw's most recent biographer, Michael Holroyd, sees it as having been central to his worldview that 'the humane and reasoned voice of the intellectual must not be lost amid the struggle of professional politicians and the rough and tumble of popular democracy'.[38] Education included the painstaking use Shaw and his fellow Fabians made of research and social analysis in order to equip themselves with a distinctive socialist alternative to the Marxist Labour Theory of Value in Jevons' Theory of Marginal Utility.

The vehicle chosen by the Fabians for the development of their new doctrines was the improbably named Hampstead Historic Society – which turns out on closer inspection to have been formed in 1885 at the instigation of the solitary anarchist member of the London Society Executive, Charlotte Wilson, under the less anodyne title of the Karl Marx Club. Shaw figured early in the life of the group as a defender of Marx, but was won over to Jevons by the advocacy of his fellow Fabians Webb and Olivier, and the Unitarian minister and economist Philip Wicksteed. In the process, he concluded that the Labour Theory of Value was untenable, and reached agreement with Webb and Olivier on the need for a government motivated by altruism and able to impose 'the will of the more moral members of society upon the parasitic'. For him, in the view of some, 'Property replaced original sin in the Evangelical scheme of things, and the sanctions of the state would have to substitute for those of the Recording Angel'.[39]

Meetings of the Hampstead Historic Society over the winter of 1887–88 discussed the development of British society from 1600 to the emergence of the Positivists, the Chartists and the utopian socialists in the early nineteenth century, on the basis of papers from Wilson, Olivier, Podmore, Shaw, Wallas and Webb. Topics a year later included co-operation, trade unionism, the women's movement and the Poor Law. The debates gave rise to specific policies through which socialism was to be given practical effect. On a less high-minded note, Alice Hoatson, who was Edith Nesbit's best friend and the London Society's assistant secretary, was reported by Nesbit to be in love with Shaw, as was Podmore to be in love with Hoatson. Hoatson subsequently had a daughter and then a son by Nesbit's husband, Bland, both of whom were raised by Nesbit among children of her own.[40] Besant and Nesbit had affairs with Shaw which to their consternation remained unconsummated.[41] So painful was the experience for Besant that 'Her hair turned white, and for several days she thought of suicide'.[42] Wilson dropped off the London Society Executive in 1897 after being worsted in debate by Shaw and Besant and – perhaps – taking the Russian anarchist, Prince Kropotkin, as her lover.[43] Pease, the London Society's third and longest serving secretary, was introduced through the group to Marjorie Davidson, whom he later married. Unsurprisingly in the circumstances, Davidson was cautioned by Sidney Webb that she might do the Fabians harm by marrying one of the more useful of their number, unless it transpired that 'Pease plus Davidson = *more* than Davidson and Pease, not, as usual, much less'.[44]

The Hampstead Historic Society has been seen by some as 'the seed-bed of Fabian attitudes and policies', and its proceedings as 'a seminar in which the most able members of the London Fabian Society put themselves through a stiff course of study and worked out their conceptions of capitalist society and the ways of changing it'.[45] Agitation and organisation through pamphlets and public lectures were the London Society's way of attracting informed public support. None of this meant that the early Fabians were necessarily as humourlessly intellectual or singleminded a group as they have sometimes been painted. As Shaw has recorded: 'It was at this period we contracted the habit of freely laughing at ourselves which has always distinguished us, and which has saved us from becoming hampered by the gushing enthusiasts who mistake their own emotions for public movements'.[46]

MIDDLE-CLASS ACTIVISM

The Fabian Basis also contained a commitment to the achievement of the Society's goals 'by the methods of political democracy'.[47] 'The distinctive mark of the Fabian Society among the rival bodies of Socialists with which it came in conflict in its early days' was identified by Shaw as its 'resolute constitutionalism'.[48] Change was pursued both nationally and through local authorities, where the Society's reputation for municipal or 'gas and water' socialism was gained. In London, the Fabians and the radical liberals joined forces in the Progressive Party to give effect to proposals for municipal reform set out by Sidney Webb under the title of *The London Programme*. The objectives of the *Programme* included publicly owned tramways and gas, water and electricity supplies. Webb was one of six Fabians who became members of the London County Council at the 1892 elections. He was chairman of the Council's London Technical Education Board, and held appointments which included membership of the Parliamentary, Local Government, Tax, Education, Housing and Water Committees of the Council.[49] Wallas, Headlam, Besant and A.W. Jephson were members of the London School Board; and Mann was the secretary of the London Reform Union. Shaw was elected to the St Pancras Vestry – a municipal body – where he briefly held the view that 'there is better work to be done in the Vestry than in the theatre'.[50] The Society's pursuit of municipal socialism supplied, in the view of some, 'Works as well as Faith, the indispensable mixture for continued as well as vigorous political action'.[51]

Most of the Society's members took the view early on that liberal and conservative bodies should be 'permeated' with Fabian thinking, so that the policies it developed could be carried forward irrespective of which party held office.[52] 'The Fabian policy', according to Shaw, 'was to support and take advantage of every legislative step towards Collectivism no matter what quarter it came from, nor how little its promoters dreamt that they were advocating an instalment of Socialism'.[53] The Fabians, Webb wrote to Pease in 1886, would win 'without being acknowledged victors, by permeation of others'.[54] Disenchantment with the outcomes of permeation later prompted members of the Society, such as MacDonald, to play key roles in bringing about the establishment of the Labour Party, which, from its inception in 1900, included the Society among its affiliates; made constitutional provision for a Society member to serve on its National Executive Committee; and ultimately, as has been seen, adopted what was – in theory at least – a predominantly Fabian platform, largely drafted for it by Sidney Webb.[55]

Such were the Society's nominal strengths that it was widely assumed to exercise a seminal and distinctive influence in Britain's public, parliamentary and municipal affairs. If the claim, as some have argued,[56] seems in excess of the Society's specific achievements, the fault may be partly attributable to Shaw's self-promotional genius for 'seizing the initiative in retrospect':

> As one of the authors of *A Campaign for Labour* he made claim to have been a founder of the Labour Party and a Fabian instrument in driving the Liberals from power; as author of the *Report on Fabian Policy* he was prepared to admit having helped to Fabianize socialism throughout Europe, and initiate the major social advances of the twentieth century. Only occasionally did he privately acknowledge some of this as 'pose' to be assumed 'whenever advisable'.[57]

Even so, for its dedicated early members – including Shaw himself – the Society possessed much more than a name to conjure with. It offered a philosophy, a process and a capacity for getting results. As will be seen, comparable attributes were to characterise its antipodean counterparts.

The Society's debut in Britain coincided with a new mood of national introspection. Consciences and religious convictions were under review as never before, along with more public questions, such as the sustainability of Britain's role in world affairs, and whether, as the conventional wisdom suggested, a cure for mass unemployment and impoverishment could emerge from the interaction of the 'invisible hand' of *laissez-faire* economics with philanthropic bodies such as the Bosanquets' Charity Organisation Society.[58] The great economic slump which overtook Britain in the early 1870s and peaked around five years later deprived huge numbers of working-class breadwinners of their livelihoods, with the result that, as Charles Booth's poverty surveys revealed in the early 1880s, 30 per cent of the population of London – reputedly the richest city on earth – was living in destitution.[59] At the same time, middle-class religious convictions came under massive attack from Darwin's insights into evolution, which succeeded in relieving many people of the consolations of Christian certainty while leaving largely intact the deep-seated consciousness of personal guilt which they owed to their sound Christian upbringing. As it seemed to Beatrice Webb, 'We lived, indeed, in a perpetual state of ferment, receiving and questioning all contemporary hypotheses as to the duty and destiny of man in this world and the next'.[60] The result, as some have seen it, was 'to transfer the impulse to self-subordinating that was so often nurtured in an Evangelical conscience from God to all mankind'.[61]

The energies which the uncoupling of guilt from faith set free were recycled through what Beatrice Webb termed 'a growing uneasiness' among 'men of intellect and men of property'. The focus for much of the anxiety was the fact that 'the industrial organisation which had yielded rent, interest and profits on a stupendous scale, had failed to provide a decent livelihood and tolerable conditions for the inhabitants of Great Britain'.[62] There were also those who deplored the waste of human resources which unemployment and poverty represented, or feared that dispossession in conjunction with democracy and the new unionism – 'distinguished by its recruiting of hitherto unorganised, or virtually unorganised, strata of working-men, by its basic maxim that solidarity gives strength, and by its association with political creeds, notably socialism' – might result in the overthrow of privilege or public order.[63] Britain's anxious self-examination was further agitated by over-the-shoulder glimpses of new and industrially powerful nations overtaking it in world markets, in ways which both called into question whether the eagerly awaited good times could be counted upon ever to return and vaguely menaced imperial security. The upshot was summarised by Beatrice Webb, when she recorded in her diary in 1884 that 'Social questions are the vital questions of today. They take the place of religion'.[64]

The responsibility for Britain's parlous situation rested, in the Fabian view, with the moral bankruptcy of the capitalist social order, which allowed riches beyond the imaginings of Croesus to become concentrated in the hands of those who had neither earned them nor were capable of putting them to productive use. The 'rent' which Fabian economic theory saw as being exacted from society by wealth was, on this basis, bereft of any legitimacy, and the proper course of action for an injured community was to tax the rich out of existence at the earliest possible opportunity, as idlers and drones. The proceeds, it was believed, would then enable acceptable minimum living standards to be enjoyed by all, in a society where consumer co-operatives in the form of municipalities would assume the responsibility for production.

The mechanisms the Fabians used to prepare themselves for the time when, as Sidney Webb put it, 'we all get into power'[65] included the debating society known as the Charing Cross Parliament. The mock legislature was formed on 15 July 1888, at Besant's instigation, and it may not have outlived her departure from the Society in 1890, when, as Pease recorded, 'she became a Theosophist, and regarded poverty and misfortune as punishment for sin in a former incarnation'.[66] Champion was Prime Minister and First Lord of the Treasury, Besant Home Secretary, Shaw President of the Local Government Board, Sidney Webb Chancellor of the Exchequer, Bland Secretary for Foreign Affairs, Wallas President of the Board of Trade and Olivier Colonial Secretary.[67] Mock bills were debated, and proceedings were reported in the style of Hansard in Besant's socialist monthly, *Our Corner*.[68] 'For the first time', it has been said, 'the leading Fabians felt, if only vicariously, what it was like to take office and present their ideas in the form of draft legislation'.[69]

What emerged from the 'perpetual state of ferment' identified by Beatrice Webb was perhaps the most homogeneously middle-class organisation in socialist history. It was axiomatic, in the Society's view, that 'middle-class professionals would play a much greater part than the working-class in achieving socialism, that they would themselves be among its beneficiaries, and indeed that their way of life anticipated it'.[70] While there is no evidence that the Society actively discouraged working-class members, it may well be that the latter found its outlook and ambience uncongenial. 'When a proletarian joined us', according to Shaw, 'he could not work mentally at the same speed and in the same way against the same cultural background as we'.[71] Society meetings took place in surroundings where working-class members were unlikely to have felt welcome or comfortable. In 1888, the meeting place was reported to be a 'spacious and lofty apartment in the Western end of London', 'brilliantly lit by a score of handsome candelabra' and 'thickly carpeted so that no footfall disturbs the solemn hush'. 'You might well imagine the scene to be laid in the Duchess of Brickbat's drawing room', the report continued, 'and fancy the company to consist of Lady Fannys and Lord Arthurs, assembled to exchange the ghastly smalltalk of fashionable frivolity'.[72]

So much was the London Fabian Society 'an overwhelmingly non-proletarian body',[73] that the house painter W.L. Phillips remained for some years its only working-class member, until his isolation was relieved by Hines, 'the intellectual chimney-sweep of Oxford'.[74] Working-class Fabians never accounted for more than 10 per cent of the membership, except perhaps in the early 1890s, when – 'for the want of any other national nucleus' – an influx of 'otherwise homeless working-class socialists',[75] including such trade unionist luminaries as Ben Tillett, Will Crooks and Peter Curran, were attracted to the Society.[76] Even then, the Society was said to be 'unhappy' with their presence, and allowed its provincial offshoots, where their numbers tended to be greatest, to drift off into the new Independent Labour Party after 1893.[77] 'As our relations were quite friendly as long as we worked in separate compartments', Shaw concluded, 'we learnt that cultural segregation is essential, and indiscriminate fraternisation fatal'.[78] Shaw's exclusive outlook and often high-handed ways were such a source of offence to labour leaders like Keir Hardie – himself a London Society member – that the two places originally allocated to the Society on the Labour Party's precursor, the Labour Representation Committee, were reduced to one at Hardie's instigation.[79] As will be seen, related attributes on the part of Champion contributed significantly to the derailing of Fabian socialism in Australia. Fabian societies have succeeded to the extent that they have been included by and in-clusive of the labour movement, and resisted separation from that movement.

The middle-class homogeneity of the Society's membership was due in part to the fact that the 'new consciousness of sin' about which Beatrice Webb wrote was not personal in nature, but rather a 'collective consciousness' of elements within middle-class Britain.[80] In part too, the early Fabians are seen by some as having exhibited a further common trait or 'rough pattern', in the form of 'a link of some kind (past or current, personal or family) with certain sections (large scale or small scale) of the Victorian commercial world; but one that was clearly severed through revulsion or disillusionment or failure'.[81] The slump of the 1870s and early 1880s was a further contributing factor. The hard times claimed middle-class as well as working-class victims, and the psychological impact on the former was generally greater because they were not accustomed to such sudden reverses or deprivation. Shaw argued that 'All men except those who possess either exceptional ability or property which brings them in a considerable unearned income, or both, stand to lose instead of win by Unsocialism; and sooner or later they must find this out and throw in their lot with us'.[82]

Closer inspection reveals the presence of two distinct groups within the middle-class majority of Society members, which differed from one another less in current status than in origins. Like Hyndmans' Social Democratic Federation and William Morris' Socialist League, which also had their inception in the early 1880s, the Fabian Society included its share of members who had been born into impeccably middle-class homes but had subsequently become alienated to the point where their bourgeois values were supplanted by a robust socialist faith. Examples included Beatrice Webb, the daughter of a wealthy railway promoter; Champion, the major-general's son who had a Marlborough education and saw service overseas as a Royal Artillery officer; Pease, who came from a prosperous family of Bristol Quakers; and Pease's fellow founder Fabian and Fabian Executive member, Frank Podmore, whose father was an Oxford don. Podmore and Pease had helped to found the Society for Psychical Research in 1882, and were members of its council. It is on record that 'it was while vainly waiting for a ghost to appear in an empty, supposedly haunted house at Notting Hill that they discussed Henry George's teachings in *Progress and Poverty*, and found they had a common interest in social as well as in psychical progress'.[83] On another occasion, Shaw slept in a haunted house in Clapham on their behalf.[84] Psychic research was a further surrogate for orthodox religion, comparable with the ruminations of the Theosophical Society, in which Besant immersed herself, or the wilder shores of seances and ectoplasmic manifestations to which the future Prime Minister of Australia, Alfred Deakin, was attracted in far-off Victoria.[85]

The novel element of the Society was the heavy preponderance of members who represented the new 'salariat' of professional and senior administrative workers, which Shaw and Webb referred to variously as the *nouvelle couche sociale*, 'intellectual proletariat', 'literary proletariat', 'black-coated proletariat' or 'professional proletariat'. An analysis of early membership discloses that:

If we think of the characteristic Fabian of the 1880s and early 1890s, we shall inevitably think of independent women, often earning their livelihoods as writers, teachers and even typists; of self-made newspapermen and writers; of self-made civil servants, political functionaries and itinerant lecturers; of clerks and professional men like T. Bolas who edited the *Practical Socialist* (the first organ of socialist reformism) 'at his chemical, electrical and technological laboratory' and J.M. Fells and E. Garcke, whose *Factory Accounts* (1888) is an early landmark in the British history of scientific management.

The Society, in summary, was made up, overwhelmingly, of not only 'the "new women" who so largely peopled Shaw's plays, but also the "new men" rising through the interstices of the traditional social and economic structure of Victorian Britain, or anticipating a new structure'.[86] The socialism of their dreams was to be, in the words of the young Ramsay MacDonald, 'a revolution directed from the study; . . . one not of brutal need, but of intellectual development; . . . in fact, a revolution of the relatively well-to-do'.[87] It is, perhaps, not surprising, in these circumstances, that they were sceptical of suggestions that an independent working-class party might be the best way for the socialist cause to be carried forward, or that the enduring intellectual alliance between the Society and the Labour Party – as opposed to their formal constitutional affiliations – was not finally achieved until after 1915.

The convergence of the two organisations, then, owed less to Fabian calculation or connivance than to the friendship between Sidney Webb and the secretary of the Labour Party, Arthur Henderson. Webb and Henderson were thrown together by their work for the War Emergency Workers' National Committee (WEWNC) – which Henderson chaired – and again when Webb replaced W.S. Sanders as the London Society's representative on the Labour Party executive. The WEWNC is remembered by its secretary, J.S. Middleton, as having been 'constantly engaged in promoting special measures, legislative and administrative, and urging them by deputations to Ministers, through the Parliamentary Labour Party, by steady press propaganda, by regional conferences, demonstrations and platform campaigns, and the regular circulation of the informative minutes of the Committee's weekly meetings to a wide network of national and local organisations and individuals'.[88]

The WEWNC's first publication – *The War and the Workers* – was prepared for it by Sidney Webb and issued as Fabian Tract 176. Webb also originated the Committee's proposals for price-fixing and rationing. A conference convened by him on the WEWNC's behalf induced representatives of building societies, ratepayers and small property owners to agree to limits on rents and mortgage interest rates, which were subsequently the basis for the government's rent restriction arrangements. Webb's untiring attention to the WEWNC's affairs gave rise to an intimacy with Henderson and his fellow Labour Party leaders which extended, as Middleton has recalled, over 'a very wide field, upon which he found the fullest scope for his amazing fertility of ideas, his unrivalled mastery of detail, and his special genius for draftmanship'.[89] Henderson is seen by some as having in part taken Shaw's place in Webb's life, vacated when Shaw's attention was diverted from politics by his success as a dramatist.[90] By 1922–23, Webb was Chairman of the National Executive Committee of the Labour Party, and he and Henderson were ministerial colleagues in the 1924 and 1929 Labour governments.

Most of the social currents which gave rise to the London Society were exemplified in the five Society members who carried its message to Australia. Marson and Sinclaire as clergymen, Champion and Besant-Scott as journalists, and Mann as a trade union functionary were all part of the so-called *nouvelle couche sociale*. The lives of all five men were influenced powerfully by their quests for a faith by which to live, which, in most cases, socialism only partly satisfied. Champion and Besant-Scott involved themselves vigorously in the Theosophical Society and the Australian Church. Mann gave serious consideration – even at so relatively advanced a point in his career as the early 1890s – to exchanging politics and the trade union movement for a clerical collar; and Sinclaire's Christian faith was retained, as will be seen, through a combination of emphasis on its social content and a theology which was idiosyncratic even by the relaxed standards of the Unitarian pulpit from which he preached.[91] Marson, Champion and Besant-Scott represented the established middle-class element in the mould of Pease and Podmore, while Mann and Sinclaire were examples – in Mann's case, extreme in character – of those who, like Sidney Webb, acquired middle-class status from humbler origins.

All five were lovers of learning, beauty and the arts, who experienced alienation from the capitalist social order around them because of its unfairness, inhumanity and ugliness, and who committed themselves – not without some doubts and deviations in the direction of more radical solutions on the part of Champion, or the ultimate defection of Mann – to achieving socialism through propaganda and gradualist parliamentary reform. Champion and Besant-Scott were prominent advocates of women's suffrage, which also enjoyed extensive support among their fellow London Fabians. Following in the tracks of the London Fabians who gave rise to organisations such as the Stage Society, they, along with Sinclaire, became key figures in the network of small literary and cultural groups – such as the Literature Club – which were active in Melbourne immediately after the turn of the century, and provided a seed bed for efforts to establish a national cultural identity (to which many Fabian-minded Victorians devoted their energies) when, as will be seen, further action along Fabian lines seemed to have ceased to be feasible around 1910.

THE FABIANS IN AUSTRALIA

Fabian socialism spread to the Australian colonies in the 1890s, with Archer's admission to the London Society, and with the formation of the South Australian and Melbourne societies. The eastern seaboard's convict settlement past had been put behind it with the cessation of transportation in 1850. The same year also saw the foundations for parliamentary democracy laid, with the Westminster parliament's passage of the Australian Colonies Government Act. The Australian population trebled in the course of the Gold Rush decade of 1851–61, and the consequent labour scarcities placed greater bargaining power in the hands of working people. Craft unionism rapidly became deep-rooted. Many of the early British unionists to come to Australia brought Chartist ideas with them – manhood suffrage, equal electoral districts, vote by ballot, annual parliaments, abolition of property qualifications for election to parliament, and payment of MPs. These ideas were shared by the key middle-class elements who became their allies in the struggle to wrest political and economic power from the squattocracy, which dominated the early proceedings of the colonial legislatures.

The outcome was a colonial liberalism whose most distinctive form was in Victoria, where the liberals adopted protectionist policies and had adherents of the stature of George Higinbotham, Charles Pearson and David Syme. Higinbotham is celebrated by Vance Palmer as the one true Athenian of nineteenth century public life – 'the democrat who did not mind the jostling in the market-place, but drew pride from the soil beneath him when he stood up in the name of the people'.[92] He was, successively, an editor of the Melbourne *Argus* who championed democratic reforms (such as the extension of the franchise) against the more cautious instincts of the proprietor of the paper, Edward Wilson; an activist Attorney-General who championed the popular will against the entrenched conservative obstructionism of the Legislative Council and the interference of the Colonial Office; a visionary royal commissioner, whose championing of non-denominational against denominational schools paved the way for 'free, secular and compulsory' education; and a Chief Justice who championed the unions against the employers in the 1890 Maritime Strike. A letter which he addressed to the Trades Hall Council on that notable occasion reads in part:

> The Chief Justice presents his compliments to the President of the Trades Hall Council, and requests that he will be so good as to place the amount of the enclosed cheque of fifty pounds to the credit of the strike fund. While the United Trades are awaiting compliance with their reasonable request for a conference with the employers, the Chief Justice will continue for the present to forward a weekly contribution of ten pounds to the same object.[93]

Pearson was an expatriate Oxford don and veteran of the seminal debates around the inception of the New Liberalism in Britain, who became in turn a lecturer in history and political economy at the fledgling University of Melbourne; headmaster of the newly established Presbyterian Ladies' College; and a royal commissioner on education and Minister for Public Instruction whose contributions to government schooling and public culture caused him to be celebrated as the father of Victorian education.

Syme was the proprietor and editor of the Melbourne *Age*; an advocate of protection for emerging colonial industries; and the 'King David' of Victorian politics, whose off-stage influence by his own account 'made and unmade' liberal ministries, to the point where, in the view of one parliamentary observer, 'Ours is not so much the Legislature of the colony as the Legislature of Boss Syme'.[94] He was also a reflective man, whose conclusions about political economy were given eloquent expression in journals of opinion and in his book, *Outlines of Industrial Science*, published in 1876. Stuart Macintyre writes that the colonial liberals spoke for the people:

They posited a national harmony of interest between the fair-minded employer and the honest artisan who dealt with each other 'in a spirit of manly independence, with no sense of subserviency or obligation on either side'. The improving selector who furnished the table of both, while swelling the demand for their output, completed a trinity of productive classes. Against them were ranged powerful and unscrupulous opponents, the squatter, the warehouseman, the absentee owner, who, as liberals characterised them, prospered by putting their privileges before the public interest. The potency of such a delineation came from its heady mixture of altruism and self-interest; the liberal crusade was at once a fight for justice and for progress since the eradication of privilege would release the productive energies of the people, enlarge their freedom and bind them in contented harmony.[95]

Prior to the emergence of the Australian Labor Party in the 1890s, labour activists and middle-class radicals mostly saw themselves as liberals; those who contested parliamentary elections did so as liberals; and the colonial labour movement relied on the Liberal Party to look after its interests in parliament. The colonial liberalism of Syme and his associates, as will be seen, gave rise in the 1880s to the New Liberalism, whose principal advocate was Deakin.

The eight-hour working day was substantially won in Australia in 1856, and by 1860 Victorian, New South Wales and South Australian colonists had achieved the combination of secret ballot, manhood suffrage and regular parliaments which still eluded their British counterparts. A further economic boom was touched off by a massive inflow of British capital, beginning in the 1870s, with public expenditure proceeding at rates up to double that in the United Kingdom, or five times greater than that in Germany. In Victoria, for example, outlays totalling in excess of forty million pounds were incurred for the railways, roads, bridges, ports and wharves, posts and telegraphs, and other facilities the colony needed in order for its agricultural, manufacturing and commercial activities to expand. Working people for the most part enjoyed an unprecedented prosperity, and the colonial legislatures were encouraged to enact the social and industrial legislation through which the reputation of Australia and New Zealand as 'social laboratories' was finally consolidated. A visit to Australia and New Zealand in 1899 prompted the young French socialist, André Métin, to coin his memorable description of colonial politics and public administration as 'socialism without doctrine'. 'Australasia', Métin observed, 'has contributed little to social philosophy, but she has gone further than any other land whatever along the road to social experimentation'. It was to the antipodean colonies, he recommended, that Europeans should turn 'to study the implementation of advanced measures, frequently debated but never actually put into practice among us'.[96]

The Melbourne Trades Hall Council was formed in 1856. It was joined by the Sydney Trades and Labour Council in 1871, by trades councils in Brisbane and Hobart in 1883, and by the South Australian United Trades and Labour Council in 1884. An Intercolonial Trades Union Congress took place for the first time in 1879 in Sydney, and a second Congress, in 1884, gave expression to nascent union aspirations for a say in the affairs of parliament by recommending the establishment of parliamentary committees. At the same time, the advent of the 'new unionism' of unskilled and semi-skilled workers was signalled by the formation of the Amalgamated Miners' Association in 1874, the Federated Seamen's Union in 1876 and the Shearers' Union in 1886. All told, the position of the unions entering the second half of the 1880s had never seemed stronger, nor their future prospects brighter. Within a handful of years, however, much the same disastrous conditions were setting in as had prevailed in Britain a decade earlier, when the London Fabian Society was formed.

Australians were thrown out of work by the great depression which reached its peak in the 1890s, just as their British counterparts had been in the 1870s and 1880s, and they experienced similar privation. The impact of the experience may well have been the greater by reason of its unfamiliarity. As Noel Butlin points out, 'This was, indeed, a "generation during which children grew to middle age without personal experience of economic depression"'.[97] The same doubts as in Britain were expressed about the worth of a social order which was unable to provide large numbers of its citizens with a proper livelihood, and the same limitations on achieving reform by means of industrial action were evident. The sense of sin imposed on elements of the middle class by its Christian origins gave rise to the same 'evangelical heritage' of 'anxiety and guilt, the need for moral redemption and a compulsion to regenerate the world', which in Australia was similarly given expression in support for the working-class cause.[98] The need for political organisations of new kinds was similarly canvassed. Labor parties were formed by the colonial labour movements in similar ways and for similar reasons, and advocacy of socialism was undertaken along similar lines, mostly by organisations independent of the party, including some in the Fabian mould. While the Victorian Labor Party, for example, included outspoken socialists such as the future MPs W.D. Maloney and G.M. Prendergast, sustained or systematic advocacy of the socialist cause was mostly conducted through a series of other radical groups whose origins predated the party. The Democratic Association of Victoria, for example, was founded in 1872, the Melbourne Anarchist Club in 1886, the Brisbane Bellamy Society and the Sydney-based Australian Socialist League in 1887, the Sydney Republican League in 1888, and the Melbourne Social Democratic League and the Georgist Single Tax Leagues in South Australia in 1889.

Organisational distinctions apart, the barriers against labour activists and middle-class radicals working harmoniously with one another were less formidable than in Britain. Colonial egalitarianism continued to promote a more ecumenical spirit within the labour movement, as did the relative absence of passionately felt class conflict. In Victoria, for example, what was initially an exclusively labour Progressive Political League – established in 1891 by the Trades Hall Councils of Melbourne, Geelong, Ballarat and Bendigo, together with the Amalgamated Miners' Association, the Australian Shearers' Union and the Social Democratic League – gave way as late as 1894 to a broader United Labor and Liberal Party, consisting of 'all trades and labour bodies and of all labour and female organisations, democratic and workingmen's clubs and of all persons who will give their adherence to the platform adopted by the conference'.[99] The adherents so enfranchised 'included not only those who had been elected as Labor members in 1892 and others of distinctly working class or radical background but also and without distinction, such indubitably non-Labor liberals as Berry, Deakin and Best'.[100] The unions and workers, in turn, in the view of some, 'continued to believe that politics was not of direct concern to them, except when directly related to industrial matters', to the point where 'It was tacitly understood that the Labour representatives in parliament should preserve the interests of the workers, but could vote with the Liberals or as they pleased on other issues'. As late as 1895, it was still possible for the United Labor and Liberal Party (ULLP) to protest to the Melbourne Trades Hall Council that Champion's establishment of the Social Democratic Federation of Victoria should be resisted as an attempt to separate the Labor forces in the parliament from their Liberal allies.[101]

The turn of the century, however, brought with it what Rickard terms 'a complete reversal of the "nineties situation"'. Powerful currents of class consciousness had been set in motion by the Maritime Strike, and a brash confidence was abroad, both industrially and politically, that the labour movement could fend for itself, independent of middle-class support or tutelage:

> No longer were the Labor members there to provide the numbers for middle-class liberalism. The Labor Party itself would now draw on the traditional resources of middle-class radicalism – the lawyers, do-gooders and reformers – when and as required.[102]

The welcome the movement had previously extended to supporters who had neither had a trade union background nor lived and worked closely enough to the working class to be able to talk the language of labour politics was replaced in the process by what was at best an uneasy tolerance. The new insistence on labour movement self-sufficiency and exclusivity was not necessarily conducive to the colonies' retaining their reputation as social laboratories or main-taining their former rate of reform. The practised scrutiny of the Webbs led them to detect during their visit in 1898 notable differences between New Zealand – where, as Sidney noted, 'There has never been any distinct separation between the old Liberal Party and the new Socialist Party' – and the Australian colonies, where the Liberal and Labor Parties were independent of one another.

'English Liberals', Sidney Webb reported to the London Society following his return to Britain in 1899, 'were fond of saying that the pretended Socialism of New Zealand did not amount to much; but a country which had just passed universal old age pensions, which fixed wages by law in every department in which the work-men choose to ask for it, which had a much more complete system of factory inspections than our own, which had absolutely stamped out home work, and which went into the money-lending business so that the rate of interest had fallen below 2 per cent directly the Act was passed, must be regarded, if not as a Socialist Government, as being at least much more advanced than our own'. By contrast, the situation of the Labor Parties in the Australian colonies struck the Webbs as being far less auspicious. In New South Wales, Sidney told the London Fabians, the leader of the 'so-called Liberal Party', George Reid, depended on the support of the Labor Party to remain in office, but 'though one would think that in consequence the Labor Party would be very powerful indeed, they seem to have attained nothing except a Factory Act and a Mines Regulation Act which resembled the legislative enactments of twenty years ago'. The liberal premier of South Australia, Charles Kingston, similarly depended on the Labor Party for support, but, in Webb's view, 'They initiated nothing, they suggested nothing to the Government, they asked for nothing and they got nothing'. 'Queensland', Webb reported, 'was the only country in the world where the franchise had gone back, the reason being that the country was under a White Terror, and the whole Government was carried on by a gang, not even of millionaires, but of failed financiers, while the Labor Party sat on the front Opposition benches and snarled'. 'In Victoria', finally, 'there were no politics, because the Government was run by a kind of solicitor, who, after a frightful financial collapse which affected nearly every body in the colony, collected the dividends for the English bondholders, and it was impossible to turn him out'. The root of Australian Labor difficulties, Sidney Webb concluded, was 'want of political education'.[103]

The Fusion of 1909 – a merger of Deakin's liberals with the conservatives – enabled the conservatives to acquire a veneer of respectability beyond their wildest dreams. The New Liberal luminaries who at that stage passed into the conservative camp were accompanied by a substantial following of loyal white-collar and middle-class supporters, whose British counterparts in many instances gravitated to the Labour Party. In Britain, the defection of Lloyd George and his followers had nowhere near so damaging an effect as that of Deakin and his followers in Australia. The rift was not repaired until well into the second half of the century, and, *inter alia*, enabled Sir Robert Menzies to perpetrate the supreme confidence trick and absurdity of Australia's political history: appropriating the title 'Liberal Party' for the new conservative movement which he resurrected from the wreckage of its conservative predecessor the United Australia Party in the mid 1940s.

Within the Australian Labor Party, the principal beneficiary from the enhanced class polarisation was the narrow labourism which Jim Hagan has encapsulated memorably:

> Like its counterpart in Britain, Australian labourism's central principle was that the capitalist state could be managed to the advantage of working men by a combination of a strong trade union movement with a parliamentary Labor Party. In Australia, labourism added three distinctive credos: protection to keep out cheap goods; a White Australia

policy to keep out cheap labour; and a system of arbitration to keep the fair employer fair.[104]

The socialists and other radicals within the party – those who, in G.D.H. Cole's memorable formulation, were members because 'it had been the party of the workers, the party of the exploited, the party of those who are determined to end the system of exploitation, and in its stead to build up the classless society of Socialism' – increasingly found themselves marginalised and ineffectual.[105] Many lapsed into passivity, abandoned politics for literary or academic pursuits, or gravitated to fringe presences in the political landscape such as the debauched and dying Victorian Socialist Party in the post-Fabian phase of its history or, later, the Communist Party. With their departures, the last barriers to labourist hegemony within the party finally crumbled.

The kind of contribution which the London Society was by then making to the Labour Party in Britain (at the instigation of Henderson and Webb) was never more sadly missed. In addition to the Society's providing, as in Britain, a bridge by which erstwhile radical liberals could pass into the Labour Party or identify electorally with it, Society members of the stamp of the 'great Fabians' – as Robert Skidelsky styles the 'Old Gang' of the Society's founder members and their closest associates – were capable of contributing formidably to the development of the internally consistent program of principled and evolutionary reformist measures which the party in Australia so conspicuously lacked. As Skidelsky notes:

> Their work schedules were forbidding. For a decade from 1885, Shaw worked eighteen hours a day, seven days a week. He exercised his faculties on socialist pamphleteering, journalism, public speaking, service on the St Pancras Vestry, writing novels and plays, and carrying on a gigantic correspondence. He believed he owed his genius to his will to work. 'Anyone', he wrote, 'can get my skill for the same price, and a good many people could probably get it cheaper'. Early in their partnership the Webbs, too, devised a punishing work plan to which they more or less kept for the remainder of their working lives. There were many lapses, particularly by Beatrice, but on the whole they thrived on it. After several weeks of non-stop work, Shaw wrote to Beatrice in 1898: 'By this time I was in an almost superhuman condition – fleshless, bloodless, vaporous, ethereal and stupendous in literary efficiency . . .'. Ten years later Beatrice could report that Sidney and she were 'living at the highest pressure of brainwork' on the most 'hygenic basis – up at 6:30, cold baths

and quick walk or ride, work from 7:30 to 1 o'clock, bread and cheese lunch, short rest, another walk, then tea and work until 6 or 6:30'. She could hardly sleep from 'brain excitement'.[106]

The upshot of all this Fabian industry and application – of the energies liberated by exchanging service to God for service to humanity – was that the British Labour Party was able to move forward, on the basis of the comprehensive and detailed policy with which it was endowed initially by Webb and Henderson, to the mighty program of reformist legislation which Attlee's predominantly Fabian government enacted between 1945 and 1951. No comparable program became available to the Labor Party in Australia until the 1960s, when Whitlam set out systematically to rectify the omission.

Meanwhile, 'intellectual' and 'academic' remained pre-eminent in the argot of the movement as terms of abuse. The contrast with other countries is instructive. Academics and intellectuals have been unpopular in other labour parties and movements – as witness, for example, in the hostility of Attlee and Ernest Bevin to a notable former chairman of the London Society, Harold Laski, or the observation once made of another former chairman, Harold Wilson, that 'Though one of the best "firsts" of his period at Oxford, he was never labelled by the most damaging of all tags in the Labour Party – he was never called an intellectual' – but the words are used within the ALP with a venom and abandon remarkable even by British standards.[107] It has remained the case until recently that, in the words of Frederic Eggleston, himself a Fabian, 'Intellectuals are not encouraged'.[108] As late as 1968, it was possible for Whitlam to be criticised by his predecessor, Calwell, for having an office 'full of long-haired academics'. Whitlam responded by pointing out that none of his staff were graduates and that one of them was bald. His wit may well have been held against him. The elephantine capacity of the movement for remembering injuries and harbouring grudges is exemplified by the fact that, in 1989, an amalgamation between the Australian Railways Union, the Australian Tramway and Motor Omnibus Employees' Association and the National Union of Railway Workers of Australia was reported to be delayed because 'some officials and members of the A.R.U. will not tolerate amalgamation with the N.U.R.W., which they still regard as a 'scab' union because of its role in helping to break a big N.S.W. strike in 1917'.[109]

WILLIAM ARCHER: AUSTRALIA'S FIRST FABIAN

It was against this backdrop of looming economic upheaval, industrial confrontation and heightened class consciousness that the Australian colonies acquired their first Fabian, in the person of William H. Archer. Archer joined the London Society from his home in Victoria in 1890, when the Society was barely six years old and numbered fewer than 200 members. The connection was maintained until 1905. Close inspection of Archer's life and career discloses that he embodied so many Fabian traits and attributes that he could be called not only the Society's Australian precursor but also something approaching a Fabian archetype.

Archer was born close to the Tower of London on 13 November 1825, the first son of a general dealer, William Archer, and his wife Sarah. In 1841, he went to work as a clerk with the Medical, Invalid and General Life Assurance Company, where the celebrated actuary F.G.P. Neison took charge of his training and introduced him to an enduring enthusiasm for statistics. Following a near fatal illness in 1847, he was converted to Catholicism under the guidance of Bishop – later Cardinal – Wiseman, and a year later found employment, along with his mentor Neison, at the Catholic, Law and General Life Assurance Company, which made him its Managing Actuary in 1850. Emigration to Australia followed in 1852, with appointment as Acting Registrar-General of Births, Deaths and Marriages for Victoria in 1853, as Assistant Registrar-General in 1853 and as Registrar-General in 1859. A foretaste of his radicalism in later life, and also of his caution, is implicit in his friendship with Raffaello Carboni, which was abruptly terminated after Carboni's arrest at the Eureka Stockade in 1854. Archer studied law at Melbourne University, and was called to the Bar in 1867. Appointment as Registrar of Titles came his way in 1868, as did promotion to Secretary of Lands and Survey in 1874.

Archer was also a holder of the Papal Order of Gregory the Great, a Knight Commander of the Papal Order of Pio Nono and a member of the 1859 and 1870 Royal Commissions on the Victorian Public Service and the 1867 and 1872 Royal Commissions on Education. However, the glittering prizes were interspersed with shattering setbacks and disappointments. In London in 1851 the directors of the Catholic, Law and General Life Assurance Company slashed the high income to which he had become accustomed as their Managing Actuary, in circumstances which he saw as reflecting a lack of loyalty to him and disregard for his advice. His distress was exacerbated by fears of sectarian discrimination. He had witnessed the outbreak of overt anti-Catholicism touched off when Wiseman became a cardinal in 1850, and it was his belief that, as an ex-employee of a Catholic insurance organisation, he would have difficulty in obtaining a position elsewhere in the industry, where the Protestant influence predominated. These considerations prompted him to speculate about a new life in Australia, where,

> as a keeper of sheep I might gain at least my lodgings, food, raiment and have the solitude of nature so favourable to the cultivation of mind and sweetness of soul. Who knows but there – removed from the temptations that have taint me here – it might be as an instrument in the hands of God for much good to the infant Empire.[110]

In the event, the move brought him great rewards but also further misfortunes which, in some instances, he may once again have attributed to sectarianism. In 1854 La Trobe's private secretary, Major Norman Campbell, was appointed Registrar-General of Births, Deaths and Marriages, the position Archer had held on an acting basis. In Archer's view, 'I was the originator of the department and formed it wholly; and the general belief was that I should have the head position'.[111] Responsibility for the administration of the 'Torrens Title' land registration system which he introduced into Victoria was lost to him in 1864, as a consequence of what he believed was a debauching of the Act 'for family and personal reasons'[112] by the Attorney-General of the day, Richard Ireland. At the pinnacle of his career, all that he had gained was finally snatched away from him. He was dismissed by Graham Berry's government as one of the luckless public servant victims of 'Black Wednesday', 8 January 1878, and was later denied the reinstatement which many of his colleagues were able to obtain.

Meanwhile, Archer was an unhappy witness to the despoliation of the service to whose creation his lifework had so largely been devoted: 'Plunder and devastation of the public service continued during the late 1870s and early 1880s, as ministers careless or ignorant of the principles of sound administration exploited it for their own purposes and others, nobler in intent but equally destructive in action, sought to redress the wrongs inflicted by their predecessors'.[113] He also had difficulty in finding himself a new livelihood:

> I tried the Bar but its ranks are crowded by younger men whose age enables them to work far harder where I cannot. I tried for the Librarianship of the Public Library and was nominated for months by

the Minister in the teeth of the Government of the State but Berry, through a political clique of the Irish faction just as he was leaving office appointed a young Irishman instead of me. I endeavoured to obtain a Police magistrateship from Sir Bernard O'Loghlen but he was afraid for reasons various to give me the office and so I left to look about me and discern if possible a way to supplement my small means so as to keep my wife and child and my mother in decency and without debt.[114]

It was not until 1887 that proceeds from the sale of a Burwood Road parcel of land enabled him to build his Hawthorn mansion, 'Alverno', and enter finally on a financially secure retirement.

The archetypal Fabian elements are plain. The middle-class credentials which rewarded Archer's single-minded upward social mobility were the same as those of his fellow London Fabians, and he belonged to the same *nouvelle couche sociale* or intellectual proletariat of administrative and professional workers. The checkered course of his insurance industry and public service career engendered in him something of the 'sense of social dislocation, financial insecurity or occupational anxiety' with which many London Fabians were familiar, and also conformed with the 'rough pattern' of 'a link of some kind (past or current, personal or family) with certain sections of the Victorian commercial world; but one that was clearly severed through revulsion or disillusionment or failure'.[115] He shared the taste for the arts and love of beauty which made some Society members reject capitalism because it was philistine and ugly, as well as the yearning for the 'simplified life' which had them 'acquiring labourers' cottages in Surrey, where they grew food, made sandals and communed with Nature'.[116] His lifelong vocation as a statistician, together with his scientific curiosity, his habit of research, the importance he attached to education and his passionate commitment to the reform of public administration were also characteristically Fabian qualities.

Archer's deeply felt Catholic faith may well have been unusual within an organisation of which it has been said that 'the service of God was transferred to the service of Humanity',[117] but it was not unique. The Society's treasurer, Hubert Bland, was a fellow Catholic, and clergymen of various denominations made up the second largest occupational category – after journalists – within the Society's ranks.[118] So much was faith a quintessential Fabian characteristic that, as some have seen it, 'Both Shaw and the Webbs tried to overcome "the death of God" by establishing new gods'.[119] Archer's wife's aunt, Agnes Nind, recorded in January, 1891, that she was 'sorry to hear that Archer had taken the socialist craze'.[120] At that stage Archer had been a Society member for some months. The fact should have surprised nobody. The way was open, at last, for him to respond freely to the promptings of his conscience. His means, leisure and social standing were sufficiently assured to allow some latitude for unconventionality.

Archer, in his role as the Fabian Society's Australian precursor, demonstrated that the economic, cultural, social and political factors responsible for the London Society's debut were also at work within the colonies. It followed that more Australian Fabians would emerge and in due course form local Fabian organisations. Archer himself seems to have taken no part in these developments. There is no indication that he joined any of the local groups or associated himself in any way with their activities. The reasons for his abstention may well have been threefold. In the first instance, the early Fabians were, as one historian has noted, 'mostly young, high-spirited people', still making their way in life. Archer, by contrast, was sixty-five when the London Society admitted him, and accustomed in every respect to the status and habits of high colonial officialdom. Socialist gatherings in Melbourne were a far cry from 'the Fabian drawing-room environment' of London, which 'effectively kept out nearly all the proletarians',[121] and it is difficult to imagine his being at ease either socially or intellectually in a meeting like the one attended by Sidney and Beatrice Webb in Melbourne in 1898, where, as Beatrice recorded in her diary:

> In an out of the way, dirty and badly ventilated place we met our 'poor relations', the believers in socialist shibboleths: a nondescript body of no particular class, and with a strong infusion of foreigners; a Polish Jew as secretary and various other nationalities (among them a black) being scattered among the audience. The chairman was the usual S.D.F. young man, with narrow forehead, bristling hair, retreating chin and dirty coat, and the inevitable red tie.[122]

Even allowing for the characteristically acerbic quality of the diarist's pen, Archer's acceptance of such associates may well have required greater adaptability than he could muster – or he may simply have felt too old to try.

Finally, while Catholics such as Bland were not unknown among the London Fabians, there is no record of them among the Anglicans, Unitarians, Theosophists, Freethinkers and adherents of the Australian Church and the Labour Church who made up the Society's colonial offshoots. If anything, the mood within the organisations Victorian Fabians established for themselves was most likely one of philosophical antagonism to Catholicism, exacerbated by the ill feeling left over from the debate on government aid to church schools – 'the oldest, deepest, most poisonous debate in Australian history', as Graham Freudenberg has aptly described it.[123] As a prominent protagonist in that debate, Archer may well have taken the view that it would be unbecoming for him to intrude where he had good reason to believe that his welcome would be less than wholehearted.

Archer's second year as a Society member was also the year the great social encyclical *Rerum Novarum* was published by Pope Leo XIII. Bruce Duncan concludes that:

> Leo placed himself close to reformist socialism and committed the Church to work for reform within existing institutions, even trade unions. Though the credit for the workers' movement belongs to the socialists, Leo endorsed it with the full force of his authority, and advanced a critique of capitalism and the demands of the workers. Catholics could no longer use the Church as an excuse for inaction.

The Australian primate of the day, Sydney's Cardinal Moran, is seen by Duncan as having welcomed *Rerum Novarum* and 'consistently supported a labour movement free of extremes, and supported the right to a just wage and trade unions'.[124] A similar approach was adopted in Melbourne, where Archbishop Carr caused the encyclical to be read in all the churches of the archdiocese.[125] Archer was perhaps the most senior Catholic ever to adopt Fabian socialism and, if he had chosen to identify himself openly with the local Fabians at this crucial point in the affairs of his church, the example might well have been followed by numbers of his co-religionists. He was also a public man, whose high standing in the eyes of his peers could have gone far towards dispelling the slightly raffish reputation which Fabianism acquired in some colonial circles as a result, as will be seen, of its association with locally controversial identities. In the event, neither of these highly desirable prospects materialised. His contribution was simply to foreshadow by his presence on the Fabian scene others of greater significance for it who came after him, and to whom attention can now be turned.

CHAPTER 2

Charles Marson and the South Australian Fabian Society

Prior to arriving in South Australia in 1889, Charles Marson was a commanding figure among the crusading band of socialist-minded Anglican clergymen whose leader was the Reverend Stewart Headlam. The socialist and Anglo-Catholic Guild of St Matthew, which Headlam established in 1877 and Marson joined a little later, aimed *inter alia* 'to promote the study of social and political questions in the light of the Incarnation'. A 'Priest's Political Programme', adopted by the Guild at the instigation of Headlam in 1884, stated that:

> Whereas the present contrast between the great body of the workers who produce much and consume little, and of those classes which produce little but consume much is contrary to the Christian doctrines of brotherhood and justice, this meeting urges on all Churchmen *the duty of supporting such measures as will tend* –
> (a) to restore to the people the value which they give to the land;
> (b) to bring about a better distribution of the wealth created by labour;
> (c) to give the whole body of the people a voice in their own government;
> (d) to abolish false standards of worth and dignity.[1]

A memorable encapsulation of the restless spirit and idiosyncratic enthusiasms with which Headlam infused the Guild – and inspired or exasperated fellow members such as Marson – is provided by the American historian Peter Jones:

> Within his chosen church (to which he remained devoted all his life) he became an implacable rebel and openly spurned his bishop. He rejected 'Protestantism', and plumped for an uncompromising form of Anglo-Catholic ritualism – though in outside life, when leading socialist marches of the unemployed, for instance, he was equally uncompromising in refusing to wear priestly garb. Constantly in trouble with the Anglican authorities over his 'High Churchliness', he never considered

leaving the faith for Rome, and he firmly repudiated papal authority. In an age of gentility and convention, Headlam campaigned on behalf of chorus girls, the popular theatre, freedom of opinion for atheists, and drink. He stood staunchly for anti-Sabbatarianism, anti-Puritanism, and anti-temperance, and gaily went to the local pub for a drink with his pupil-teacher disciples. His fight for secular education deeply upset some of his own clerical supporters, and his bohemianism irritated many of his severe Fabian socialist colleagues (not Shaw, of course). Scarcely having met the man, Headlam went bail for Oscar Wilde when all of self-righteous middle-class England was against him; and as a London County Councillor, he fought the London County Council.

Jones further credits Headlam and his followers with having been more alive than earlier Anglican socialists 'to the need for eradicating class consciousness, snobbery and elitism, and for smashing the upper-class Tory image of Anglicanism'. Headlam in particular is seen as having 'wished chiefly to make the Anglican church more honest by disestablishing it'. 'The hierarchy', Jones notes, 'was not slow to "purge" political or theological heresy in the late nineteenth century', with the result that 'Headlam was constantly being dismissed and never rose above the status of a curate; he finally gave up all hope of ever being beneficed and was able to hold services only when friendly clergymen invited him'.[2] Similar setbacks were experienced repeatedly by Marson, both in Britain and in South Australia.

In the eyes of some, Marson manifested 'truly saintly qualities'.[3] His political life – like that of Headlam – richly exemplified the linkages of the day between Christians, socialists and the Single Tax followers of Henry George. Service in London as a settlement worker and member of the Charity Organisation Society in the early 1880s, as a curate in the heavily working-class district of Soho from 1882 to 1884, and as a rector in Whitechapel from 1885 to 1886 alerted Marson to the depths of urban poverty documented by the research of Charles and Mary Booth. His supervisor in Soho was a notable Guild colleague, the Reverend W.E. Moll, of whom a contemporary noted: 'No parson in England has done so much for the cause of socialism'.[4] Moll was a prominent adherent of the Single Tax cause and a High Church sacramentalist who allowed Headlam to say Mass from his pulpit when others had been closed against him. A term as a village curate at Orlestone in Kent from 1886 to 1889 introduced Marson to rural poverty. The result was that his mission in life became to 'battle for the Have-nots against the Haves'.[5]

By 1884 the Guild's gospel of sacramental socialism ('the belief that the best proof and witness of the socialism of Christ is the Holy Sacraments of the Church – especially Baptism and the Mass') and the Single Tax was being spread in centres as widely separated as Folkestone, Liverpool, London, Preston, Northampton, Plymouth, Wellingborough and Oldham. Guild members demonstrated in support of the unemployed outside the Royal Exchange; socialism was advocated at public meetings organised by the Guild; and the Guild Council presented a memorandum on socialism to the 1888 Lambeth Pan-Anglican Conference. Leaflets and broadsheets were issued, and letters on behalf of the Guild appeared regularly in the newspapers. A Guild journal – the *Christian Socialist* – was established, and was joined shortly by Headlam's *Church Reformer*, which Shaw regarded as 'one of the best socialist journals of that day'.[6] Membership of the Guild peaked at around 400, with four branches in London and others in centres such as Oxford. Marson became the founder and sole member of the Guild's South Australian branch and, following his return from the colony, president of a branch in Bristol.

Marson and Headlam were also founder members of the Land Reform Union, which was formed in 1883 to promote George's proposals for the nationalisation of land through the imposition of a single tax on land values. Action was required, according to George, because 'land was the source of all wealth, and all inequalities were caused by the fact that a few men monopolised the birthright of the people'.[7] In 1884 the Land Reform Union became the English Land Restoration League, with Moll as a prominent member of its committee. Marson and Headlam apart, the instigators of the Land Reform Union included fellow Guild members such as the Reverend Henry Carey Shuttleworth and the Reverend John Elliotson Symes; future fellow Fabians such as Harry Champion and Sydney Olivier; and the Unitarian Church's Reverend Philip Wicksteed, whose influence, as noted earlier, prompted Shaw to abandon Marx in favour of Jevons. Champion became secretary of the Land Reform Union, and Shaw was an early recruit. Champion's socialism has been attributed to the chance reading of a pamphlet by George, while he was on leave from his regiment in America.[8] Shaw credited George's book *Progress and Poverty* with his conversion to 'the economic basis' from 'the overthrow of the Bible, the higher education of women, Mill on Liberty, and all the rest of the storm which raged about Darwin, Tyndell, Huxley, Spencer and the rest, on which I had brought myself up intellectually'.[9]

The Guild of St Matthew and the Land Reform Union adopted as their official organ the *Christian Socialist*, which Champion edited until 1884, when his place was taken by Marson. Marson's articles for the *Christian Socialist* assailed targets such as the Irish Union, which he described as 'the union of thumb and thumbscrew'; the 'low-minded and over-pampered scoundrels' who jeered from the windows of their West End clubs at the passing Fabians and their fellow protesters during the "Black Monday" riot in February, 1886; and the Established Church, which he saw as 'an interesting piece of archaeology' condemned alike by 'political sanitation and moral health'. A further broadside anticipated the acute concern for the suffering of the Australian Aborigines which he exhibited later in South Australia:

> To supply blacks with soda water and blue pills is not the end of our duties towards them. Our efforts to cheat, rob, murder and enslave them require as much denunciation as the fact that we dram, drug and syphelize them.

English colonial policy was lambasted for being uncaring about indigenous populations and for sending them missionaries, 'Bible in one hand and gun in the other'.[10]

The Single Tax movement was, in part, the intellectual seed bed in which the earliest Fabians were nurtured, and it was through the Land Reform Union that many of them were introduced to one another. In the sense of having brought prospective Fabians together in the same group for the first time, the Land Reform Union perhaps rivals the meetings in Edward Pease's rooms in Osnaburgh Street in 1883–84, to which, as will be seen, the Society's origin is more directly attributed. Land Reform Union members who became London Fabians included the Society's inaugural secretary, Frederick Keddell; the Eton schoolmasters, James Joynes and Henry Salt; Salt's wife, Kate, who was also Joynes' sister and – like Edith Nesbit – one of Shaw's longtime confidants; and Sidney Webb, who was persuaded to join by Shaw. Joynes is best remembered as a Social-Democratic Federation activist and the co-editor – along with the militantly anti-religious Belfort Bax – of Champion's Modern Press monthly *Today*. He resigned from his position at Eton after he and Henry George were arrested as suspected Fenian organisers during George's 1882 Irish lecture tour. The vegetarian Salt – described by Shaw as 'the mildest man that ever defied society' – followed his example in 1885, as a protest against having to work with 'cannibals in cap and gown', a protest the headmaster, Dr Warr, attributed to 'the incendiary combination of socialism and *legumes*'. Joynes' premature death in 1894 was likewise attributed by his detractors to vegetarianism. Salt outlived him, to become co-founder of the Humanitarian League and editor for a quarter of a century of the League's journal, 'dedicated to the abolition of blood sports, corporal punishment, the death penalty and the commercial vulgarisation of the countryside'.[11]

Marson joined the London Society in 1885 as one of its earliest members, and Headlam was a member from 1886 until his death in 1924, serving as an executive member from 1890 to 1891 and 1901 to 1911, and helping to draw up the 'Basis' of the Society in 1887, when, according to Sidney Webb, his persistence secured the inclusion of 'the declarations which were afterwards considered most extreme'.[12] However, neither in Britain nor in Australia were all Single Tax and socialist groups necessarily on such amicable terms as the Land Reform Union experience suggests. Henry George saw lurking behind socialism 'spectral horrors of state regulation', and similar fears were voiced in Australia by the best known of his antipodean followers, Max Hirsch. In the eyes of some socialists, the Single Taxers in turn constituted simply an aberrant subset of the broad collectivist movement, whose development had in some inexplicable manner been arrested, so that they were unable to countenance any form of nationalisation other than that of land.

No such reservations troubled Marson or Headlam, for whom Georgist and socialist convictions were part and parcel of one another. Marson's absence from the meetings in Pease's rooms which gave rise to the London Society may well have been due solely to the demanding character of his new duties with the *Christian Socialist*. The *Christian Socialist* in turn gave rise in 1886 to the establishment of the non-denominational Christian Socialist Society, which reflected in part a conviction among Marson and some other Guild of St Matthew members that, while it and other Christian socialist groups of the day were operating on a missionary basis: 'none of them are striving to convert those to the common faith who are non-sacerdotal Christians'. The Society's manifesto reads accordingly that 'The Society, then, is independent of all theological views, and welcomes as members all who desire to make self-sacrifice for men the rule of their lives, and to work as brothers one of another, who are bound to subordinate their private advantage to the good of the commonwealth and of mankind'.[13]

The Society met for the first time on 21 June 1886, and branches were formed in Bristol later that year; in Liverpool and Glasgow in 1887; and in Leicester in 1891. Among those who became members were Reverend John Glasse, whom Sidney Webb described as one of the two most influential socialists in Scotland, and W.H.P. Campbell, who succeeded Marson as editor of the *Christian Socialist*, from 1887 to 1890. Weekly public meetings at the Industrial Hall in Bloomsbury were instituted. A Special Propaganda Fund was established, and the Society became a major advocate of the doctrines of the American socialist and 'ethical idealist', Laurence Gronlund. Gronlund's major work – *The Co-operative Commonwealth* – had been extensively edited by Shaw for a British edition under the imprint of Champion's Modern Press, which Gronlund had promptly repudiated. Marson was able to report within six months of the inaugural meeting that the Society had become 'a greater success even than we dared to hope'. Headlam addressed meetings for the Society, but he remained resistant to making the Guild of St Matthew a more ecumenical organisation. Further friction between Headlam and Marson resulted from the fact that, while Headlam leaned to the Liberals and adopted a patronising attitude to working-class organisation, other Guild members such as Marson were anti-Liberal and wanted to see a working-class party seated in parliament at the earliest possible date. A rift was developing, which, as will become plain, brought about a serious weakening of the Guild, and caused Marson to be seen by some as its *méchant garçon*.[14]

Further attributes credited to Marson by associates included a defiance of every form of ecclesiastical convention, and a wisdom and erudition such as prompted Paul Stacey, the author of the preface of the 1930 edition of Marson's *God's Co-operative Society*, to note: 'I cannot remember any casual five minutes' conversation with him that would have been called ordinary; everything he said either informed, arrested, pleased or amused . . . he let light in all around'. His 'sardonic frivolities' were noted, as was the 'characteristic mordancy' with which he dismissed less adventurously-minded fellow Anglicans as 'ever learning but never coming to a knowledge of the truth'.[15] He was, in the view of a further observer, 'Not a man to hide his light under a bushel, nor to allow anyone to eclipse it;

he compelled attention, as much by his caustic wit as by the cogency of his arguments'. He excelled, it is said, 'In ridiculing ideas and habits out of existence'.[16]

While such a larger-than-life figure naturally created 'an impression on many of his contemporaries the power of which it is impossible to exaggerate',[17] he was also bound to attract critics and enemies. Some regretted his failure to deal with the bishops and his fellow priests 'more in the manner of the Fabians when dealing with capitalist politicians, ignoring their absurdities and prescribing what they ought to do'.[18] His 1884 appointment to a curacy at Petersham was prematurely cut short when he was 'kicked out by a drove of Tories as a seditious heretic'.[19] The Orlestone appointment was terminated when his Anglo-Catholicism gave rise to a situation where 'the dread of the Scarlet Woman was now added to the fear of the Red Flag'.[20] By late 1888 both his bishop and the patrons of the Orlestone church were of the view that Marson should again move on. It became known early in the following year that he had accepted another curacy in the Adelaide suburb of Glenelg, where his invalid brother Frank would accompany him in search of a healthier climate, and that they would be joined at a later date by his fiance, Clotilda Bayne. The decision cannot have been easily reconciled with his deeply felt attachment to London: 'How I love it – the smell of garlic and cooked stuffs, and petrol, and the rush of life; there is no place in the world like Soho'.[21]

MARSON IN AUSTRALIA

Marson's South Australian sojourn began when he was curate of St Peter's Church in Glenelg; he later served at St Jude's in Brighton and St Oswald's in Parkside. A contemporary account describes him as 'being in appearance about eighteen years of age'. 'He has prominent features, and is a great smoker', the writer went on, 'his pipe and himself being almost inseparable'.[22] His 'large, mobile mouth, grey eyes with an indescribable twinkle, and rich, husky yet musical voice' were irresistible, it is said, 'to most people of all classes'.[23] His qualities as an outspoken social critic, willing polemicist and deliverer of impassioned sermons were also shortly made plain. Such was the experience of hearing him preach that:

> You sat and shivered as blow after blow demolished the moral foundations of your father's income. References to the servant question made

you thankful that your own were not in the church; denunciations of Protestantism made the necks in the pew in front of you grow deep purple, and the whole service meant such an explosive mid-day dinner table that it remains in your memory like a nightmare.[24]

The wider community sat up and took notice when, within a few months of Marson's arrival, he entertained an Aborigine to tea. The colony's treatment of the Queen's Aboriginal subjects was a source of grief and outrage to him. 'Constant massacres and venality and contempt', he believed, had left the blacks with 'Their tribal organisation broken up, their game all killed, their lands annexed . . . their sons made slaves of, and all by people who talk about the love of Christ and profess piety'. At a service for Missionary Sunday, he 'got wild and said just what came uppermost – reproach, jest, entreaty and appeal' before a congregation which 'hung on the words, were impressed, but angry'. 'God grant', he noted afterwards, 'It may stir some of the audience to a more chivalrous participation in the Catholic life – of rebellion and reconstruction'.[25]

Further attention was attracted when Marson delivered a paper on the defects of state education which astonished his fellow members of the colonial clergy 'by the freedom of the utterances, the unconventionality of the diction and the unexpected smartness of the arguments'.[26] 'Stuffing machines for the poor and for their instructors', Marson argued, were separated by 'a great gulf' from 'universities and their training schools for the rich'. Their teachers, in his view, were 'pitiable creatures whose minds have been banged into official dullness by blinding showers of rules, codes and regulations'. The 'utter badness palmed off on the poor' was evident, as he saw it, in a course of study where 'all subjects requiring most thought and nimbleness of wits come last, ie. educationally the list is upside down'. The measures required to remedy the situation included, he believed, 'state-paid education from top to bottom', such as would 'draw into State schools all the more thoughtful parents, and would set such parents zealously struggling to better national education' and 'fuse classes and give the unity between men which it effects in Switzerland'; abolition of 'the mischievous system of payment by results' in favour of putting 'casual, constant and unexpected visits by examiners in the place of the formal fiasco now endured'; and the introduction of gymnasia, music and gardening or swimming into every school.[27]

The appearance of this material in the columns of the *Advertiser* prompted a flood of replies, and Marson was encouraged to give expression to further strongly held opinions. One subsequent polemic – defending the good name of barmaids – showed a greater familiarity with hotel interiors than might have been expected among clerical circles in Adelaide. A second attempted, in similarly trenchant terms, 'to give a death blow to that Puritanism which induced and induces parents to give their children only what are known as "good" books to read on the seventh day, and justified the playing of a game of cricket or tennis after church'.[28]

Radical opinion in the colony initially regarded Marson with reserve, and was quick to pounce when his name appeared in an English church periodical over an article construed as conveying that 'Our public life is corrupt, our buildings are shoddy, our youths are pale, slight and undisciplined, our birds are songless, our flowers scentless'.[29] If anything, the summary understated Marson's initial distaste for his new surroundings. A letter to his fiance read, in part, 'Private life is hideous and hypocritical. The largest profession of piety is allowed to be made by people of equally large and equally open profligacy'.[30] Time, however, gave rise to a mellowing on both sides, such that a handsome apology on behalf of the radicals was offered over the signature of 'Quiz', in the journal of the same name:

> There is, for instance, the boisterous parson – an assertive and dog-matical creature, who rams his opinions down your throat willy-nilly. Shall I confess that I at one time believed you to belong to this objectionable class? Then there is the sensational parson who adopts the extremist methods of advertising himself and his work, and I am ashamed to own that I was once inclined to consider you a sensationalist. I was mistaken.[31]

Marson's clerical superiors were less forgiving. 'Tiring', it is said, 'of the strain of working with a curate who always seemed to be in hot water', the rector of St Jude's, Canon French, declined to renew his appointment when it expired in June, 1891.[32] His subsequent period at St Oswald's in Parkside was no less stormy. *Quiz* reported on 17 July 1891 that 'He has already so shocked many of the Low Church people of the community that several vow they will not enter the place of worship again so long as he is in the pulpit'. 'The great points in dispute', the report continued, were 'the lighting of candles and the number and depth of reverence of the bows made by the new pastor'. Marson's religious obligations in other respects were taken no more lightly. A Kent Town Literary Society meeting where he was to lecture took place in a Wesleyan church hall and commenced with a prayer from its president, who was also the Wesleyan incumbent. Marson demurred. As a priest, he pointed out later, he was 'quite willing to dance, eat, drink, run and walk with Turks, Jews, infidels and heretics', but he could not pray with them.[33]

THE GRAND DESIGN

Marson's involvement in South Australian radical politics shows that he was ahead of his fellow London Fabians by a quarter of a century in acknowledging that any attempt to reconstruct the social order along socialist lines would be totally dependent on the labour movement and the Labor Party. The task he set himself was to play an antipodean Sidney Webb to the Arthur Henderson of leading local unionists, such as Charleston and McPherson, who joined the South Australian Fabian Society and also became London Society members. Further unionist Fabians included W.O. Archibald, who was an executive member of the Railway Service Mutual Association prior to taking his place beside McPherson in the Legislative Assembly and ultimately becoming a Member of the House of Representatives and a federal minister; Tom Price, who was a Stonecutters' Union secretary and UTLC delegate and became the first Labor premier of South Australia; and George Buttery, the Adelaide bookseller who, prior to his arrival in South Australia, had sat beside Marx as a fellow delegate to the Council of the International Workingmen's Association.

A sixth unionist Fabian – the Society's second president, R.S. Guthrie – was South Australian secretary and federal secretary of the Federated Seamen's Union of Australasia, a UTLC delegate for the Seamen's Union, president of the UTLC, the founder secretary-treasurer of the Federated Council of Australasian Labour Unions – later the Australian Council of Trade Unions – and a Member of the Legislative Council. His parliamentary career culminated as a senator in Canberra. This impressive concentration of the cream of South Australia's trade union leadership recalls the accolade coined in another context by the British Social Democratic Federation leader, H.M. Hyndman: 'as promising and capable a set of men as ever threw in their lot with an advanced movement'.[34]

Looking back on his South Australian associates on his return to England in 1892, Marson recalled in a letter to the *Church Reformer* that the South Australian Fabian Society had from the first 'widely gone in for labour members'. Since the Liberals were distinguishable from the Tories only because they possessed 'simulation and adroitness', Marson argued, the question was, 'Are we to conceal our differences and permeate? Or are we to act in the open?'. 'Permeation', he continued, 'is a dangerous game, and especially dangerous for middle-class socialists', since 'We are only half-washed from bourgeois slush, and if we do not keep quite clear of the whole mud-bath, we soon end by wallowing again in dirty contentment, amid the approving grunts of our friends and relatives'. Labour members, in his view, were essential because 'No one else can be trusted, just at present, to grapple with our plutocratic society; no one else knows so well where the boot of poverty pinches the toe of labour'. 'Since we want working-class legislation', it followed, 'We had better get, as soon as we can, working class legislators, and since we want socialist legislation we had better get socialist legislators'. The South Australian Society, Marson concluded, was enjoying a far greater proportional power than its London counterpart, in 'reaping the reward of its honesty'.[35] As has been seen, his active courting of working-class recruits – albeit trade union functionaries – to the Society would have been viewed by many in London as heretical. Shaw for one maintained throughout a lifespan of exceptional length that, in order for the Fabians to keep 'their ancient intellectual leadership in the Socialist movement', they had to remain 'a minority of cultural snobs and genuinely scientific socialist tacticians, few enough to be negligible in the electoral count of noses, and with no time to spend on the conversion and elementary Socialist education of illiterates and political novices'.[36]

DAVID CHARLESTON

The South Australian Society's sources of support were not restricted to its unionist adherents, but included the Single Tax Leagues and the broader radical constituency of the colonial Forward Movement. Charleston was an activist in all three spheres and may well have been partly responsible for linking Marson with them. When Marson arrived in South Australia in 1889 Charleston was president of the United Trades and Labour Council. By the time of Marson's departure for England three years later he was one of the three United Labor Party MPs whose election to the Legislative Council in 1891 had given the Labor Party representation in an Australian parliament for the first time. A Cornishman by birth, a marine engineer by trade and a follower of the Single Tax doctrines of Henry George by conviction, Charleston had arrived in South Australia in 1884, with a solid record of involvement in the affairs of the British trade union and land reform movements. He was also a Rechabite who figured prominently in the colonial temperance movement; an outspoken advocate of women's suffrage and the president of the Working Women's Trade Union for tailoresses and seamstresses; the chairman of the Eight Hours Protection Society; an energetic supporter of the Homestead League which sought to alleviate unemployment by settling workers on rural land; and one of the first UTLC members to become a Justice of the Peace.

Early evidence of Charleston's willingness to transcend the narrowly trade unionist perspectives implicit in his capacity as an Amalgamated Society of Engineers delegate to the UTLC was forthcoming in episodes such as the inclusion of the Employers' Union in his presidential toast to 'kindred associations', on the occasion of the retirement of the UTLC secretary W.A. Robinson in 1890. What was termed his Single Tax 'bias' caused offence to some, as did his invitations to reporters from Adelaide's more conservative daily, the *Register*, to attend his meetings. While Buttery, his successor as president of the UTLC, told an audience of 10,000 at the great maritime strike meeting in 1890 that 'It was no use complaining of bad laws, unjustly and inequitably administered, for the labouring classes had the power in their own hands to alter them' and 'The next fight would be at the next election',[37] Charleston's election-night speech a year later expressed the more conciliatory hope that 'now the Labor Party was represented there would be no more recourse to the barbarous system of strikes, but that their difficulties would be adjusted by intelligent and honourable means' and that 'a new era was dawning – not an era of selfishness and individualism, but of co-operation'.[38]

Charleston's interpretation of socialism similarly laid emphasis on co-operation. 'Those engaged in an industry', he told members of the Australian Natives' Association, 'must control the capital machinery used in that industry, and by being freed from exploiters in the shape of employer and interest receiver, the products will be theirs to be divided between them according to the service each has received in the production'.[39] 'The principle of progressive taxation', he said in parliament, 'was to equalise things by giving greater opportunities to the greater number'.[40] His convictions may well have been the firmer for being based, in part, on firsthand observation. As in its sister colonies, the South Australian government accepted the responsibility for roads, railways and water conservation – together with the provision of advances for the settlement of Crown lands – a situation which has been characterised by Métin as *le Socialisme sans Doctrine*.[41] Charleston's familiarity with such projects – socialist in their form, as Métin argued, if not necessarily in their inspiration – rendered him the more receptive to Marson's Fabian message. He was among the South Australian members who followed Marson into the London Society in 1892, and his membership was maintained until 1911, when all but one of the group had long since resigned or been excluded.

THE LABOUR MOVEMENT

Charleston's passage from the UTLC presidency to the parliament coincided with a watershed in the wider affairs of the colony's labour movement.[42] Hitherto, carriage of the political activities of the United Trades and Labour Council had largely rested with the Parliamentary Committee established by the UTLC in 1885 as a means of lobbying and disseminating publicity. A platform – including payment of MPs; imposition of a tariff for protective rather than revenue purposes; increase in the current land tax; extension of employers' liability to merchant seamen; introduction of a factory and workshops act; and a mining on property act – was adopted by the UTLC at the parliamentary committee's recommendation on 21 January 1887. Reference to socialism of any sort was conspicuous by its absence, but the committee drew widely on examples from Europe and America, and Charleston is credited by some as having been 'certainly one obvious transmitter of such ideas'.[43]

The omission of socialism from the platform reflected, in part, the labour movement's fundamental moderation. At the 1887 and 1890 Legislative Assembly elections, UTLC support was directed to such liberals as broadly endorsed its platform. 'If returned', it has been noted, 'they were expected to safeguard the interests of workingmen by voting against legislation considered detrimental to labour's cause and to promote them by urging the initiation and passing of favourable measures'.[44] As one close observer of the period has pointed out, working-class people's discontent about the drudgery of their labour and the paucity of their pay did not assume a radical or purposeful form until the agitators among them opened their eyes to the possibility of change.[45] South Australia, however, had produced no counterpart for the fiery William Spence, who led the shearers to victory over the station owners in New South Wales in 1888. No homegrown William Lane had raised a local following for dreams such as those which were later shattered in the Utopian communities established by followers of Lane at Cosme and New Australia in Paraguay.

The ascendancy established in New South Wales by the new unionism of unskilled and semi-skilled workers had no parallel within the UTLC, where the relatively conservative craft unions – concerned primarily with protecting the welfare and privileges of the skilled workers who made up their memberships – remained predominant. Backing the more enlightened forms of capital was, in the view of the majority, the best means available for improving wages and the conditions of work. Challenges to the conventional industrial and political wisdom were correspondingly unpopular. In 1889, for example, Charleston's Single Tax sympathies resulted in pressure on him to step down prematurely from his UTLC presidency. The defeat of J.N. Birks as a ULP candidate at the 1894 elections was similarly attributed by some to Birks' being a Single Taxer, and was used to justify the reimposition of arrangements which limited ULP preselection to candidates from organisations which were eligible to affiliate with the UTLC.[46]

An article in the *Weekly Herald* for 30 November 1894 argued that 'The United Labor Party surely ought not to feel so strong that it can dispense with any section, or that it can in the end gain anything by limiting its own field of choice',[47] but two weeks later, on 13 December, a plebiscite supported the more restrictive option by 1,291 votes to ninety-nine. The result reflected the grip on the party of a cautious craft unionist liberalism – averse alike to electoral risk and ideological contagion – but the plebiscite would not necessarily have been opposed by the Fabians. Marson may well have expressed the view of the South Australian Society in his *Church Reformer* article:

> It is a good bit of class legislation we want, to counteract the class legislation now on our Statute books. *When this has been achieved, and there is something like equality*, then it will be absurd to choose or reject a candidate because he has learnt or not learnt any trade or profession or craft other than law-making.[48]

Meanwhile, consideration was given by the Parliamentary Committee as early as 1886 to the UTLC's raising funds for the support of direct working-class representation in parliament. The passage of legislation providing for payment of MPs for a single parliament in 1887 and its extension on a permanent basis in 1890 – together with the defeat of the 1890 Maritime Strike and its strengthening, in relative terms, of the 'new unionism' – were catalytic in finally bringing the earlier era to its end. A meeting convened by the UTLC at the Selborne Hotel in Pirie Street, Adelaide, on 7 January 1891, then agreed that a Legislative Council Elections Committee – which shortly became the Council of the United Labor Party of South Australia – should be established. Committee members included the parliamentary committee of the UTLC, together with the secretaries of the Maritime, Building and Iron Trades Councils, the South Australian Democratic Club, the German Workingmen's Association and the North Adelaide Workingmen's Social and Patriotic Association. Campaign funds were raised and a plebiscite of members of committee affiliates selected a slate of three candidates – Charleston, his future fellow Fabian, Guthrie, and A.A. Kirkpatrick – whose election as what was characterised by some as a 'Labour Wedge' within the Legislative Council in May 1891 marked the parliamentary debut of the ULP.[49]

JOHN McPHERSON

A further meeting, to select ULP candidates for the 1893 Assembly elections, was convened on 11 July 1891 by the secretary of the Legislative Council Elections Committee, J.A. McPherson.[50] McPherson was shortly to join Marson and Charleston in ensuring that their South Australian Fabian Society gave practical expression to the indivisibility of the socialist and labour causes. Like Charleston, he was a relative newcomer to the colony from Britain, where his apprenticeship as a printer had been served with the Free Press Printing and Publishing Company in Aberdeen. The positions to which he was elected within his union, the South Australian Typographical Society, included vice-president, president and delegate to the UTLC. Within the UTLC, he rose to be general secretary and secretary to the committee responsible for the construction of the Adelaide Trades Hall, and within the ULP he became party secretary and parliamentary leader. At the peak of his career, he was concurrently either the secretary or president of his union, the UTLC and both the organisational and parliamentary wings of the ULP, in a combination perhaps unparalleled in either prior or subsequent labour movement experience. 'He was', in a contemporary view, 'an indefatigible worker, and was endowed with no small measure of organising talent, while he rapidly made himself master of the forms and requirements of Parliamentary practice', to the point where he achieved recognition as 'an "old hand" with whom it was by no means safe to trifle'.[51]

Further positions held by McPherson included initiator and inaugural secretary of the Working Women's Trade Union (which Charleston chaired); member of the State Children's Council; and publisher – as chairman of the Co-operative Printing and Publishing Company – of the party journal, the *Weekly Herald*. Familiar at first hand with unemployment following an 1888 strike at the Adelaide *Register*, where he worked as a compositor, he believed, it was said, 'in conciliation being tried first and in making strikes the very last resource in settling trade disputes', while 'When once the strike was entered upon, against what he considered to be an abuse, he was the last man to admit defeat'. His efforts to resolve the Maritime Strike were recognised through the presentation to him of a purse of sovereigns. In parliament the issues to which he devoted special attention included shops and factories legislation, the introduction of a graduated land tax and opposition to the alienation of further crown land. He was a supporter of the introduction of votes for women in 1893–94, and campaigned energetically but unsuccessfully for the early closing of hotels. Reflecting in part, perhaps, the Fabian influence, he placed the Liberals on warning that the ULP regarded them as having become too conservative, and would in future throw its weight behind legislation which corresponded with labour policy, irrespective of the side of the House from which it originated. 'He lived and worked', it was further said, 'to find solutions for many of life's graver problems, and especially those affecting social relations and the right of the great masses of the people to more leisure, comfort and happiness'. His death from cancer in 1897, at the age of thirty-eight, was seen by some as being attributable in part to his grief over a falling out of the former unionist Fabians and Charleston's subsequent withdrawal from the ULP.

SINGLE TAXERS

Charleston's Single Tax convictions made him a major spokesperson for the South Australian Single Tax Leagues, whose emergence may well have contributed to Marson's choice of the colony as his new home, and, perhaps, to Charleston's introduction to Fabian socialism. The British popularity of the Single Tax stemmed in part from the fact that the grinding poverty in Ireland and much of rural England was attributed by many to absentee landlords. Similar discontents agitated South Australia, where a 'pale imitation' of the systematic colonisation doctrines of Gibbon Wakefield's National Colonisation Society[52] required the local authorities to refrain from selling land at the low prices set by market forces at the time of settlement, in favour of prices high enough to ensure that the buyers were men of substance. The profits, Wakefield and his followers believed, could then be used for bringing out poorer colonists from Britain, to develop on behalf of the proprietors the land which they were unable to afford for themselves. In the event, however, the plan's expectations were largely frustrated. Much of the land was bought by absentee *rentiers*, whose efforts to develop their holdings were minimal. The workers, whose livelihoods the activities of the landowners were to have provided, found themselves instead impoverished by chronic unemployment and underemployment. Resentment of 'the wrongs, the hardships and injustices' inflicted by the system on its victims[53] gave rise in about 1890 to the proliferation of Single Tax Leagues in Adelaide and its suburbs, as well as to demands for the introduction of the Single Tax in order to bring about land nationalisation.

For practical purposes, any differences between the socialist and Single Tax camps in South Australia were inconsequential. Uprooting the monopoly of land was vital, the Leagues' members argued in their journal, the *Pioneer*, because 'Then, and then only, will the way be clear for socialism'.[54] The arrival of *Fabian Essays in Socialism* from Britain in the second half of 1891 drew from the same source the accolade that 'This collection of essays and lectures represents the principles, aims and purposes of the modern Socialistic school of reformers in such a way as to disarm all factious opposition'. It was the view of the *Pioneer* that 'A tone calm and dispassionate, a humanitarian spirit of noble endeavour combined with sound logical reasoning and treatment will make these essays a valuable addition to the library of every student of social science'.[55] The plaudits of the Single Taxers would have pleased the editor of the collection, Shaw, whose postscript to the Jubilee Edition in 1948 defined the purpose of the essays as 'to rescue Socialism and Communism from the barricades, from the pseudo-democracy of the Party System, from confusion with the traditional heterodoxies of anti-clericalism, individualist anti-State republicanism, and middle-class Bohemian anarchism; in short, to make it a constitutional movement in which the most respectable citizens and families may enlist, without forfeiting the least scrap of their social or spiritual standing'.[56]

The program advocated by the *Pioneer* in its issue for 11 July 1891 resembled in every significant respect that which was promulgated subsequently in South Australian Fabian Society Tracts and other publications. The components included – in addition to 'National-isation of Land by gradually increasing the Tax on all Unimproved Land Values, and the general abolition of all Taxes on Thrift and Industry' – such Fabian preoccupations as 'Nationalisation and working of all such branches of industry which are in their nature now or may some day become monopolies, viz, Railways, Post and Telegraphs, National Irrigation and Waterworks, Harbors, Mines and Forests, etc.',[57] together with adult compulsory education, social security, and the municipalisation of gas, markets, waterworks and tramways.

Fabian Society members were made welcome in the columns of the *Pioneer*, where Society Tracts on topics such as *What Socialism Is* and *Some Objections to Socialism* first made their appearance. Further hospitality on the part of the *Pioneer* was extended for protracted controversies involving Fabians, including, as will be seen, a notable exchange of polemics between the Society's A.W. Rayment, a tailor in the copper-mining town of Kapunda, and Hirsch. The cordiality was not one-sided; Society luminaries of the stamp of Charleston and Guthrie were as much at home on Single Tax League platforms as on those of the Society itself, and the Society's lectures and publications gave prominence to Single Tax thought. A letter published in the *Pioneer* over the signature 'A Fabian Socialist' concluded: 'Let us then – Socialists and Single Taxers – brothers in the sacred cause of God and Humanity – unite our forces and fight shoulder to shoulder against all the powers of evil which, unvanquished, will inevitably wreck our civilisation'.[58]

THE FORWARD MOVEMENT

The Single Tax Leagues in turn linked Charleston with the Forward Movement, whose leaders included such notable pillars of non-conformist opinion as the Reverend Hugh Gilmore. Gilmore's adoption as minister for the North Adelaide Primitive Methodist Church shortly prior to Marson's arrival in Adelaide had led to the establishment of the ecumenical Christian Commonwealth group as a means of helping the poor, the unemployed, the sick and those newly arrived in the colony. A Society for the Study of Christian Sociology had also emerged, and it would have been in character for Marson to have involved himself in both bodies – not least, perhaps, as compensation for the failure of the South Australian Branch of the Guild of St Matthew, whose sole member he seems to have remained. Gilmore became a notable first president for the Adelaide Single Tax Society, whose lecture on Single Tax thought at the Victoria Hall on 24 April 1891 prompted the chairman Sir George Grey to observe: 'I have never heard an address so eloquent, arguments so forcible, or seen an audience so moved'. It was Gilmore's strong belief that the introduction of the Single Tax would constitute the means for an orderly and peaceful transition to socialism. His death in October 1891 robbed Marson of a valuable colleague who might otherwise have figured prominently in the South Australian Fabian Society's affairs. The *Pioneer* grieved that 'when he left us he was the central figure of South Australian life, and the tremors of sorrow for his untimely end were felt in the remotest corners of the colony'.[59]

More generally, Gilmore's passing was a major setback to the 'earnest, well-meaning reform groups' of which the Forward Movement was constituted.[60] The religious roots of Forward Movement thinking – and the group's influence within the labour movement – were strikingly reflected by the assertion of the United Labor Party journal, the *Weekly Herald*, that 'We cannot recognise any other than Christian socialism, which necessarily must work for order, and not disorder, for right, and not wrong'.[61] A further charac-teristic was the courtesy and mutual tolerance which enabled adherents to exchange ideas amiably at Mrs J. Medway Day's 'Friday

afternoon gatherings for helping on the Forward Movement', and
to sing in harmony what is seen by some to have been the movement's
favourite hymn:

> The land, the land, 'twas God who gave the land;
> The land, the land, the ground on which we stand;
> Why should we be beggars with the ballot in our hand?
> God gave the land for the people.[62]

The outlook of the Forward Movement was encapsulated in a
lecture on the 'new political economy' delivered by Gilmore in
March 1891. The challenges facing South Australia, in his view,
were the achievement of social equality; the abolition of sectional
interests; and enabling parliament to legislate in the public interest,
through the introduction of majority rule. The new political
economy, his lecture concluded, 'believes that the glaring inequalities
which are at once the disgrace and the menace of our nineteenth
century are not of Divine origin, but of human intervention, and
it seeks to show how they can be overcome'.[63] As in the case of the
Land Reform Union nearly a decade earlier, the values of the
company in which Marson now found himself were 'faith in land
reform, God and parliament'.[64]

LUCY AND JAMES MORICE

The Forward Movement provided the South Australian Society with
middle-class radicals of the stamp of Lucy and James Morice. Lucy
was the niece and constant companion of the influential writer,
preacher, reformer and feminist Catherine Spence. It is said of her
that 'Pretty, poised and sociable, Lucy read avidly and developed an
idealistic vision of a just society; she frequently despaired of its
realisation'.[65] Her formative years were shaped powerfully by the
Unitarian faith and radical politics of her immediate and extended
family circles, and on 20 March 1886 she became the bride of a fellow
radical – the newly-appointed Librarian of the South Australian
Parliament, James Morice, who had worked as a clerk for the South
Australian Survey and Crown Lands Department following his
arrival in the colony from Britain in 1877. The Unitarian service
at the family home in Glenelg marked the beginning of a long-
lasting, mutually supportive and socially constructive partnership
in the best tradition of such other notable Fabian couples as the
Webbs, the Shaws, the Peases, the Wallases and the Oliviers. As

Beatrice Webb confided to her diary in 1935: 'Have there ever been five more respectable, cultivated and mutually devoted, and be it added, successful couples – the ultra-essence of British morality, comfort and enlightenment – than the Peases, Shaws, Wallases, Oliviers and Webbs, who founded the Fabian Society during the first half-century from 1883?'.[66] The Morices were on visiting terms with Marson and his wife Clotilda, following their marriage on 20 May 1890 – where Marson's composer friend and future fellow London Fabian Cecil Sharp served as best man – and it may well be that their embracing of the Fabian cause was a direct result of Marson's influence.[67] It was a source of pride to Lucy Morice that, as she once told an interviewer, 'In our home we have almost every printed line of Shaw'.[68] She and James were natural co-founders of the South Australian Fabian Society, which Marson saw as being required in the colony where his hopes for the future were now invested. James Morice became the Society's inaugural secretary.

Further interests to which Lucy actively devoted herself while she was a South Australian Society or London Society member included the Woman's League, which she established in conjunction with Catherine Spence in 1895 in 'an effort to educate women politically and to form a real Woman's Party to work for the interests of women and children';[69] the all-women South Australian Co-operative Clothing Co., which she and Spence established as an anti-sweating venture in 1902; the Kindergarten Union; the School for Mothers Institute; and the Women's Political Association, which she initiated in 1909 at the instigation of her sister Fabian from Victoria, Vida Goldstein. All Lucy Morice's ventures reflected Forward Movement concerns, and it may well be that they served in part as avenues through which she was able to gain wider audiences for Fabian policies and philosophy. The report of a Women's League meeting on sweating in July 1896 refers to Lucy Morice's reading of a Fabian Tract to the League four weeks earlier. The title of the Tract was *Sweat, its Cause and Cure*.[70] Other founder South Australian Fabians who may well also have been Forward Movement adherents included Walter H. Baker, William S. Bickford and Arthur F. Pearson.

THE SOUTH AUSTRALIAN FABIAN SOCIETY

Marson launched the South Australian Society in 1891, with an initial membership of seven. It may well have been no coincidence that this was the same number of South Australians as gained admission to the London Society the following year. Marson, Charleston and the Morices apart, those who were members of both bodies in 1892 were Baker, Bickford and Pearson, and their example was followed by McPherson in 1893.[71] Once again the overwhelming preponderance of Webb's *nouvelle couche sociale* is apparent. Prior to becoming a member of parliament, Charleston held the position of clerk of works for the Roads Board at Hackney Bridge and superintended the installation of the Australian Copper Company's plant at Moonta.[72] Pearson, who succeeded James Morice as the Society's second secretary, was the manager of George Robertson & Co., booksellers, and later an Unley municipal councillor. Bickford was a Glenelg councillor, and Baker the proprietor of a pharmacy in Parkside and a member of the Royal Society of South Australia and the Council of the South Australian Pharmaceutical Society. A further Society member, George Dankeld, was a Kensington butcher who served on the Kensington and Norwood Council prior to his election to parliament in 1905 for the state seat of Torrens, and in 1912 for the federal seat of Boothby.

Marson, it seems plain, regarded the South Australian Society as a direct extension of the parent body he had left behind him in Britain. The first South Australian Tract – an adaptation of the London Society's Tract 4, *What Socialism Is*, which was issued as a separate publication by October 1891, after being printed initially as an article in the *Pioneer* – carried the attribution 'South Australian Branch Fabian Society's Tracts – No. 1'. The question arises of whether, and if so how, branch status was conferred by the London Society in the face of its otherwise unswerving refusal to take responsibility for – or in any way approve – such overseas bodies as 'sprang up and called themselves Fabian'. The South Australian Society was almost certainly the first Fabian body outside Britain, preceding the Bombay Fabian Society of 1892, and it is at least likely that the issue of whether overseas groups were to be accorded recognition had at the time neither been considered nor foreseen.[73] In such circumstances, branch status may have been approved arbitrarily by the London secretary, Pease, through an administrative decision independent of the executive. Alternatively, Marson may have interpreted agreement by the London Society to the South Australians' adapting and republishing its tracts as an implicit conferral of branch status, or adopted it unilaterally, on the basis of his 'special relationship' with the relatively few London activists who were his seniors in the Society. Irrespective of which explanation is correct, the use of the attribution 'South Australian Fabian Society' for subsequent Tracts suggests strongly that the situation was promptly regretted and rectified, and the general opposition to overseas branches may well have applied as of that date.

A report delivered to the Society by Marson on 16 April 1892 disclosed that numbers had grown to thirty-seven, while in the first six months of the Society's existence four Tracts had been published and sixteen lectures delivered in Adelaide and its suburbs. The forty-six members who made up the Society at its 1893 Annual General Meeting included two municipal councillors and four MPs. The Working Women's Trade Union rooms at Victoria Square West provided a venue for regular monthly meetings, which were held throughout 1892 and 1893, while in 1892 there were local groups of Society members among the largely working-class populations of Port Pirie and Port Augusta. The Society was said to have 'plenty of cash',[74] and a postscript to *What Socialism Is* announced accordingly that 'Copies of the "Fabian Essays" will be sent gratis to any Institute, Public Library or other institution applying to the Hon. Secretary'.[75]

POLITICAL EDUCATION BY LECTURING

In 1893 the London Society received reports from South Australia that 'five or six [members] are constantly lecturing on Socialism and similar subjects'.[76] Once more, Marson was drawing on the London model. Lecturing was an activity to which the London Fabians attached major importance. William Clarke, a prominent figure among their number and a Fabian essayist, observed of the Society ten years after its inception: 'It is in lectures that its work has largely consisted'. A report commissioned by the executive from a special committee in 1911 confirmed that lecturing 'was still the most effective form of political education', and took the view that its function was 'to act as a medium of education, propaganda and discussion on socialist and other issues, for the benefit not only of members but also of the public at large'.[77] The London Society's first lecture was given on 25 January 1885, when J.G. Stapleton spoke on 'Social Conditions in England with a view to Social Reconstruction or Development'.[78] A lecture subcommittee of the executive decided in 1888 that the formal business of the fortnightly meetings for Society members should be followed by lectures on the case for and against socialism. These were begun on 21 September by Sidney Webb, repeated by request at Cambridge and Leicester, and ultimately edited in 1889 as the famous *Fabian Essays in Socialism*. Their success also gave rise to an annual series of Fabian Autumn Lectures which continued well into the new century.[79] The essays lasted even longer, and are still in print. Shaw's preface to the fourth edition in 1931 described them as 'inextinguishable'.[80]

The number of lectures delivered annually reached an initial peak of around 3,340 in 1892 and 1893 – after 700 in 1889 and 324 a year earlier – then peaked again between 1908 and 1914, when it is estimated that 'the quantity was greater than ever before'. In the case of London, platforms were sought predominantly from such radical groups of city workmen as liberal associations, radical clubs, secular societies, co-operatives, working-men's colleges, debating clubs and trades councils, while local branches of the Society were given guidance on how to achieve maximum effect from lecturing through the pages of *Fabian News*.[81] Special efforts such as the Lancashire Campaign of 1900 were mounted to bring Fabian lecturers in front of provincial audiences and the Hutchinson Trust legacy which the Society received in 1894 was used in part to fund touring lecturers, one of whom was the future prime minister, Ramsay MacDonald.[82] The Charing Cross Parliament debating society of the late 1880s was in part a response to the need for leading Fabians to improve their skills in public speaking, as were the elocution courses which Shaw organised for the Society in 1892 and the Speakers' Class which was established in 1912.

Marson apart, the South Australian Society's lecturers included an indefatigable Congregational Church minister, the Reverend J. Reed Glasson, and the Wesleyan Reverend G.E. Rowe. The 9 July 1892 issue of the *Pioneer* noted that 'There are very few men in Australia more capable of expounding Socialism or more conversant with socialist thought than Mr. Glasson',[83] and Glasson was zealous in living up to its accolade. A lecture on 'The Progress and Position of Socialism', delivered for the Unley and Parkside Branch of the Single Tax League on 7 June 1892 was followed by a series of six addresses on 'Christian Socialism', with topics including 'The Twofold Mission of Christ', 'The Awakening of the Churches', 'Problems of Poverty', 'Socialism Christian and non-Christian',

'Competition and Co-operation' and 'Incentives and Rewards', while on 1 December 1892, he was reported as speaking at Port Pirie on 'Socialism. What It Is and Is Not'.

Rowe, for his part, had no hesitation in telling the congregation of the Wesleyan Church at Prospect in February the same year that the triumph of the ULP meant the downfall of 'individual mammonism' and 'the rise of a new social era'.[84] He also lectured for a number of trade unions on 'The New Crusade'. Marson, Glasson and Rowe were not the only Adelaide clergymen of the day willing to speak out in favour of Single Tax or socialist thought. The Reverend S. Fairey, the Reverend James Bickford, the Reverend A.C. Sutherland, the Reverend J. Day Thompson and the Reverend A.N. McDonald were reported by the *Pioneer* between June and December 1892, as bearing public witness to the socialist implications of the Christian message. It is likely that some of them followed the example of their colleagues Marson, Glasson and Rowe in becoming Fabian Society members.

A further regular speaker for the Society was Rayment. The *Pioneer* numbered him among its most prolific contributors, and regularly carried advertisements for his pamphlets, *The Rights of Labor* and *The Phenomenon of Interest*. Addresses by Rayment, such as those on 'Compensation' at the Democratic Club on 20 September 1891, and on 'The Rights of Labor and How to Obtain Them' for the Adelaide Branch of the Single Tax League the following night, were punctuated by more sustained efforts, such as his prolonged and spirited controversy with Hirsch in the *Pioneer*, and the lecture series on 'Land, Labor, Capital and Co-operation', which he gave for the Fabian Society over three successive nights (5, 6 and 7 March 1892) at Marson's St Oswald's Schoolrooms in Parkside, the Democratic Club and the Norwood Town Hall respectively. Later that year, the topics and speakers for successive monthly meetings of the Society at the Working Women's Trade Union Rooms were, on 2 July, a discussion of the first Fabian essay; on 6 August, Charleston on 'Exchange, Value and Wages'; on 3 September, Guthrie on 'Land Taxation'; on 1 October, Guthrie on 'Wages'; on 5 November, the Society's Annual General Meeting; and on 6 December, Guthrie (for the third time in four months) again on 'Wages'. Speakers who addressed the Society in 1893 included W.H. Pope on 'Capitalism', Buttery on 'The Social Outlook', Archibald on 'Referendum', Glasson on 'Some Thoughts on the Growing Unrest', Rayment on 'The Unemployed Problem' and Charleston on 'Aims of the Fabian Society'.

ROBERT GUTHRIE

Guthrie took over the presidency of the Society at its Annual General Meeting on 5 November 1892, and the Society participated vigorously in Labor's campaign at the 1893 House of Assembly elections, where Price and Archibald were successful. Their seats were not the only reward the Society received for its efforts. The annual report for the year ended January 1894 noted that 'quite a number of Fabians were successful at the poll in the elections for the House of Assembly in April, and in no single instance was there a failure', while 'In municipal matters our propaganda is beginning to be felt, and in several municipalities our program is all but accepted'.[85]

Guthrie's accession to the presidency was a triumphant vindication of the trade unionisation of the Society which Marson had so consistently pursued. When Guthrie decided to leave the sea in 1887 and to settle in South Australia, the labour movement gained one of its most notable pioneers, and his fellow seamen gained an organisation which was seen by some as 'a monument to himself which will be remembered for generations'.[86] His concern for the welfare of sailors and the organisation of maritime industry was prompted by his years of service before the mast – largely in China, where in the course of one memorable year he was wrecked in three successive ships. His knowledge of the appalling working conditions within the industry was encyclopedic.

The 1906 Royal Commission on the Navigation Bill – in whose proceedings Guthrie was prominent following his election to the Senate in 1903 – concluded that 'The condition of the seaman is little better than it was 50 years ago, although the shipping world in other respects has been revolutionised'.[87] His efforts as secretary of the South Australian Branch of the Federated Seamen's Union of Australasia, as the union's federal president and as a member of the state and federal parliaments were consistently directed at correcting these deficiencies, and gained him a reputation for being 'perhaps without a peer in the splendid work he did for the betterment of seamen's conditions'.[88] The Navigation Act which resulted from the Royal Commission was widely known as 'Guthrie's Bill', and Guthrie himself was often referred to as 'Australia's Plimsoll'. Further recognition of his qualities and achievements was reflected in his appointment, in 1902, as founder secretary and treasurer of the Federated Council of Australasian Labour Unions (the forerunner of the Australian

Council of Trade Unions). Like Charleston, he was a justice of the peace, a temperance campaigner who achieved senior office within the Independent Order of Rechabites, and a supporter of the Homestead League. His *Australian Dictionary of Biography* entry reads in part: 'It is said of him that "He was true to his mates", and he had many of them'.[89]

THE FABIAN TRACTS

The attention devoted by the South Australian Society to Tracts and other publications again exemplifies the role played by the London Society as a model for Marson's activities. That the early London Fabians were gifted drafters of pamphlets and administrative projects is acknowledged even by the Society's more acerbic critics.[90] The number of Fabian Tracts and leaflets distributed at particular points in the Society's history has been described as a more important measure of Fabian influence than the size of its membership. The Society's origins as a response to widespread and persistent poverty were reflected in its choice of topic for the first Tract: *Why are the Many Poor?* Tract 2 – written for the Society by Shaw as *A Manifesto* – raised, *inter alia*, the notably un-Fabian proposition subsequently adopted by Society members on a majority vote, that 'We would rather face a Civil War than such another century of suffering as the present one has been'. Tract 3 was *To Provident Landlords and Capitalists: A Suggestion and a Warning*, again from Shaw, and, as has been seen, Tract 4 was *What Socialism Is*, attributed to Charlotte Wilson and others, and adapted by the South Australian Fabians as their inaugural publication. The circulation of Society leaflets peaked at between 300,000 and 350,000 in 1891–92, during the Fabian campaign for the London County Council. Fabian Tracts peaked at a level in excess of 150,000 a year or so later. A leaflet by Pease, *How Trade Unions Benefit Workmen*, sold widely within the labour movement for a lengthy period, as did Tract 82, *The Workmen's Compensation Act: what it means, and how to make use of it*. Tract 5, *Facts For Socialists*, was another bestseller, as were Tract 42, *Christian Socialism*; Tract 76, *Houses for the People*; Tract 78, *Socialism and the Teaching of Christ*; and Tract 109, *Cottage Plans and Common Sense*. The publishing program reflected the image of the Society in the minds of its members as 'a body for the study of socialist problems and the publication of the results of the study'.

'If there was a dilemma at all for the Society', a principal writer on
the topic asserts, 'it was whether to make its principal concern the
scientific investigation of social and socialist problems at the higher
level, or to devote itself mainly to "educating the masses" '.[91]

Any dilemma Marson and his South Australians may have
perceived the issue to present was resolved firmly in favour of
educating the masses. The South Australian Fabian Society's First
Tract - *What Socialism Is* - was, as has been seen, an adaptation
to local conditions of the London Society Tracts 4 and 13. South
Australian Fabian Tracts 2 and 5, *Questions for Parliamentary
Candidates*, were adaptations of London Society Tract 24; South
Australian Fabian Tract 4, *Questions for Candidates for Municipal
Office*, was an adaptation of London Society Tracts 26, 27 and 28;
and the leaflet *Vote! Vote! Vote!* was an adaptation of London Society
Tract 43. Only South Australian Fabian Tracts 3, *Some Objections
to Socialism*, and 7, *Land Values Assessment Bill (Part XIX)*, appear
to have been original contributions. In each case the intention was
education rather than research.

A further distinguishing quality of the South Australian Tracts
was the precedence given to the issue of land over the issue of poverty.
In place of the London Society's initial attention to the reasons for
poverty, 'South Australian Branch Fabian Society's Tracts - No. 1'
reflected in its opening passage the embittered character of local
feeling over land which so closely united the colony's Fabians and
Single Taxers:

> We have already parted with eight and a half millions of acres, and so
> absolutely have we thereby delivered ourselves over bound hand and foot
> into the hands of these landowners that 66 absentees hold no less than
> £2,377,016 worth of land in the City of Adelaide alone, and their per-
> mission is required before we may build or live thereon . . . Out of every
> 64 persons in the colony, 56 are disinherited and own no land, while
> only one in 64 owns more than £1000 worth.[92]

Alienation of land, together with monopoly ownership of industrial plant and privileged access to education, were seen by the South
Australian Fabians no less than their Single Tax associates as
underpinning an inequality which owed nothing to 'personal merit
or demerit'. *What Socialism Is* posed the question 'What do you think
of it?', and argued in response:

> An ordinary man thinks it is bad and unjust and cruel. If you are rich
> you perhaps think it is a good thing that it fosters emulation and

enterprise, and prevents things from stagnating at a dead level. If you are poor, or know anything of your neighbours, you know well that it fosters only despair, recklessness and brutality among the very poor; meanness, envy and snobbery among the middle classes; arrogance, wastefulness and callousness among the rich. Great poverty means disease and ugliness, drunkenness and violence, stunted bodies and darkened minds. Great riches means flunkeyism and folly, insolence and servility, too often bad example, false standards of worth, and the destruction of all incentive to noble and useful work in those who could best educate themselves for it. Great poverty and great riches side by side mean the perversion of industry to the production of frippery and luxury, while wholesomeness and useful foods and clothes and dwellings are not possessed by all; while education, music and the arts, learning and refinement are apt to be left out of the count.

Socialists, the pamphlet concluded, should 'try to get the land and machinery made the property of the whole people, to free all education, and to secure the whole product of his work to the worker'.[93]

SOCIALISM AND THE SOUTH AUSTRALIAN FABIANS

The Society's advocacy of socialism was pursued in its Tract 3, *Some Objections to Socialism Considered in the Light of Common Sense.* The Tract appeared initially in the *Pioneer* between 6 February and 5 March 1892, as a three-part series over the byline of 'A Member of the S.A. Fabian Society'. It was the author's view that socialism no longer had to contend generally with religious objections, since the churches had begun to realise – 'rather late in the day' – that the Christian message obligated them to 'at least inquire into any means suggested for the amelioration of the lot of the toiling and starving millions'. Instead, the Tract singled out first, as 'one of the commonest and silliest' objections to socialism, 'the belief of "superficial people" that "Socialism is a system devised without a proper consideration of human nature; and that the natural depravity and selfishness of the people must render it unworkable"'. In fact, it was argued, the reverse was the case, with socialism being needed precisely in order to curb 'that very depravity and selfishness', so that:

The selfish person who wishes to heap up riches for himself, or to collect more than he has rightly earned, will not have, as now, all the Powers of the earth, the law courts, the police and if necessary the soldiery, enlisted in his service, though paid by the whole people. On the contrary, he will have every one in the community against him, because it will be in every one's interest that no one else shall get more than his share of the good things, and that he does his fair share of work in return.[94]

The second objection to socialism identified in the Tract was that it would stop progress and take away the incentive for hard work 'because every one will be so happy and comfortable that no one will want to improve his own or the world's lot any more'. This was refuted by the Tract, on the grounds that fame and job satisfaction had greater importance than wealth as motivators for work, creativity and progress, while 'the smart businessman's capacity is woefully wasted now, for instead of being used for the perfecting of the supply of goods to the people it is simply used to get as much out of the transfer of goods from the producer to the consumer as possible, and often absolutely in preventing a full supply when the goods are required'.[95] Finally, the Tract highlighted a third objection to socialism in the contention that socialist enterprises such as the post office and the railways could not be made to pay, which was rejected because, in the Tract's view, any surplus of earnings over expenses represented a withholding of a part of the labour value involved from workers or consumers. It was the Tract's conclusion that, when all the objections to socialism 'are once looked fairly and square in the face in the light of reason and common humanity, they immediately wither up and show themselves for what they are – inconsequent fallacies only fit to be consigned to the limbo of unmasked bogies and exploded superstitions'.

A further statement of the South Australian Fabian position was set out in the address on *The Rights of Man; and How to Obtain Them* which Rayment delivered to the Adelaide Branch of the Single Tax League on 21 September 1891, and later had distributed as a *Pioneer* article and a privately printed pamphlet. Rayment saw the root of society's troubles in the fact that 'Under our present social arrangements a working man, unless it be an exceptional case, does not get what he earns; the remainder goes to swell the incomes of those who earn little or nothing'. This was morally wrong, in his view, because 'No matter whether it be the portion of wealth which is intended for consumption or the other portion of wealth which is intended for production, it is labour that produces it, and it is labour that is the rightful owner'. Moreover, Rayment believed, the practical consequences in terms of overproduction – and therefore unemployment – were disastrous:

What is called overproduction is not overproduction at all; it is under-pay. The value which a working man gives in his labour is greater than the value he receives in the shape of wages; hence the increasing stocks on the one hand and the deficiency of purchasing power on the other.

These considerations led him to argue strongly for 'State Socialism', which he saw as a situation where:

> The instruments of production and exchange, instead of being owned by separate individuals or separate companies of individuals competing against each other to the injury of all concerned, are thus owned by the State, that is to say, by the people collectively, and the stocks as they are produced are distributed by the State, not for profit but for use and convenience. Instead of things being made to sell, they will be made because people want them, and the quantity produced will be regulated by the demand.[96]

The Society's point was reinforced by reproducing in full in each of its pamphlets the Basis adopted by the London Fabians in 1887, with its eloquent opening passage:

> The Society consists of Socialists. It therefore aims at the re-organisation of Society by the emancipation of Land and industrial Capital from individual and class ownership, and vesting of them in the community for the general benefit.[97]

Marson, for his part, was unequivocal. In his address to the South Australian Society on 6 April 1892, he advised its members to be vigilant against 'quack nostrums for the social disease', among which he included 'especially any measures that may be, and probably will be, brought forward with a view to bursting up monopolies'. It was his strong view that, as evolutionary socialists, Fabians should concentrate on capturing monopolies for the good of the community as a whole, in preference to killing them off, which he condemned as a 'reactionary step'.[98]

ELECTIONS: FABIAN POLICIES AND PUBLICATIONS

Most of all, however, the publications of the South Australian Society sought to reinforce the Society's identity of purpose with the labour movement, by stressing policies which were also those of the UTLC and the ULP, or were calculated to appeal strongly to working-class voters. *Questions for Parliamentary Candidates* – Tract 2 – pressed for graduation of Income Tax and Death Duties and the abolition of duties on tea, cocoa, coffee and kerosene. Land, the

Tract argued, should be nationalised, along with mines and the manufacture of major items for state use, such as locomotives and water pipes, while gas, electricity and the tramways should be owned by municipalities. Municipalities, in the Tract's view should also be empowered to own markets, build rental housing and compulsorily acquire land for letting out as small tenancies and allotments. A statutory eight-hour working day was advocated, as was a Liens Act to protect workingmen's wages, a Workshop and Factory Act, legislation restricting the employment of children in industrial occupations, the use of day labour by public authorities (in preference to employment of contractors), the offer of publicly funded scholarships and the introduction of age pensions. Electorally, the Tract favoured the enfranchisement of women, proportional representation, £50 candidature deposits, the abolition of the Legislative Council and, in its place, provision for holding referenda.

Questions for Candidates for Municipal Office – Tract 4 – sought, in addition, employment by municipalities of enough inspectorial staff to enforce laws for the sanitation of houses, workrooms and factories; electric lighting of streets; night meetings of councils so that working people could take part in their proceedings; and the inclusion of particulars of municipal receipts and expenditure in annual reports distributed by councils at the lowest possible price. The second *Questions for Parliamentary Candidates* – Tract 5 – added to these demands the establishment of state farms to absorb the unemployed; opposition to the Land Grant principle for the construction of railways, harbours and other public works; and the raising of council revenues by taxation of the unimproved capital value of land. *Vote! Vote! Vote!* – circulated at the time of the 1893 Legislative Assembly elections – introduced as further requirements opposition to 'the influx of Aliens, such as Syrians, Afghans, Chinese and other Asiatics, into the Province', a state bank of issue; and a system of state insurance. This unnumbered Tract was introduced disingenuously with the claim that 'This is an Election leaflet; but it is not a Party leaflet. It applies to you, no matter what your politics are. It does not ask you to vote for any particular candidate, but only to use your vote somehow'. 'Choose your side according to your conscience', the Tract continued, 'And strike the one blow that the law allows you'. An appropriate concluding note was struck with the query 'How will you feel if you neglect to vote, and find, the day after the poll, that the candidate who best represents your interests is beaten by one vote?'. The theme of the achievability of social reform by parliamentary and constitutional means was also given emphasis in *What Socialism Is*:

> Parliaments, with all their faults, have always well served the class of the majority of their members. The English House of Commons served the country gentlemen well before 1832. Since then it has served the capitalists and employers, who won a majority at the Reform Bill, and our Parliament has faithfully served the squatters and the speculators and the rich traders in turn. It will serve the workers equally well if they choose.[99]

PARLIAMENTARY PERFORMANCE

In the event, the Society's hopes were disappointed. While its unionist core was a formidable sextet whose phase of Fabian activism was undertaken when each member's influence within the industrial movement was at its zenith, their fervour appeared to wane rapidly once they were in parliament. Irrespective of whether they ultimately turned their backs on the labour movement – like Charleston after a fracas with Price in 1897, and, as will be seen, Archibald and Guthrie over conscription in 1916 – or, like Price, held high office on the movement's behalf, they gave rise to little legislation which could not equally well have originated with Kingston's Liberals (or with the Cobdenite Liberals their London counterparts in some instances regarded as no better than the Tories, but still hoped to permeate). Their parliamentary careers were devoid of any action which could be construed as advancing the reconstruction of the social order along socialist lines. Guthrie introduced the Marine Board and Navigation Bill 1891, the Marine Board Bill 1894, the Tramways Bill 1895, the Merchant Seamen Bill 1896, the Boiler Explosions Bill 1896, and the Steam Boiler Bill 1897, and Archibald introduced bills dealing with free libraries, moneylending, workers' compensation and rent, but in ideological terms these measures were all indistinguishable from the legislation of the ministries of Kingston and earlier Liberal leaders. Archibald – perhaps the group's most effective parliamentary performer – was a member of six commissions and select committees. Charleston sat on select committees on legislation for the duplication of a private tramway between Adelaide and Unley, and on the unemployment problem, and Guthrie and McPherson sat on a shops and factories investigation committee. Their contributions, in the view of some, had some success in moderating the views of their more conservative colleagues.[100]

It is held similarly by some that, in the case of the Chinese Immigration Restriction Act 1891, the Education Act 1891, the Conciliation Act 1894 and the Factories Act 1894, 'the U.L.P. vote, giving added strength to the Liberal bloc in the Legislative Council, was the force without which neither would have been passed', but these were government measures, of a purely liberal origin and nature. Far from foreshadowing the capture of monopolies, which Marson advocated – or their killing off, which he feared – such references to socialism as occurred in parliamentary debate were of so general a character as to amount to no more than 'philanthropy by the State, mutual assistance by its individual members, equality of opportunity for all, moderation, "gradualism" and a certain readiness to compromise'.[101] Price in a sense spoke for the group as a whole, when, at a London business dinner in 1908, he 'confessed to certain changes of opinion, and went so far as to say that he was not so radical as he used to be and that in London he does not know what his politics are'.[102]

TOM PRICE

Price's confession may well have come as no surprise to his erstwhile fellow Fabian, Charleston, whose departure from the ULP in 1897 Price in part prompted. The son of an alcoholic father, 'whose intemperance kept the home in a continuous state of poverty',[103] in 1883 Price was obliged by ill health to abandon his prosperous business as a contracting stonemason in Wales in favour of the warmer climate of South Australia. As a workman on the new parliament house in Adelaide, and subsequently a Railways Department clerk of works and foreman, he was introduced to the colonial labour movement, where his skills as a debater, Methodist lay preacher, Sunday-school teacher and temperance campaigner gained him the confidence of his workmates and established firm foundations for his future political career. His election to the Legislative Assembly by a one-vote majority at the 1893 elections ushered in a period where his outspoken advocacy of a better deal for impoverished and otherwise downtrodden people, and his condemnation of the Legislative Council as a 'House of Landlords' made up of 'the bosses of the destiny of South Australia', branded him in the eyes of some as a dangerous demagogue.[104] A contemporary account recalls that: 'Certainly in those days he lived up to the character; fiery in spirit, ready tongued, versatile in argument, he spared no person or thing that antagonised the party which he represented, and thus he gained a reputation for harsh intolerance'.[105]

Price's Fabian convictions were likewise freely and forcefully put forward. Expressing the hope that a Tory MP who had read the Fabian essays would benefit from the experience, he declared:

> The socialism that I believe in at the present time . . . is a nobler conception of our duty to each other, and the higher ideal of life than the mere making of money; it claims a truer basis of mutual relationship than the mere cash nexus which Carlisle writes about. It fights against the supremacy of greed, which in these days so overshadows and retards the striving after goodness, and it pleads that men and women shall have a right to live lives befitting men and women.

'I believe', he told parliament on another occasion, 'not in revolution, but in gradual progress – indeed in the Fabian system of going slow'.[106]

Even so, Price's influence among the unionist Fabians was ultimately disruptive. Charleston's undoing stemmed from his complaints that an independent Labor MP, E.A. Roberts, along with a Joseph Salmon, had worked against him at the elections for the Federal Convention, and counter charges by Roberts and Salmon that Charleston was disloyal to the party. A party inquiry found in favour of Charleston, but the matter was reopened when Price claimed that he was a traitor, who had sold out the ULP for personal advantage. Price's attack occurred when Charleston was already under fire for infrequent attendance at caucus meetings, for support of a pastoral Bill exempting forty-year crown leases from land tax, and for alleged shortcomings in the investigation of hospital malpractice charges while serving as a member of a parliamentary committee of inquiry. It was Price's further contention that Charleston had supported the establishment of the malpractice inquiry in the first place, as part of a discreditable deal to avert an extraordinary election which might otherwise have cut short his parliamentary career. Charleston promptly resigned from the party and the parliament on the grounds that his honour had been impugned, and was re-elected at the subsequent by-election, despite the publication of a damaging telegram from Kingston, which read in part:

> At the late Federal (Convention) elections, you deliberately tried to split the Liberal vote so that by its wasteful distribution your personal

solid following might secure your election at the expense of Messrs McPherson, Batchelor and McGregor. . . . You admitted all of this to me after the election in your King William Street office. . . . You were proud of your tactics. . . . You stand self-confessed as having treacherously wrecked the joint Labour prospects to secure your own election.[107]

Charleston's interpretation of socialism has been characterised as 'more advanced than that of his colleagues',[108] and he was lauded personally by the *Pioneer* as being among 'socialists of the true type', who would 'do well to continually force upon their colleagues the imperative necessity of first and foremost throwing open to all alike the natural opportunities for wealth production'.[109] However, his powerful commitment to conscience and principle was not necessarily conducive to a sustained advancement in public life. The upshot was that the ULP lost its most effective socialist advocate at the point when its need for him was most acute. Irrespective of whether or not this was intended by Price and Kingston, it is unlikely to have disappointed them.

The episode suggests strongly that, even at so early a point in Price's parliamentary career as 1897, his reputation as the 'stormy petrel'[110] of the ULP had not inhibited him from forging close links with the Liberals, whose governments relied on ULP support from 1893 to 1901, and who in turn served under Price as premier in the coalition government which gained office at the 1905 elections and was returned with an increased majority following the dissolution of both houses of the parliament on the issue of Legislative Council reform in 1906. The achievements of the coalition included setting in train negotiations with other states on a Murray River agreement and the transfer of the Northern Territory to the Commonwealth; a new Factory Act with more wages boards, and penalties for strikes and lockouts in defiance of their determinations; and the establishment of a Government Produce Export Department. Even so, in the judgement of many within the labour movement, 'Rather than any gradual advance to socialism, the public sector was designed to assist capitalism and Price showed himself to be a sound administrator of private enterprise',[111] and by 1903 he had begun to describe himself openly as a liberal.[112] His attitude would have saddened Marson, whose hopes for the South Australian Fabian Society had included that it would deflect the unwelcome attentions of the liberals from the nascent ULP.

GORDON CHILDE'S VIEW

In the interpretative framework first proposed by Gordon Childe – and characterised ironically by some as the 'Doctrine of Primal Socialist Innocence and the Fall' – the parliamentary records of the unionist Fabians constitute a defection from the socialist and Single Tax ideals to which their loyalties had previously been given.[113] The failure of the group to pursue any sort of collectivist program – together, as has been seen, with the ultimate 'ratting' of the survivors from the ULP ranks – figures, in Childe's model, as the inevitable consequence of the exposure of a party of poorly educated working men to the alien environment of a parliament created by their ruling-class adversaries and reflecting ruling-class practices and prerogatives. Such men, it was argued by Childe, would inescapably be seduced from the class of their origin by the rarefied and comfortable setting to which they found themselves translated. Legislation aimed at social equality and redistributive taxation, he concluded, would be eschewed by them as much because privilege had blunted their sensitivity to the need for it as because they feared forfeiting electoral support. 'The Labor Party', it followed, 'starting with a band of inspired socialists, degenerated into a vast machine for capturing political power, but did not know how to use that power when attained except for the profit of individuals'.[114]

Childe's analysis, however, makes insufficient allowance for the characters of those concerned. In the case of Price, observers may perhaps agree to differ, but nothing about Guthrie or Archibald lends credence to the notion that their working-class identities were any less firm at the conclusion of their careers than at the outset, while Charleston remained a London Fabian Society member even after his ULP membership and service in parliament were long behind him. What the three men attempted or overlooked in parliament may well have been a function less of any diminution of their commitment to socialism than of an increase in the intensity of their trade unionist values and priorities. At a time of widespread economic and social privation and industrial exploitation, the need to pursue specific, practical and achievable ameliorative measures in effect crowded out the necessarily millennial socialist aspirations for whose advancement the parliament appeared to provide little opportunity.

In addition, the unionist Fabians increasingly found themselves over-extended as parliamentarians and party activists because, while the ULP had been incomparably the most successful of South Australia's political groupings in mobilising an extra-parliamentary organisation for campaign purposes in the early 1890s, this advantage was eroded by the party's opponents' adopting its example and, in some instances, perhaps improving on it. Like the Red Queen in *Alice Through the Looking Glass*, the ULP found itself obliged to run faster and faster at elections, as much for the sake of retaining past gains as of making new ones. The energies its Fabian parliamentarians were able to deploy – initially to the Society's affairs, and later to such ideological legacy as may have been left behind it – were correspondingly reduced. McPherson was seen by many as having literally worked and worried himself into an early grave,[115] and the same may have been the case with Price. The impression overall is of men who were simultaneously exhilarated and exhausted by the weight of the responsibilities which had so unexpectedly been thrust upon them, and the public attention to which they had become exposed.

Finally, the South Australian Fabian Society's demise in itself further impaired such stimulus for the development of a mutually supportive socialist culture within the labour movement as was available in circumstances where the inroads of a new unionism relatively more sympathetic to the socialist cause was less marked than in New South Wales or Victoria, and the dominance of liberal-leaning craft unions remained relatively entrenched.[116] Far from being able to tap any significant measure of peer group support, socialists within the labour movement met a certain hostility to any form of departure from a liberal or labourist orthodoxy preoccupied overwhelmingly with its industrial agenda (as has been seen, in the pressure on Charleston for a premature abdication of his UTLC presidency and the aftermath to Birks' 1894 election defeat). In summary, such apostasy as the unionist Fabians may be held to have perpetrated was a consequence less of pressures operating on them from outside the labour movement, as Childe would have supposed, than of those they experienced within it. By the time Price entered on his term as premier, the subordination of socialist aspiration and advocacy to labourist pragmatism within the parliamentary ULP was for all practical purposes complete. The root of the problem – to repeat Sidney Webb's conclusion on his return to Britain from Australasia in 1899 – was a 'want of political education' which Marson had had insufficient time to correct.

THE DEMISE OF THE SOUTH AUSTRALIAN FABIAN SOCIETY

The London Society's *Fabian News* recorded in May 1893 that 'At the annual meeting of the London Society the record of the progress and activity of the South Australian Fabian Society was received with much applause'. Fourteen months later, in July 1894, there was a further reference to 'this flourishing society',[117] but in the London Society's 1896 annual report it figured only as 'one of two Fabian Societies in Australia, of which we have no recent news'.[118] The last recorded action by the South Australian Fabian Society appears to have been the republication of its 1893 leaflet, *Land Values Assessment Bill (Part XIX)*, as Tract 7 in 1895.[119] The Society's winding-up was effectively finalised in 1902, when the parent body in London discontinued the memberships of Guthrie, Pearson, Baker, Bickford and James Morice, on the grounds of their failure to respond to a series of three subscription reminders.[120]

Marson was by then virtually forgotten. He returned to Britain in the second half of 1892, a victim of the asthma which was to bring his life to a tragically premature end twenty years later. 'To desert the post seems treason', he noted prior to his departure, 'but after all one must look for signs of Divine guidance and these beckon me away'.[121] The Society he had created withered in the absence of his charismatic presence. Events, in effect, had brought about a premature termination of the partnership of his Sidney Webb and the Arthur Henderson of his unionist Fabian associates, and, in its absence, the self-defeatingly divergent courses of labour activists and middle-class radicals were resumed. The bonds between Society members which he had instigated were attenuated gradually – to the point of invisibility – an attentuation marked initially by the falling out of Price with Charleston. The habit of evangelical Fabianism, on whose inculcation his passion and energy had so freely been lavished, succumbed ultimately to disuse. The decline illustrates vividly the ability of liberal and labourist outlooks to reassert themselves, in the absence of a credible socialist alternative that is forcefully and consistently argued from a trusted source.

Marson's enduring legacy to those who came after him remains his clear demonstration that middle-class radicals and labour activists could work together successfully in the hope of bringing about a reconstruction of Australian society along socialist lines, and such class complications as might attend relationships between them could be overcome. The need to bind together the Fabian and labour causes governed his actions in every respect throughout his stay in South Australia. To this end, he actively sought out and embraced a level of working-class involvement in the South Australian Society which Fabians in Britain would mostly have regarded as inexpedient or inappropriate. The Society likewise embraced the United Trades and Labour Council and United Labor Party platforms, as was evidenced by the Tracts in its *Questions for Candidates* series, and campaigned actively in their support, as was indicated by its annual reports. The upshot was that the Society included a higher proportion of leading trade unionists than any other Fabian body on record; concerted its activities wholly with those of the UTLC and the ULP; and did nothing which might alienate labour support. A model for antipodean Fabian organisation was established, which Marson's immediate successors – Champion and Mann, who launched organisations along Fabian lines in Victoria over the next ten years – might usefully have emulated. The absence from their activities of a comparable approach or set of principles was to exact a heavy price.

CHAPTER 3

Harry Champion and the Melbourne Fabian Society

The decline of the South Australian Fabian Society around 1894 coincided with calls for the establishment of a Fabian Society in Victoria, which gave rise to the Melbourne Fabian Society in 1895, the Fabian-in-all-but-name Social Questions Committee in 1905, and the Fabian Society of Victoria in 1908. The major cause was hard times – and frustration within the labour movement – on a scale beyond any the colony had previously experienced. The speculative boom of the 1880s had soared to its peak in 1889, faltered the following year and then fallen away precipitously through 1891's drying up of British capital inflow in the face of reports of fraud and failure; 1892's further fall in the price of wool and the closing of all but three of the trading banks in 1893, to the ignominious trough of 1894–95.[1] The intervening period saw investment, consumption and employment follow one another down in a vicious spiral of assured mutual attrition. The number of workers in manufacturing industry in Victoria, for example, fell away between 1889 and 1894 from 57,432 to 41,000. The value of manufacturing output fell from £22.3 million to £13.9 million and the number of residences constructed fell from 3,525 to 1,041. Property lenders facing imminent collapse, for example, called in their loans from developers, who in turn defaulted because they were either under-secured or unable to raise book values from the forced sale of their assets, leaving both parties bankrupt or otherwise inoperative. Employees of the building and construction firms which relied on the developers for work lost their jobs, which in turn reduced purchases of the products of local industries, causing further labour to be shed.

Both small and large investors were seared by the fallout from the speculative excesses to which the community had been incited by its often fraudulent or near-fraudulent land banks and other fringe financial intermediaries. Leading citizens were exposed as having involved themselves in embezzlement and other breaches of trust. Retired people lost the nest-eggs which were their sole source of income. Factory gates closed. Shops put up their shutters: 'general unemployment followed. The provident suffered with the improvident and for the whole community the winter of 1893 was miserable and desperate'.[2] Expansion was confined to soup kitchens and the centres from which charitable organisations and municipalities distributed free clothing and fuel. The 1894 report of the Melbourne Ladies Benevolent Society documented the provision of weekly relief throughout the year for 2,295 cases numbering 6,889 individuals, of whom many were 'elderly or aged single women who, in the changed condition of the colony find it impossible to maintain themselves', while a South Melbourne food depot provided bread, meat and vegetables twice a week for 800 people, the majority of whom were 'women and children, the husbands having gone into the country to look for work'. It was noted, in the latter case, that 'Among the sufferers are people well brought up, but who refuse absolutely to come here. They would rather starve than accept charity'.[3]

The recovery that took place over the next decade was neither adequate nor unmarred by further episodes of recession. Employment levels fell again in 1902, as did real wages.[4] A house-to-house survey conducted by the Social Questions Committee in 1905 established that, in the industrial districts of Melbourne, 'over five thousand adults, and a similar number of young people, were unemployed, and that very much real poverty existed'.[5] The predicament in which many found themselves is exemplified by a letter which appeared in the *Age* on 21 March 1906:

> Sir – I am a native of this country, 40 years of age, married and have contributed to its taxes in no niggardly fashion, and now, after leading an honest life and working hard as traveller, canvasser and clerk, etc, find it impossible to get employment. In your Saturday's issue there were no fewer than five advertisements from capable young men offering £5 and £10 for billets. . . . As I am half-starved, I would willingly do any kind of work for shelter and food.

The activities mainly responsible for the colony's earlier, spectacular economic expansion – home building, capital formation and the pastoral industry – remained depressed until around 1910.[6]

The economic downturn conferred important industrial relations advantages on employers, which were exploited as early as the 1890 national Maritime Strike. Faced on that occasion as they supposed, or purported to suppose, by the menacing solidarity of 'the Confederated Labour Unions' – a term attributed to the super-intendent of the Australian Agricultural Company, Jesse Gregson – the employers met and defeated it with a solidarity of their own.[7] Further victories were achieved at the expense of the shearers in 1891 and 1894, the Broken Hill miners in 1892, the Victorian railway workers in 1903, the Sydney tramworkers in 1908 and the New South Wales coalminers in 1909–10. The Maritime Strike taught the employers the value of organisation and united action, but the weaknesses inflicted on the unions by the availability of free labour and their difficulty in effectively concerting action obviated any need for the lesson to be applied until the new century. The employers then moved decisively, with new organisations to target the labour movement both industrially and politically. The year 1901 brought a flurry of new employer initiatives. In Victoria, for example, the Employers' Union of the 1880s gave way to the higher powered, overtly political Employers' Federation. Rural conserva-tism acquired a focus, through the Kyabram-based Citizens' Reform Association movement, with 210 branches and 15,555 members. The conservative Australian Women's National League blossomed suddenly, as did the conservative Farmers, Property Owners and Producers League.[8]

The assumptions behind the employer strategy proved to be sound. The nascent anti-union, anti-socialist mood of middle-class Australia was crystallised, entrenched and given institutional expression. The 1902 elections confirmed 'Iceberg' Irvine as Victoria's first conservative premier since Patterson almost a decade earlier. Such was the hold of anti-unionism on public opinion that his ruthless crushing of the striking railwaymen a year later gave him 'his finest hour' when 'Melbourne paid homage to the Iceberg'. Meanwhile, opportunities for the betterment of wages and working conditions stemming from the 1896 Factory Act provided workers with a powerful incentive to become union members. Total trade union membership in Australia increased between 1901 and 1911 from 97,174 to 364,732.[9] Both capital and labour had reason to conclude that they were in better shape at the end of the decade than at its beginning. Feelings on both sides were harder, and the lines between them were more clearly drawn. The concepts of 'Labour' and 'anti-Labour' were branded irrevocably on the national consciousness.

THE VICTORIAN PARLIAMENT

In parliamentary terms, the hard times turned the electorate towards the security and reassurance of leaders and governments whose dominant characteristics – irrespective of party – were staidness and caution. What was generally perceived as unsatisfactory handling of the Maritime Strike and rising unemployment brought about the defeat of the coalition government of 'Constitutionalists' – as the conservatives at the time described themselves – and Liberals under Deakin and Duncan Gillies in October 1890, on the motion of Deakin's fellow Liberal, James Munro, who replaced Gillies as premier. Deakin – the one truly luminous presence in a largely mediocre caste – then chose to remain out of office until the end of the decade. The 'independent and private member', as he now styled himself, had shared the financial misfortunes of his fellow colonists. 'With the rest (though among the last to yield)', as he later recalled, 'I plunged into the boom, losing all the money my father had available'. A further blow to his pocket and self-respect followed, with the collapse of the City of Melbourne Building Society, whose board he had chaired. The 'long and bitter experience' of restoring the family's fortunes and repaying his creditors entailed a return to practice at the Bar, where his energies were in part absorbed by the preparation of his controversial defences of the notorious murderer known as 'Baron Swanston', and of Syme in the libel action brought against him by an erstwhile Commissioner of Railways. Even so, his freedom from ministerial responsibilities and the need to conciliate more conservative coalitionists enabled him to turn his attention increasingly to expanding the horizons of the New Liberalism, and pushing forward the drive for federation. 'During the 1890s', as J.A. La Nauze notes, 'he did more for the causes he believed in than he could have done in office'.[10]

Meanwhile, Munro's retirement prior to the 1892 elections paved the way for another Liberal, Shiels, to be premier from 1892 until 1893, and a Constitutionalist, Patterson, from 1893 to 1894. Both were 'grossly incompetent leaders', who 'failed to take stern measures, lest their parliamentary majorities be affected, to cope with, or ameliorate, the disastrous deterioration of the national economy', with the result that George Turner – a Liberal elected to the Assembly for the first time only in 1889 – became premier with a mandate from his party 'to rescue the colony from chaos'.[11] Turner's five-year term of office

– the longest of any Victorian premier to that date – is widely regarded as a period when the adoption by a drab leader of an administrative style of government virtually unimpeded by party divisions brought about an exodus of Victoria's more adventurous and restless spirits 'for other colonies and new opportunities'.[12] An alternative view holds that Turner was 'the man of the hour', who 'battled hard to produce balanced budgets by stern economy and rigid parsimony to the approbation of an admiring public'.[13]

Irrespective of where the balance may lie, what can never be taken away from Turner and his ministers is that their 1896 Factory Act and its confirmatory and amending Act of 1900 were among the most important measures ever enacted by the Victorian parliament. The legislation – in the adoption of which the National Anti-Sweating League together with Deakin, Champion and Champion's fellow Fabian, Strong, played major parts – gave statutory effect to minimum wage requirements and enabled wages boards to be established on the motion of either the Assembly or the Council. 'The prospect of bringing new trades under the Act', as John Rickard points out, then became 'a powerful incentive for dead unions to rise from the grave, and for new unions to be created'.[14] The self-confidence of the Trades Hall Council, largely shattered by the years of depression, was in part restored, and secure foundations were set in place for the explosive growth in trade union membership and the labour vote which marked the opening decade of the new century.

Turner lost a vote of confidence in 1899 and was replaced briefly by his former fellow Liberal McLean, but became premier again after the 1900 elections until 1901, when he made way for Peacock. The collapse of Peacock's government the following year opened the door for the conservatives, under the leadership of 'Iceberg' Irvine, who took office on an anti-socialist, anti-labour platform which was given expression in his bludgeoning of the railway strikers. The succession to the premiership of Bent, Irvine's Railways Minister, after Irvine's resignation in 1904 on the grounds of ill health, con-firmed the arrival of a new conservative ascendancy which outlasted the decade. Irvine and Bent were direct beneficiaries of the conclusions about unity and organisation which the employers had drawn from their Maritime Strike experience. The events of 1901–2 showed plainly that much of middle-class opinion would welcome what the New South Wales conservative leader, Joseph Carruthers, summarised as 'a coalition of all parties opposed to Caucus Labour in politics'.[15]

The arrival of the Fusion in 1909 was what much of the middle class had been demanding for the greater part of the decade.

Coming up from behind the Liberals and Constitutionalists to match and ultimately exceed their respective numbers were the new Labor members. The setbacks of the early 1890s brought home to the labour movement that it needed both to pursue by parliamentary means those goals which industrial action failed to deliver and to avoid having the resources of government turned against it by its conservative adversaries. This realisation precipitated a break with the prior desultory and dilatory practice of throwing labour support behind the occasional politically ambitious union functionary and such middle-class candidates as identified themselves with the union cause. When the Progressive Political League was formed in 1891, five Legislative Assembly members returned at the 1889 elections joined it, and organised themselves into a parliamentary Labor party under Trenwith's leadership, which became the United Labor and Liberal Party in 1894. Eleven Labor members were returned at the 1892 elections, seventeen in 1894 and fourteen in 1897, so that between 1894 and 1897, the party nominally controlled a fifth of the vote on the Assembly floor.[16] The Liberal leaders of the 1890s could mostly count on the support of this substantial minority where the survival of their governments was at stake, but such support was given less and less willingly as the decade went on, and the procrastination of Turner on issues such as the old age pension, the State Bank and Legislative Council reform strained the friendship.

The closing years of the century were marked by repeated efforts to establish a proper party organisation. In 1896, the party dropped 'Liberal' from its title and adopted a new platform and structure. A further overhaul in 1901 saw it renamed the Political Labour Council. Heightened class consciousness on the part of workers and the impact of the wage fixation system on union membership after the late 1890s also worked in the party's favour. Between 1901 and 1910, the Labor vote quadrupled (going from 12% to 48%). No Labor government took office in Victoria during the period, but firm foundations for the future were secured. The state's part in the unexpected Labor triumph over the Fusion at the 1910 federal elections indicated that the years of preparation and waiting might be approaching their end.

The Victorian Labor Party which waited in the wings for office in 1910 was not and had never been a socialist body. The Melbourne

Trades Hall Council which gave rise to it in the early 1890s was stamped indelibly with 'the liberalism of the respectable, thrifty, God-fearing Victorian craft unionist'.[17] The unionist MPs who made up the overwhelming majority of party members – including, after the 1894 elections, six former THC presidents – carried with them into parliament a characteristically liberal belief in the harmony and compatibility of labour and capital, such that 'Though a temporary cleavage between the owner and employee may have occurred, it was understood that this was not the normal state of affairs'.[18] Socialism, as it seemed to them, had little to offer for a society which was already enjoying such notable benefits as the eight-hour working day and tariff protection for its manufacturing industries, with the hope of further prizes to follow. The rough egalitarianism of colonial life afforded no justification, in their view, for socialist rhetoric about a class system which they firmly believed had been left behind them in the Old World, along with a host of other objectionable and outmoded practices and prejudices. It is therefore no cause for surprise that an analysis of the party as a whole at the time when Turner was premier discloses 'little to indicate that the majority of members of this strong minority group were anything other than Left-wing Liberals'.[19]

Even so, in the view of some, 'The absence of strong organisations of unskilled workers, and the traditional links between the Victorian craft unions and middle class radicalism, meant that the suspicion of intellectuals and of socialist theorising, strong elsewhere, was not so evident in Victoria'.[20] Irrespective of the significance of these considerations earlier on, their effect was drastically diminished in the course of the 1890s, to the point where, by the end of first decade of the new century, it had, for all practical purposes, vanished. An autarchic, 'ourselves against all others' mood had taken hold of the union movement and – consequently – the Labor Party. What has been characterised by some as the party's 'ruthless indifference to the fate of sympathisers, however radical, outside its ranks'[21] was associated increasingly with the belief that in the parliamentary sphere only working-class MPs could be trusted to represent working-class interests faithfully. In this way, ironically, the same heightened sense of working-class identity which played so large a part in Labor's rise also, in some respects, further diminished the possibility of a role or influence in its affairs for the middle-class socialists who looked to it for the fulfilment of their dreams.

Meanwhile, as will be seen, far from the Fabians accommodating themselves to these emerging realities, they allowed themselves to become instead the unwitting instruments of their own undoing.

THE VICTORIAN FABIANS

HARRY CHAMPION

Marson's erstwhile fellow member of the Land Reform Union and the London Fabian Society, and his predecessor as editor of the *Christian Socialist,* Champion – 'Harry' to his friends in Britain, but for no obvious reason 'Hyde' to those in Australia – visited the Australian colonies on a fact-finding mission in 1890 and returned to establish a home for himself in Victoria in 1894. Champion's father and grandfather had been army officers in India, where Champion was born at Poona on 22 January 1859. His father, Major-General James Hyde Champion of Sir John Mitchell's column, 'received a letter telling him of the birth of his son and heir' while on a hunting trip in another part of the country.[22] Sent away at the age of four to England, he completed officer training at the Royal Military College in Woolwich, thus refuting the belief – later attributed by him to his headmaster at Marlborough, Canon Farrar – that it would be quite futile for him to be sent to university, but that he might possibly make a fairly competent ploughboy.[23] He was commissioned in the Royal Artillery in 1878; invalided home from the Afghan War with typhoid in 1881; and, following his recovery, became adjutant of a unit in Portsmouth.

His formative years inculcated in him a capacity for leadership, but also, perhaps, made some contribution to the darker side of his nature, which was wayward, self-opinionated, swashbuckling and dangerously prone to adventurism. St John Irvine – a Fabian himself, and secretary of the Stage Society, an independent group with a heavily-Fabian membership which is credited with having 'helped make it fun to be a Fabian' – describes him as 'a brilliant, restless man, who could not remain faithful to a scheme long enough to obtain a result from it'.[24] He was, in Shaw's view, 'so extraordinarily ready with a practicable plan in every emergency that if the plan could only have remained the same for half an hour he would have been the greatest general of his age'.[25] More prone to be guided by his own conscience and inclinations than by the dictates of a group loyalty or solidarity – to command rather than cajole – he never wholly succeeded in reconciling the values of his upper middle-class origins with those of the working class whose hero he briefly became. His marriage on 9 August 1883 to the twenty-eight-year-old Juliet Bennett was cut short by her death three years later, in circumstances where references on the death certificate to alcoholism and heart failure invite the interpretation that happiness had eluded them.[26] The socialist novelist and journalist Margaret Harkness is seen by some as having tried to revive or continue a subsequent 'close and possibly intimate' relationship by following him to Australia in 1894, but without success.[27] When Champion married for the second time in 1898 in Melbourne, it seems to have been in response less to the attractions of the bride than to those of her politically influential family. It may well be that his capacity to receive and return love or experience empathy had been impaired by an insufficient exposure to parental love prior to his departure from India for school in Britain. He was solitary, perhaps, even in the company of the working-class leaders who became his closest associates.

Champion's turbulent character and career may well also have been owed to the Urquhart blood he inherited from his mother and paternal grandmother. The Urquharts were a Highland family with a reputation for eccentricity. The MP for Aberdeen, Dr Hunter is credited by Champion's sometime friend and mentor, H.M. Hyndman, with the observation, 'Oh, Urquhart blood in him – that accounts for it all'.[28] A study by the labour historian Henry Pelling reads in part:

> It would not be difficult to find precedent for much of his behaviour in the career of Sir Thomas Urquhart, the translator of Rabelais, who is reputed to have died of laughter on hearing of the restoration of Charles II; or in that of Captain John Urquhart, 'the Pirate', who as a Jacobite commanded a privateer in the service of the King of Spain, and made enough by way of booty to be able to repurchase the family estates in Scotland. Still alive when Champion was born, and even more of an influence on his career, was David Urquhart, the Turcophil, who is best remembered for having converted Karl Marx to the view that Palmerston was in the pay of the Russians, and who spent much of his time attempting to persuade working men to take an interest in foreign affairs.

'From Cavalier and Jacobite to Tory radical and "Tory Socialist"', Pelling concludes, 'the tradition of high principle combined with personal recklessness seems to trace a direct hereditary course'.[29]

Champion's convalescence from typhoid was put to good use. A friend – probably his Marlborough contemporary and future Social Democratic Federation comrade-in-arms, R.P.B. Frost – introduced him to the nature and extent of poverty, as exemplified in the East End of London.[30] His discovery of Henry George's *Progress and Poverty* was followed up with an extensive study of political economy, through the work of such writers as Adam Smith, Mill, Ricardo and Marx. The upshot, as he later recalled, was that 'Gradually, step by step, I was driven to Socialism, and also to the conclusion that I must leave the army'. 'On the 17th of September, 1882', his account continues, 'I handed in my resignation to my commanding officer, and the next night I was preaching Socialism on Clerkenwall Green'.[31] He also became co-proprietor of the Modern Press in Paternoster Row, in partnership with another Fabian-to-be, J.C. Foulger, whose journal, *Modern Thought* – seen by some as 'a parish magazine for the unorthodox' – gave rise in 1891 to the establishment of the Progressive Association.[32] The Modern Press produced pamphlets and periodicals for the range of radical and socialist groups whose meeting places included the Cyprus Teashop adjacent to the firm's office. Champion and Foulger became the first publishers to issue Shaw's work in book form, when Champion's enthusiasm for prize fighting prompted the production of 2,500 copies of *Cashel Byron's Profession* in 1886.

More even than the Land Reform Union in 1883 or Pease's Osnaburgh Street meetings in 1884, the establishment of the Progressive Association marked the start of the Fabian Society's gestation. The seminal significance of the occasion is acknowledged by Shaw in a designation of the association's founder, Foulger, as 'the genuine original Fabian'.[33] An initial circular from the Association declared that 'The Progressive Association is neither theological nor anti-theological, but is founded on what is conceived to be the widest workable basis, namely that Man may by his honest efforts promote the highest good and happiness of the human race on earth'.[34] Champion joined, as did the future 'Sage of Sex', Havelock Ellis, who was studying medicine following a sojourn as a teacher at the Sparkes Creek and Junction Creek schools in New South Wales, and 'had renounced Christianity after reading James Hinton's *Life in Nature*, which not only advocated sexual freedom but also offered a mystical doctrine to reconcile the scientific concept of the world with divine illumination'. Other Progressive Association members who later achieved Fabian prominence included Pease, Podmore and Percival Chubb – 'a lapsed Anglican alternating between ethical enthusiasms and depression over his own unworthiness and the dreary worldliness of his poorly paid work at the Local Government Board', who had adopted as his mentor and father confessor the charismatic wandering scholar Thomas Davidson.[35] Ellis and Foulger were joint secretaries of the Association until 1884, when Ellis' position was taken over by Chubb. Norman Mackenzie notes in an essay on 'Percival Chubb and the Formation of the Fabian Society' that, not dissimilarly from the Fabian Society:

> There were to be lectures and meetings 'devoted largely to questions of human conduct, and the advancement of man's condition and ideal'. There were to be campaigns for improved housing and other sanitary measures and for 'advances in Physical, Mental and Moral Education' . . . The association also proposed to prepare and distribute pamphlets, to support parliamentary measures which it approved and to oppose those it disliked, and to 'run classes of an attractive kind' for young people 'to teach such views of life as will make them worthy citizens of their own, and fit parents of the next generation'.[36]

A subsequent toughening of the Progressive Association's outlook is suggested by a resolution – discussed by members during the winter of 1882–83 and attributed by Mackenzie to Champion – which reads in part:

> While believing in the necessity for social reconstruction, the Progressive Association considers that such reconstruction, to be either permanent or beneficial, must proceed by only such revolutionary means as are consistent with the natural development of the community, and that social development can only advance side by side with individual development. The Association looks for a more equable distribution of labour and wealth, thus placing within the reach of all classes (and doing injustice to no class) the attainment of the full development of individual activities. It will therefore be prepared to support measures for bringing the means of production within the control of the community, and for the organisation of labour, both by the state and in the form of Co-operation. As a preparation for these Social changes the Association will support compulsory education, moral, physical and intellectual (including technical education) and seeks by voluntary efforts to spread information regarding Social subjects.[37]

The tensions between ethical and political reformers implicit in the wording of the resolution are seen by Mackenzie as having given rise to a continuing debate over subsequent months, and as ultimately prompting Chubb's approach to Pease, from which the Fabian Society directly stemmed.

In October 1883, Pease invited Champion to his house in Osnaburgh Street to discuss the establishment of yet another organisation, dedicated, in this instance, to 'a single, strenuous, intellectual and communal existence through which its members might find their way to a natural religion'. The instigator was Chubb, whose imagination had been fired by Davidson with the vision of 'a really fresh start, an altogether more vigorous and determined effort to cast off the works of darkness and put on the whole armour of light'. Interventions by Champion – who was accompanied to the first meeting by Joynes and Frost – were largely responsible for steering the initial proceedings away from Chubb's spiritual preoccupations in the direction of a commitment to reformist propaganda. Proposals for the establishment of a utopian colony in southern California or a residential commune in London were rejected at his insistence. The preparation of rules for a new organisation was delegated to a drafting committee which he chaired, and in whose proceedings Pease and Podmore played leading parts. 'Pease and Podmore', Davidson was advised by Chubb, 'were "not of the right fibre" '. 'There was too much anxiety for "doing" ', in the opinion of another participant, when 'our first aim was to "be" something ourselves'.[38]

The outcome, in the event, was not one new body but two: the Fellowship of the New Life (a title Champion objected to on the grounds that it was 'bumptious')[39] and the Fabian Society. Holroyd sees the Fellowship as having attracted the aspiring saints and the Society 'the world-betterers whose religion became socialism'. Shaw characterises the intentions of the two groups as having been respectively 'the one to sit among the dandelions, the other to organise the docks'.[40] The saints were the poorer stayers, and by 1898 the Fellowship was extinct. In the course of its relatively brief lifespan, a lecture program was implemented, a quarterly journal called *Seedtime* was produced, and the more enthusiastic elements within the group resumed the effort to give effect to their principles which Champion's opposition had interrupted, through the establishment of Fellowship House as a co-operative household at 29 Doughty Street in Bloomsbury. A majority of the Fellowship members – including, for a time, both Chubb and Davidson – were also Fabians, and those sharing the 'interesting menage' in Doughty Street included Sydney Olivier and the young Ramsay MacDonald, who was invited to address the fellowship, stayed to join it and ultimately served for a year as its secretary.[41] His predecessor in the position – Edith Lees, who married Havelock Ellis after his affair with the notable South African feminist and novelist Olive Schreiner was over – was also a resident of the Doughty Street property. 'Fellowship', she concluded from the experience, 'is Hell'. Champion may well have anticipated her sentiments in the wider context. For him, it is said, 'nothing useful seemed likely to come out of such woolly discussions and constitution-mongering, and he soon dropped out'.[42]

Champion's involvement over so brief a period in the affairs of the Land Reform Union, the Progressive Association, the Fellowship of the New Life and the Fabian Society exemplifies his lifelong, tireless devotion to networking. There is a pattern in his affairs of constantly joining groups or creating them, and acquiring new associates. The 1908 interview with him which appeared over his signature as his 'Unconventional Biography' in the Melbourne literary journal *Trident* describes him as 'a man who has shaken hands with Victor Hugo, and knows everybody worth knowing in England, from Robert Browning to John Morley, from Cardinal Manning to Bernard Shaw'. He may well have been a member of and office bearer in more organisations than any other labour movement leader of his generation. In 1884, the editorship of the *Christian Socialist* was handed over by him to Marson, and Foulger's *Modern Thought* was replaced by the Modern Press with a new 'Monthly Magazine of Scientific Socialism' titled *Today*. The changes signalled a greater militancy and deeper political insight on his part, commensurate with the deepening desperation of the times for the working people to whose well being and advancement his life was now wholly dedicated. While no doctrinaire Marxist, he had joined the Marxist Democratic Federation in 1883, at the point where it was renamed the Social-Democratic Federation (SDF), and had become its secretary. 'On Whit Monday, 1883', as he later recalled the occasion, 'a memorable meeting was held in an underground room at Palace Chambers . . . before we left the room we were the Social-Democratic Federation, and I was the hon. sec.'[43]

The SDF was linked inseparably in the public mind with the paradoxically bourgeois appearance and insurrectionary utterances of its founder and most prominent member, Henry Myers Hyndman – the frock-coated, high-hatted, cricket-playing, Eton-educated,

Cambridge-trained stockbroker and journalist whose *England For All* introduced Marxism to English readers. Other SDF activists included Champion's Land Reform Union associates, Joynes, Salt and Frost; the Fabian executive members Pease, Bland and Frederick Keddell; William Morris, Edward Aveling and Marx's daughter, Eleanor, who established the Socialist League after a falling out with Hyndman; Edward Carpenter, whose gift of three hundred pounds enabled the SDF to launch its fire-eating weekly journal, *Justice*; working-class militants such as Tom Mann and Will Thorne; their unionist colleague, John Burns, who broke with the SDF in 1899 and was president of the Local Government Board in Asquith's Liberal government; and – ultimately – the Labour Party luminaries-to-be George Lansbury and Ernest Bevin. Champion spoke widely from SDF platforms, and gained Hyndman's respect as a comrade-in-arms to whom the leadership of the SDF might ultimately be handed on. As Shaw assessed the situation in October 1884, 'But for Frost and Champion, who, though nominally Hyndmanites, practically boss the whole Federation between them by sticking together and working, the whole body would have gone to pieces long ago'.[44]

The springtime phase of Champion's Land Reform Union and Progressive Association days was now behind him. By 1884 Britain had begun to move into recession. Shaw saw 1886 and 1887 as having been 'years of great distress among the working-classes – years for street-corner agitators to marshal columns of hollow-cheeked men with red flags and banners inscribed with Scriptural texts to fashionable churches on Sundays, and to lead desperate deputations from the Holborn Board of Guardians to the Local Government Board office and back again, using stronger language at each official rebuff from pillar to post'.[45] In place of their former 'drawing-room Socialism and scientific politics', Champion and the other SDF leaders found themselves addressing mass meetings of the unemployed. On 8 February, 1886 – "Black Monday" – a crowd of 100,000 converged on Trafalgar Square for a rally against free trade. The rally was taken over by the SDF and, after fiery speeches from the four SDF leaders – Champion, Hyndman, Burns and J.E. Williams – Champion proposed a march to Hyde Park. 'At that moment', as he later recalled, 'a hussar in the crowd tied a red handkerchief to a riding whip, and handed it to Burns; and we went marching away with this historic red handkerchief as our oriflame'.[46]

However, the windows of some of the great London clubs were broken as the crowd passed down St James' Street, and shops in Mayfair were broken into and looted. Four days later, Champion and his three colleagues found themselves under arrest on charges of sedition. Such was the excited state of public opinion and establishment outrage, Champion later claimed, that if the trial had been held immediately they would probably have been given twenty-year prison sentences or hanged. In the event, bail was granted and an adjournment secured. When the court reconvened a month later, feelings had cooled off and the defendants were acquitted.

Champion passed through the ordeal of uncertainty unscathed. He was also unchastened. Even prior to the acquittals he was making speeches which amounted to an overt call for revolution. Hyndman and other leading SDF members pleaded with him to moderate his rhetoric, but they were ignored. An article published over his name in *Justice* in August 1886 reads in part: 'In the face of our modern arms of precision and quick-firing guns, barricades are of no use. To be successful in street-fighting, we must have either better weapons or the positive assurance that the soldiers will refuse to obey their officers'.[47] A possible alternative, the article argued, might be the use of dynamite squads. Even so, not all the more extreme statements attributed to Champion necessarily reflect the spirit and circumstances in which they were made. Shaw's *The Fabian Society: Its Early History* quotes an apparently inflammatory declaration by Champion to a public meeting that 'If the whole propertied class had but one throat he would cut it without a second thought, if by doing so he could redress the injustices of our social system'.[48] A subsequent account by Shaw of the same incident – from his essay 'Sixty Years of Fabianism', in the Jubilee edition of *Fabian Essays* – adds a revealing qualification: 'While we were gasping at this outburst he rushed to the edge of the platform and, pointing down at the Press table, shouted: "Look! They are all scribbling as hard as they can, though they have not put pen to paper when I was talking sensibly" '.[49]

Champion was not, moreover, incapable of changing his mind. At the 1885 general election he had partnered Hyndman in fielding SDF candidates for the London seats of Hampstead and Kensington. The result was a fiasco, with the SDF winning thirty-two and twenty-seven votes respectively, and Hyndman and Champion brought under savage attack from both SDF members and radical circles generally for having funded the campaign with 'Tory Gold' from Maltman Barry, a former member of Marx's First International who was widely supposed to have taken on Tory affiliations. Barry, according to a contemporary account, was 'the most Marxian of Tories and the Toryest of Marxians'.[50] Hyndman defended accepting funds from him with the classical quotation *Non olet* ('It does not smell')[51] – but Annie Besant responded scathingly to the SDF's subsequent call for revolutionary measures: 'What is your revolutionary strength in London; may we not gauge it by your fifty votes or so, bought and paid for with Tory Gold?'[52] In 1887, as evidence mounted that direct action was doing little to advance the SDF's objectives, prospects for a parliamentary road to socialism became more attractive to Champion. Whereas in 1886 he had argued strenuously in favour of confronting official indifference to the plight of the unemployed through a protracted occupation of Trafalgar Square, his attitude a year later had become one of outright opposition. Socialism, he now insisted, could best be advanced by the establishment of a Labour Party, in alliance with the trade unions and the Labour Electoral Committee which had been established in 1886 by the Trade Union Congress.

Champion's position was increasingly at odds with majority opinion within the SDF, where Hyndman was a longtime critic of the unions and direct action still enjoyed widespread approval. The Maltman Barry episode had left a deep-seated distrust in the minds of many of his former supporters. A botched attempt to bring together in a single organisation the less extreme elements of the SDF, the Socialist League and the Fabians prompted the reproach from Hyndman that he had 'upset us all here and lost our regard and friendship by more than mere political misunderstanding'.[53] The episode marked the suspension of a close personal friendship which both Hyndman and Champion had valued highly. Years later, in 1921, a letter written by Champion to Hyndman on the occasion of his eightieth birthday evoked a time when 'You used to come down to the pleasant little place at Cookham, and walk in the quiet evening back and forth on the village green, while you declaimed about everything going shortly to the devil'. 'It seems', Champion's letter continued, 'you were not so bad a prophet after all, and if I live another seventeen years, I shall be able to wag my flowing beard, and amuse the children with tales of the brave old days when Socialism (of our kind) was the property of only a dozen of us'.[54]

Champion's position as secretary of the SDF had to be surrendered, and the satisfaction he was able to gain from his other SDF work was undermined by the critical attitude of those around him to his methods. The drifting apart became an estrangement and finally, in November 1888, he was expelled.

Any pangs the break caused Champion are unlikely to have been lasting. The prospect of pursuing socialism by parliamentary means had already for all purposes crowded out his earlier insurrectionary dreams, and had prompted him to serve briefly as the Metropolitan Section Organiser for the predominantly trade unionist Labour Electoral Association, which replaced the Labour Electoral Committee where his enthusiasm had initially been aroused. Furthermore, his thinking about how best to advance the socialist cause had again undergone a significant change. The notion that any new working-class party should be independent not only of the Liberals, but of the unions themselves had captured his imagination in the course of a seminal conversation with the Irish Nationalist leader, Parnell.[55] Following the Mid-Lanarck by-election in April 1886, he had struck out with Keir Hardie and others to form a self-styled National Labour Party, which shortly became the Independent Labour Party (ILP), and adopted the weekly paper he had recently established – the *Labour Elector* – as its official organ. Champion, Hardie and Tom Mann had thrown themselves energetically behind a policy of intervening actively in by-election campaigns, where the threat of fielding ILP candidates was held over the Liberals and Tories in an attempt to have them pledge support for specific reforms such as the eight-hour day. At the same time, fierce attacks on the Liberals were featured regularly in the *Labour Elector*, so as to further alienate workers from the local Liberal Associations in which traditionally their allegiance had so largely been invested. It was therefore no inconsiderable figure which the SDF cast adrift from its ranks in November, 1888, but rather a natural leader whose political popularity was at its peak – who commanded the limelight of public attention, addressed public meetings virtually every night of the week, and had been, as he later modestly acknowledged, the model for the heroes of as many as seven popular novels.[56]

Meanwhile, Champion was developing the distinctively 'Tory socialist' convictions to which expression was given in the series of seminal articles which appeared over his name in the *Nineteenth Century* between 1888 and 1892, and in his book, *The Root of the*

Matter, which was published in Melbourne in 1895. Socialism, as Champion saw it, was about supplanting capitalism with the philosophy and practice of co-operation, which, in turn, he equated with ownership by the state. He identified in capitalist competition the root cause of the chronic unemployment, 'sweating', starvation wages and other injustices and indignities whose prevalence so deeply stirred the consciences of Fabian Society members and socialists generally. Pending socialism, he believed, it was necessary for the worker interest to be defended by an interventionist and regulatory approach to industrial issues, as opposed to *laissez-faire* economics and free trade in their classic Cobdenite liberal mould.

The British Empire – as it seemed to Champion, in the light of these factors – was well placed to implement protectionist policies because its boundaries encompassed so wide a range of soils and climates as to enable it to be economically self-sufficient, and he identified closely with those who saw in the Empire the makings of an irresistible force for freedom and progress on the world scene. While his conclusions were not shared by the majority of his fellow socialists, whose thinking was derived predominantly from liberal doctrines and who, in many cases, were former Liberal Party members, their impact on the wider fabric of British political thought was far-reaching. The proposals for working-class housing and limitation of working hours which Lord Randolph Churchill put forward at Walsall in July 1889 are thought by some to have owed something to Champion's thinking. By Champion's account:

> One day I was told that Lord Randolph Churchill would like to see me, and I accordingly called on him. This was shortly after the break-up of his party. He was going to speak at Wolverhampton the next day. He asked me to tell him what the best things in our programme were, and I explained it all to him, speaking particularly of two points – the housing of the working classes, and the eight hours day. Then I read the reports of his speech a couple of days later; I found he had calmly appropriated both ideas, and had made them the strongest planks in his platform.[57]

Further instances may have included Joseph Chamberlain's 1903 Birmingham speech proposals for binding together the Empire with a system of preferential tariff protection, using the proceeds to fund welfare measures and, in the process, revitalising British agriculture and industry; and, perhaps, Alfred Deakin's support for factory legislation, imperial federation and the 'New Protection' as it came to be debated in the early years of the Australian parliament.[58]

In as much as the social reforming activism that Lloyd George and Winston Churchill thrust upon the Asquith government in the middle of 1908 was a direct response to the 'revived protectionism and aggressive Toryism' which Chamberlain bequeathed to his party,[59] Champion can be seen to have had a hand in shaping both ends of the political spectrum. His combination of socialism and imperialism was in no sense unique among his socialist contemporaries. Similar sentiments were espoused from within the London Society by its treasurer, Hubert Bland, and from within the Social-Democratic Federation by Hyndman. It was Shaw's view, at the time of the Boer War, that 'a Fabian must necessarily be an Imperialist, because Fabian Socialism and Imperialism both were based on a sense of the supreme importance of the Duties of the Community, with State Organisation, Efficient Government, Industrial Civil Service, Regulation of all private enterprise in the common interest and the dissolution of Frontiers through international industrial organisation'. The Society could hardly complain if it was perceived by many as supporting – or at least tacitly endorsing – the imperial cause. Empire loyalties later played a key role in the establishment of Champion's links with Australian politicians of the stamp of Deakin and Latham.

The Independent Labour Party's advocacy of the eight-hour day was accompanied by an equal interest in exposing through the columns of the *Labour Elector* the cruel, unhealthy and exploitative conditions which prevailed in workplaces such as those manufacturing chemicals for Brunners' and matches for Bryant and May. It was natural, therefore, when the London dockers went on strike in 1889, for their leader, Ben Tillett, to turn for help to the *Elector* office. The upshot was that Champion, Mann and Burns were on hand constantly for the next seven weeks, administering the strike fund, supervising the picketing and keeping up the morale of the strikers with a rhetoric which, in Champion's case, echoed the revolutionary fervour of his Trafalgar Square utterances. Champion was also the source of more practical assistance. His efforts discredited claims by the employers that the docks were operating on a 'business as usual' basis. In the words of his *Trident* article: 'One day, I put on blue dungarees, and dirtied my face, and rammed a slouch hat over my eyes; and, by the aid of an accomplice at the Dock gates, I got into the enemy's camp, and strolled about. It didn't take me many minutes to see that the Dock Companies had been committing terminological inexactitudes'. He was similarly instrumental, by his own account, in obtaining the intervention in the strike by Cardinal Manning, which contributed so largely to its successful outcome: 'It was suggested to me that he, with his enormous influence, might be able to act as a mediator, and I went to see him about it. I found him immensely interested, and the result of our interview was that he took up the matter with his usual energy'.[60] At Manning's instigation, a conciliation committee was established, and agreement to most of the strikers' demands was obtained.

The reward for Champion and his associates was that they were elevated for a time to the status of working-class heroes. However, at the point where it seemed that Champion's hopes for socialism might be realised, his position was undermined by further charges stemming from the 'Tory Gold' affair and his association with Maltman Barry. The real aim of the *Labour Elector's* aggressively anti-Liberal policies, his critics now claimed, was less to bring about the new labour party which he purported to advocate than to split the labour element within the Liberal Party, to the advantage of the Tories. Further association with Champion became, in the view of key figures like Hardie, more likely to impede than to advance the goals which they shared with him, and it was with some relief that he was seen to accept a commission to report on labour matters for *The Times* and the *Nineteenth Century* which involved extensive travel in Germany and Australia. A fracas in the course of the Victorian segment of his fact-finding tour now ended for ever his prospects of office or influence, and gravely prejudiced the chances of Fabian socialism playing an effective role in the affairs of the colonial labour movement.

Champion's arrival in Melbourne on 12 August 1890 was followed three days later by the start of the national Maritime Strike which rapidly became a watershed in Australia's industrial and political history. The supposed issue behind the strike was resistance by the shipowners to the affiliation of their ships' officers with the THC. In fact, a significantly broader group of employers had resolved to confront what they believed – or purported to believe – was the 'menace' of the 'Confederated Trade Unions', in an economic climate which unexpectedly (and probably unbeknown to the unions) had become favourable to the employers' success. Given Champion's reputation as a pioneer of labour representation and a Dock Strike veteran, it was only to be expected that the colonial unionists would look to him for outspoken support of their struggle, and when he addressed the THC at its meeting on 22 August 'The acclamation with which he was greeted lasted for some minutes, and was succeeded by three cheers, most heartily given'.[61] The THC's sense of betrayal was correspondingly the greater when Champion's later reservations about the dispute became public.

The strike, in Champion's view, was ill-conceived because the employers saw themselves as men with their backs against the wall; because the depressed state of the colonial economy made it unlikely that the stated aims of the unions would be achieved; and because the arrangements available to the unions for co-ordinating their actions were not equal to the demands which he foresaw would be made on them. It followed, he believed, that the affiliation of the ships' officers with the THC should be surrendered in the interests of securing a reconciliation of the unions with the employers; that the strikers should be meticulous in keeping their actions within the law; and that an inquiry to determine responsibility for the dispute should be held. A £20,000 loan sought by the unions from their British counterparts should be refused, he argued subsequently, in a telegram to Burns, because it could not prevent the 'absolute failure' of a dispute which had been 'grossly mismanaged'.[62] 'Ten times the amount', he wrote, in an incisive analysis of the episode for the *Nineteenth Century*, 'would not in any way have influenced the result': the strikers were 'an army of lions, led by asses'. If the London Dock Strike had been 'Labour's Austerlitz', the Maritime Strike was the movement's Moscow, and he counted himself lucky to have witnessed both.[63]

Not surprisingly, Champion's strictures placed him at loggerheads with the entire labour movement. The Sydney Trades and Labour Council refused him the chance to put his side of the story, on the grounds that he was 'a person hostile to the Labour cause'.[64] The Melbourne THC resolved that 'owing to the injury Mr Champion has done the labour cause, we decline to hear him'.[65] The revulsion against his actions was not confined to Australia: a meeting of the London Trades Council, chaired by his longtime associate and friend, Mann, denounced him roundly, while at the same time repudiating 'any representative capacity Mr H.H. Champion may have assumed in Australia, he never having been a workman, or at any time authorised to speak on behalf of the workers of this country'.[66] Calls on Burns and Mann to disown him were made through the columns of *Justice*, and by the London representative of the Australian unions, John Fitzgerald.[67] Overall, an enduring impression was created that the failure of the strike had been, in part, a direct consequence of his intervention. A less impetuous figure than Champion might have kept his conclusions to himself. One more closely attuned to working-class values would have swallowed them and taken his stand shoulder to shoulder with his comrades against the class enemy. By failing either to practise prudence or respect solidarity, Champion finally and irrevocably burned his boats. Neither in Australia nor in Britain was the confidence of the labour movement extended to him again. When he left Australia for England in mid-1891, it was with implacable union hostility both behind and before him.

The reception which awaited him at the political level was no less frigid. The stigma of Maltman Barry and 'Tory Gold' still lingered, and Champion unwisely gave it new life by arranging funds from an undisclosed source for the candidacies of Burns and Hardie at the 1892 general election. At the same time, his own general election campaign in the South Aberdeen constituency was marred by the circulation of a letter from Australian unionists describing his part in the Maritime Strike debacle, and he found himself relegated to coming in third in the poll with a meagre one-sixth of the vote. An attempt to revive the *Labour Elector* in January 1893 fell foul of suspicions that once again the bills were being paid by Maltman Barry. In April the same year a letter repudiating Champion was published over the signatures of a majority of the members of the Independent Labour Party Council, and by the year's end he had become so peripheral a figure as to suffer the indignity of being lampooned in a parody of 'The Man Who Broke the Bank at Monte Carlo', which the Manchester ILP marketed under the title 'The Man Who Wants to Buy the Labour Party'. The precipitate decline in his political fortunes was matched by failing health, and he was advised that his chances of recovery depended on moving to a warmer climate. Having heard himself censured by the second annual conference of the ILP to the hearty applause of his former friends and comrades, he decided that such career prospects as might remain open to him could best be pursued in Melbourne, and it was for there that he set out in search of a new start in 1894.

THE BESANT-SCOTTS

Champion was welcomed back to Victoria by his friends Ernest and Mabel Besant-Scott, who had arrived in the colony two years earlier. Ernest Scott was the son of a Northampton civil engineer; born in 1867, he adopted as his hero and role model the great freethinker and radical Charles Bradlaugh, who was the town's member of parliament. As a pupil and later a pupil-teacher at St Katherine's Church of England School, he saw Bradlaugh repeatedly refused his place in the House of Commons on the grounds of his atheism. In due course an atheist himself, he resigned his teaching post because he was unable in conscience to perform the religious duties it required of him. The offer of a position as a journalist on the *Globe* took him to London in the late 1880s, where he joined the Fabian Society – possibly at the instigation of Bradlaugh's companion and confidant Annie Besant, who had befriended him – and was introduced to Champion.[68]

An account of Besant-Scott's distinctively Fabian view of socialism survives in an article he contributed to the March 1896 issue of the *Australian Herald*. What he characterised as 'single and other taxes, franchises, land laws, factory acts, philanthropies innumerable, strikes Titanic, tears, oratory, lamentations, Parliamentary wrestlings and all the janglings of churches, societies and federations, with their creeds, programmes and manifestoes' would be 'ineffectual and vain', he argued, 'unless the earnest reforming be directed intelligently along the lines of Socialist evolution'. 'In place of anarchical competition, with its myriad evils', he continued, socialism desired 'to substitute a system of collective ownership of the whole of the means of production', but its attainment, as he saw it, would not be brought about 'all at once at any time' but 'little by little'. The 'Socialising of legislation', in his view, was the true policy, and 'the introduction of the Socialist principle wherever possible, in municipal and State matters' was, he concluded, 'the surest and safest method of bringing about the end in view'.[69]

It was Annie Besant again, in all probability, who encouraged Scott to interest himself in theosophy, the doctrine of divine revelation which had been originated in New York in 1875 by Helena Petrovna Blavatsky. Besant, by Shaw's account, had 'found herself the fifth wheel of the Fabian coach, and left it to succeed Helena Petrovna Blavatsky in India as queen of the Theosophists plus

educator and moderniser of native Indian policy'.[70] Her platform
skills and unflagging energy were to make her the Theosophical
Society's most effective proselytiser. Scott and Besant's militantly
feminist daughter, Mabel, were married in July 1892 and, in conformity with the common feminist practice of the day, they adopted
the family name of Besant-Scott. A week after the marriage they left
London for Melbourne, where they set up house in Jolimont and
Ernest Besant-Scott became a reporter for the *Herald*.

The choice of Melbourne for their new home may well have been
motivated by a belief – either on Annie Besant's part or their own
– that Victoria would provide rich opportunities for evangelical
activity on behalf of the Theosophical Society. Much of their time
and energy in the months following their arrival in the colony
was devoted to advancing the theosophical cause. When a senior
theosophist, Mrs Isabel Cooper-Oakley, lectured in Melbourne in
1893, she was their house guest in Jolimont, and they became charter
members of the Melbourne Theosophic League founded during her
visit. Ernest Besant-Scott edited the movement's Australian journal,
the *Austral-Theosophist*, and Mabel contributed articles to it on
topics such as the leading members of the Society as she had come
to know them through her mother in Europe. The couple then
assisted Annie Besant in the establishment of the Australasian
Section of the Theosophical Society, during her lecture tour of
Australia in 1894, while at the same time becoming active participants
in the mostly middle-class subcultures where Victoria's intellectually
and culturally more adventurous spirits intermingled and their
organisations overlapped.

Faced with the working-class hostility which the Maritime
Strike had engendered, Champion took full advantage of the access
to the more congenial and receptive circles of colonial opinion
which the friendship of the Besant-Scotts afforded him. Following
in his friends' footsteps, he became active, in particular, in the
Australasian Section of the Theosophical Society and the Australasian Church, while, on his own initiative, he embraced the colonial
co-operative movement. Given that there is no record of his having
any interest in theosophy prior to his arrival in Melbourne, it seems
likely that he was introduced to it there through the Besant-Scotts.
His fascination with ideas may well have led him to be attracted
by the glittering presence among the theosophists of his future
Fabian associate, the young Bernard O'Dowd (also a fellow activist

in the Australian Church)[71] and the pantophile element of his complex personality may similarly have been receptive to the presence of political luminaries such as the future prime ministers, Alfred Deakin and Edmund Barton.[72] Much of the Besant-Scotts' and Champion's time and energy was devoted to advancing the theosophical cause, and there is a sense in which it can be seen to have figured for them as a dry run for their Melbourne Fabian Society venture. The Australasian Section of the Theosophical Society was among the first of the many local organisations in whose activities Champion figured prominently. He founded an Ibis Lodge of the Section in honour of Annie Besant, with Deakin as secretary; spoke widely on theosophical topics from other platforms; and defended theosophy against its critics in the columns of his new weekly paper, the *Champion*. The Ibis Lodge, based in the Melbourne suburb of Prahran, faithfully reflected his reformist conscience and philosophy. The characteristically bold Champion stamp was plain in the Lodge's decision to move beyond the usual theosophical routine of classes and lectures, by establishing a theosophical Sunday School and contemplating plans for a labour bureau, a holiday home for children at Mt Macedon and a program of visits to prisons and hospitals. No less characteristically, the grand design was abandoned before it could be put to the test, when his attention was distracted by the prospect of new and more promising vehicles for reform in the Melbourne Fabian Society and the Social Democratic Federation of Victoria, and the theosophical connection was summarily dropped. The episode recalls again the erratic, impetuous side of Champion's character, which in so many instances compromised the associates whose causes he set out to advance.

JOHN ROSS

Theosophy, the Australian Church and the co-operative movement were Champion's sources for the remaining members of the inner circle of the Melbourne Fabian Society. The Theosophical Society contributed John Ross, the Australian Church the Reverend Charles Strong and Thomas Palmer, and the co-operative movement Walter A. Hamilton. The Society's indigenous recruits, like their expatriate mentors, conformed closely to Archer's Fabian archetype. The white collar salariat character of the group was demonstrated by the fact that Ross was a journalist and lecturer, Strong a clergyman, Palmer a teacher and Hamilton a member of parliament and former trade union functionary. Ross's status as a sometime Master of the Austral-Temple Lodge of the Theosophical Society, and the adherence of Strong and Palmer to the Australian Church doctrines – which so many of Strong's clerical colleagues regarded as heretical – were further relevant characteristics. Strong, Palmer and Hamilton all expressed views which clearly demonstrated their alienation from the contemporary commercial world on the grounds of its unfairness and inhumanity, while Ross may well have experienced an aesthete's revulsion from its ugliness and insensitivity.

Ross was born on 27 April 1857 and, at the outset of his working life, reported courts and local councils for the *Argus* to supplement his meagre earnings as an apprentice proof-reader. His work as a journalist was accompanied later by lecturing in voice production at Melbourne University and, later again, adjudicating for the leading elocution competitions in Australia and New Zealand and examining in elocution for bodies such as the Victorian Education Department, the London School of Music and the Music Society of Victoria. A passion for public speaking in all its forms placed him squarely in an area of major interest to the early Fabians, who valued lecturing as 'the most effective form of political education practised by the Society',[73] and worked constantly at improving their platform skills through mechanisms such as the Charing Cross Parliament debating society and the Society's various public-speaking classes. Given that Ross's training in London came from the tragedian Creswick, and that the wide range of London theatre acquaintances he made included celebrities of the stamp of Sarah Bernhardt, it seems likely that his circle also included such theatre-world Fabians as Shaw, Harley Granville Barker, Charles Charrington and Frederick Whelen. If so, it may well have been in their company that his introduction to Fabian socialism was gained, and, perhaps, that he first met Champion, who was a further ardent theatre-going Fabian. Ross was also a *litterateur* of note, who associated himself with Douglas Slade in the preparation of Slade's pioneering anthology *A Century of Australian Song*. A reverence for the work of Adam Lindsay Gordon – whom he had had pointed out to him as a child in Melbourne – was apparent in his 1885 biography of Gordon, *The Laureate of the Centaurs*, and again when he initiated an annual pilgrimage to Gordon's grave.

THOMAS PALMER

Colourfulness of a more sombre and serious stamp characterised the career of Thomas Palmer. His delivery of the Melbourne Fabian Society's first public lecture took place at a point where he was fast becoming the era's foremost educator and also one of its human tragedies. Palmer, as much as any London Fabian, epitomised the Society's archetypal ' "new man" rising through the interstices of the traditional social and economic structure'.[74] His socialist convictions may also have been attributable, in part, to the 'rough pattern', to which earlier reference has been made, of 'a link of some kind (past or current, personal or family) with certain sections (large scale or small scale) of the Victorian commercial world; but one that was clearly severed through revulsion or failure'.[75]

Palmer's advancement was won the hard way, by what the *Australasian Schoolmaster* described as 'sheer force of character and close application to the study of his profession'. Born the son of an Irish plumber in Ballarat in 1858, and educated at the Ballarat Common School, he worked as an apprentice lithographer and draftsman before deciding, at the age of seventeen, that his future was in teaching. His training college course was completed with first class honours in 1876, and part-time study at Melbourne University gained him his BA in 1881, his MA in 1884 and his LLB in 1887. His initial posting was to Williamstown State School – where he concluded that 'the Education Department offered but little scope for men of advanced thought'. He subsequently held positions as senior master at Mr Alex Sutherland's Carlton College, proprietor-principal of the South Melbourne College – where 'so great was his success as a teacher that winners of State School scholarships and students from all parts of Victoria flocked to him';[76] proprietor-principal of the University High School – where he enjoyed 'the largest school roll and the highest results and longest list of honours of all colleges and grammar schools' – and headmaster of Wesley College.[77] At the same time, however, financial difficulties dating from the early 1890s dogged his footsteps, and ultimately he was caught embezzling £1000 from Wesley College funds. At that stage, as the College historians have wryly observed, he 'quietly left the school he had done so much to rehabilitate, and went to South Africa to rehabilitate himself'.[78]

While education was Palmer's livelihood, it was also seen by him as a means to wider social ends. Victoria's early politicians had ranked as statesmen, he believed, because they saw that 'universal education was a necessary complement to universal suffrage, and that an uneducated democracy could not possibly exist'. The 1867 Higinbotham Royal Commission on the operation of the Common Schools Act had, in his view, 'been right to put forward a land tax as the way to place education on a secure footing, and Victoria was the poorer for their recommendation not having been adopted'. Without such a tax, he argued, education was at the mercy of 'a Parliament composed in part of men who cannot be called statesmen, and whose highest principle is temporary expedience'. This was exacerbated, as he saw it, by the attitudes of parents, who treated education as something to be bought 'just in the same manner as a pound of sugar or a yard of linen', and the schoolmaster as 'merely a shopkeeper with certain goods for sale at so much per quarter'.[79]

WALTER HAMILTON

Hamilton's status as the only trade unionist member of the Melbourne Fabian Society's inner circle, probably reflected the fact that, as an MP and Victoria's foremost practical co-operator, he was influenced more strongly by Champion's outspoken support for the co-operative movement than by the THC's hostility towards Champion. Born on 10 March 1863 at the Glenelg farm and vineyard his grandparents had taken up on their arrival in South Australia from England in 1836, he was educated at Mr F. Caterer's Glenelg Grammar School.[80] Following his sixteenth birthday, he worked on his father's farm for two years, winning ploughing contest prizes on three occasions. He was then apprenticed to a Glenelg coach-building firm, became a journeyman coachbuilder in Adelaide, Melbourne and Traralgon, and was awarded coach-building prizes at the 1887 Traralgon Agricultural Show.[81] Hamilton joined the Journeymen Coachbuilders' Society in South Australia in 1884 and, as the Society's Victorian Branch Secretary between 1887 and 1889, received a golden locket from his fellow unionists on his resignation, for having lifted membership from forty to 200. Moving to a job with the Bendigo Rolling Stock Company in 1889, he established a Bendigo Branch of the Coachbuilders' Society and became secretary of the Bendigo Trades and Labour Council and the Eight Hour Day Committee.[82]

The PLC selected Hamilton as its candidate for the Sandhurst seat which he contested unsuccessfully at the 1892 general election and at an 1893 by-election before winning it in 1894. The fact that the Single Tax was in each instance a major plank of his election platform probably attracted Champion's attention to him, as did his role as the founder of a co-operative bakery in the Ironbark area of Bendigo. So successful was the project under Hamilton's management that:

> It was found necessary to get new and larger premises. A piece of land was bought in the Mount Korong Road, opposite the old premises, and there one of the most commodious bake-houses in the colony has been erected. It is two stories in height, contains two ovens, a bread room, yeast room and all other accessories of a first-class bakery, and adjoining are an eight-stall stable and a manager's residence and offices. The land and buildings, to say nothing of the plant, are now worth a thousand pounds.[83]

As a co-operator, Hamilton would have had no difficulty in feeling comfortable either with his fellow union officials (some of whom established union-based co-operatives for the supply of commodities such as boots and basic foodstuffs) or with the Fabians, who were friends and eloquent advocates of the co-operative movement. Beatrice Webb wrote the definitive account of the movement – *The Co-operative Movement in Britain* – and, as late as 1916, Sidney Webb's seminal essay, 'Towards Social Democracy', singled out co-operation and municipalisation as essential ingredients of a socialist society.[84] It was only later that some Fabians entered into their Faustian bargain with the state as 'the missing prime mover, the massive actor and legislator necessary to deal with intractable social problems',[85] and were led away from the search for more practical applications of the six co-operative principles, via the infatuation of the ageing and despairing Webbs with Soviet communism, to the sterile shoals of Herbert Morrison's statutory corporations.

Hamilton's Single Tax affiliations, however, had become a political liability in Australia, and made him suspect in the eyes of more THC-oriented ULLP colleagues such as John Hancock, a former secretary of the Melbourne Typographical Society and THC president who became the first labour member of the Legislative Assembly.[86] As Bruce Scates illustrates, there was a stage during the early 1890s when the Victorian Single Tax League – like its South Australian counterparts – had worked with energy and conviction in the mainstream labour movement.[87] Between 1889 and around the middle of 1892, branches of the Progressive Political League invited Single Taxers to address their meetings; prominent unionists – albeit in the capacity of 'private citizens' – sat on the platforms of the public meetings at which Henry George spoke during his tour of Victoria in 1890; at least two PPL branches – Hawthorn and Toorak – were represented by prominent Single Taxers on the PPL Central Committee; and the PPL's 1892 election platform received public endorsement from the VSTL. However, the association of labour and liberal elements in the United Liberal and Labour Party following the mediocre performance of the PPL at the 1892 elections brought to the fore the fact that the Single Taxers' almost universal support of free trade was incompatible with the protectionism of the labour and liberal camps. By December 1892, Single Taxers such as Hirsch were sharing platforms with the conservative Free Trade Democratic Association and, in the course of the following year, such sympathies with them as may have lingered within the THC were finally alienated by their increasingly strident free trade and anti-labour rhetoric. Well before the decade was over, the egregious Hirsch and his associates had made the Single Tax politically irrelevant.

The tensions within the labour camp between Single Taxers and their critics surfaced in Hancock's attack against Hamilton in the Legislative Assembly on 23 July 1895. A report of Hancock's comments from the *Champion* reads in part:

> Certain gentlemen had tried to get into Parliament as Single Taxers. When these gentlemen found they could not get into Parliament as Single Taxers, they assumed the garb of Protectionists, and in some cases, even joined the Labour party. Up to the present time, he was happy to say, he had received nothing but congratulations on the attitude assumed by the Labour party, but he had never heard anything but condemnation of the attitude taken up by the renegade members of the Labour party. (Mr HAMILTON – 'Who are they?') He would leave that to be answered by the honourable member for Sandhurst (Mr HAMILTON), who knew to whom he referred. 'Let the galled jade wince'. Above all, the Committee must be careful of the Single Taxers in any shape or form. The Single Taxers cropped up on both sides of the House, and there was no class of politician more unreliable. Single Taxers were found voting for free-trade and associated with men who would blush to be seen in their company when it became known what they really wanted, namely, the single tax and confiscation.[88]

Champion's response to Hancock's outburst said more by far for his loyalty to Hamilton, his new-found associate, than for any capacity to keep clearly in focus the pressing need to build bridges with the labour establishment which Hancock so clearly personified. 'Hamilton', he wrote in the *Champion*, 'is a thinker and a student; a man who gives up his leisure to the hard work of directing schemes for the benefit of workers. He is small in stature but big in mind'. 'Hancock', by comparison, was 'a parrot and a blind partisan; a man who spends his spare time wagering on low suburban racecourses, rubbing shoulders with petty bookmakers, spielers and the usual riff-raff of such places':

> He has much more regard for a sporting dead bird than a social dead beat. He is big in body but small in mind. Let us 'be thankful that oblivion covers so much; that all carrion is by and by buried in the green earth's bosom, and even makes her grow the greener'.[89]

Ironically, Champion too was in the process of shedding the millennial hopes he had invested in the Georgist faith in his days as a Land Reform Union member and editor of the *Christian Socialist*, although his commitment to a land tax was unimpaired. A year later, in 1896, he likened what he described as 'the rather futile Single Tax League' to those sincere enthusiasts for apple and nut diets who believed their fad to be a panacea for all physical and spiritual ills.[90]

CHARLES STRONG

Strong – whose central credo has been defined as echoing Ruskin's declaration that 'Government and Co-operation are in all things the Law of Life, Anarchy and Competition are the Law of Death'[91] – may similarly have seen himself as having nowhere else to go, and he had good reason for 'revulsion or disillusionment' from the commercial world, whose wealthy scions among his Scots Church congregation had rejected his concern for disadvantage in all its forms, just as most of his fellow members of the Presbyterian clergy had rejected his liberal theology. Born the third son of a Presbyterian minister at Dailly in Scotland on 26 September 1844, and educated at the Ayr and Glasgow academies and Glasgow University, he was appointed assistant minister at Dalmellington in 1867. He was minister at Greenock's Old West Kirk in 1868 and at Glasgow's Anderston parish in 1871. In 1875 he accepted a call to Melbourne.

Hitherto, the expression of Strong's social conscience – shaped as it was by first-hand observation of poverty in Dailly's mining community, and the profoundly liberalising social and theological influence of his Professor of Divinity, John Caird – had been heavily in the *noblesse oblige* mould of paternalistic service to the poor, which emphasised advice and moral suasion to the exclusion of more practical forms of assistance. John Caird's better known brother Edward, the Professor of Moral Philosophy at Glasgow and a key proponent of the new liberalism in Britain, has been seen as exercising an indirect influence on New Liberals in Australia (including the young H.V. Evatt) through proteges such as Henry Jones.[92] In Melbourne, Strong preached instead to his new parishioners that 'their religion was of little value to them unless they saw it as an obligation to serve their fellow men and especially those in need and those nearest to them'.[93] A personal example was set by his involvement in such organisations as the Australian Health Society, the Convalescents' Aid Society and the Society in Aid of Mental Hospital Patients, while his views were given further amplification in his frequent articles for William Henderson's independent and liberal-leaning *Presbyterian Review*.

Unsurprisingly, such developments gave rise to disquiet within a congregation which was remarkable, in the view of one perceptive contemporary commentator, 'chiefly for the individual and aggregate worth of its members'.[94] Conservatism – albeit ostensibly theological – was no less entrenched among Strong's clerical colleagues. In the minds of many his liberal views were tantamount to heresy, while he himself was regarded as an apostate. Moreover, it has been suggested, his ecclesiastic detractors found it easier to think badly of him because their congregations were dwindling while his continued to grow. Be this as it may, the disparate wellsprings of anti-Strong sentiment coalesced in 1877 in attacks of mounting ferocity which first brought about a breakdown in his health so severe as to require lengthy recuperation in Scotland, and then laid siege to his Scots Church incumbency. Strong's support for the Sunday Liberation Society and his supposed collusion in the preparation of a controversial lecture on religion and science which Higinbotham delivered to the Literary Society on 1 August 1883 added fuel to the fire.[95] In November 1883, the Assembly of the Presbyterian Church of Victoria called on him to appear before it and explain himself. His response instead was a letter of resignation from his pulpit, which read in part, 'Allow me to say that I have done my best to serve what seemed to me the best interests of the church and of religion while here, that I have preached and tried to practise what I believe to be the essential doctrines of the Gospel, and that when I find that I can no longer remain a minister of the Presbyterian Church or sign her standards, I hope to have the moral courage to leave it'.[96] The laying-down of his office was accepted by the Assembly, and he again set sail for Scotland.

Prior to Strong's departure, a meeting of 2000 of his supporters, chaired by the Lord Mayor of Melbourne in the Melbourne Town Hall, had signalled its outrage over his treatment at the hands of the Assembly and handed him a purse of £3000, together with an illuminated address. The occasion was indicative of the esteem which his first six years in Victoria had won for him among the colony's citizens. The same depth of public support was instrumental twelve months later in securing Strong's return to Melbourne, where he resumed his delivery of sermons at the Temperance Hotel, before audiences which were seen to consist of 'the wealthy, the fashionable, the dissident, the intellectuals and many of the merely curious'. On 11 November 1885, a meeting of the Temperance Hall venture's backers decided that a new Australian Church should be formed, and Strong accepted their invitation to become its first minister. On 19 March 1887, the foundation stone was laid for a new church building, which opened its doors the following December. A statement of the new body's ideals and principles read in part:

> The Australian Church aims at being a comprehensive Church, whose bond of union is the spiritual and practical rather than creeds or ecclesiastical forms. It recognises the principles that where the Spirit of the Lord is, there is liberty, that 'by one Spirit are we baptised into the one Body and that it is hurtful to truth, honesty and spiritual life to hamper either minister or people by imposing on them the interpretation of the Gospel or the theologies handed down from olden time'.[97]

The Australian Church was also a base for the expansion of Strong's program of social and charitable activity. Even so, bodies such as the Melbourne Creche Society, the Collingwood Working Men's Club and the jaw-breakingly named Social Improvement, Friendly Help and Children's Aid Society (which the church formed as a means of grappling with social issues) could by their nature make only limited contributions to the comprehensive socialist vision which informed material like his leading article for the April

1894 issue of the Church's journal, the *Australian Herald*: 'Th.:re will be no amassing of large "fortunes" in the hands of the few: capital will be available for the use of all honest workers; public spirit will take the place of selfish interest; and a freer, healthier and happier, because more generous, way of life will be within the reach of all'.[98] Unfortunately, no happier outcome eventuated from the ill-fated Village Settlement Movement, which Strong launched in conjunction with Canon Tucker in 1892. The ULLP was preoccupied with industrial issues, which Strong generally supported, but could not accept as exhausting the real agenda of items of community concern, and there was no other organisation within the colony committed to bringing about social reform. It was natural, in such circumstances, that he should warmly welcome the arrival in Victoria, and subsequent involvement in the Church's affairs, of London Fabians such as Besant-Scott and Champion, and that he should associate himself with Champion in a range of activities which included not only the Melbourne Fabian Society but also the Australian Co-operative Society, the Australian Criminology Society and the National Anti-Sweating League.

Champion, in his turn, was a prolific contributor to the *Australian Herald* before establishing the *Champion*. He also lectured for church groups such as the Literary Society, and conducted classes in economics and politics for the Collingwood Working Men's Club. The advantages he gained in return may well have included his introduction to the Goldstein family. After proposing unsuccessfully to Vida Goldstein – as some suppose – Champion married her sister Elsie in 1898, and shared various homes with the Goldsteins for the rest of his life. The Goldsteins' links with the Australian Church were severed around the turn of the century in a conversion to Christian Science which was characteristically thorough. As Leslie Henderson points out, 'Having once embraced this religion they would want nothing further to do with hospitals or any other medical matter. Their religion became for them just exactly what a religion should be – the ruling force of their lives to which all else was subordinate'.[99] This rejection of orthodox medical care may well have had unhappy consequences for Champion, whose political activities were frequently interrupted by ill health. He had had typhoid fever during his military service in Afghanistan, and his subsequent afflictions are said to have included epilepsy, tuberculosis and – according to Havelock Ellis, although disputed vigorously by Elsie

Goldstein – venereal disease.[100] While it is not clear whether any or all of the Goldsteins joined Champion's Melbourne Fabian Society, Vida lectured subsequently for the Social Democratic Party of Victoria,[101] and was a member of Sinclaire's Fabian Society of Victoria.[102]

WOMEN'S SUFFRAGE

The bonds between Champion, Besant-Scott and Strong drew strength from another characteristically Fabian source. All three were active members of the colonial women's suffrage movement. As has been seen, 'emancipated and presumably middle-class women' accounted for between one-fifth and one-sixth of the London Society's membership at the time of the Melbourne Society's inception, with the result that, as one observer noted, 'It is not surprising that the only amendment ever carried to the Fabian "Basis" was one in favour of women's suffrage'.[103] Strong was an early supporter of the suffrage cause. He declined the offer of a position on the inaugural committee of the Victorian Women's Suffrage Society in 1884 on the grounds that his energies had to be devoted entirely to the establishment of his Australian Church, but four years later addressed the first annual general meeting of what has been seen by some as 'the more politically-assertive, social purity oriented' Australian Women's Suffrage Society, and became a vice-president of the National Society for Women's Suffrage when it was formed in 1892.[104]

Besant-Scott followed his academic inclinations – and, no doubt, the urgings of his suffragist wife, Mabel – by undertaking a study of the atmosphere of rebellion against conventional marriage expectations which the women's movement was held to be prompting,[105] while Champion's characteristically catholic involvement in the affairs of the Prahran Branch of the Victorian Women's Suffrage League, the League itself and the United Council for Women's Suffrage (UCWS) was pursued with his customary vigour. Contemporary reports suggest that the establishment of the UCWS in 1894, as an umbrella organisation for the other suffrage groups, may well have been undertaken at Champion's instigation, and his position as its 'parliamentary secretary' – presumably with liaison duties – was retained until ill health obliged him to surrender it in 1901. His views on suffrage were set out in detail in his pamphlet, *The Claim of Woman*. The *Champion* featured a notably enlightened column on issues of special interest to women, under the title of 'The World of Women', and the journal was acknowledged following its demise as having done more for the suffragist cause than any other paper.[106]

None of this meant that Champion and his associates were necessarily immune to gaffes or massive insensitivities, as illustrated by Champion in an article on the London Society in Strong's *Australian Herald*:

> In Mr Sidney Webb, it has an indefatigable and accurate collector of statistics, whose summaries have been published far and wide. His wife, who was Miss Beatrice Potter, has some talent of the same kind, and lends assistance.[107]

Three of a series of five lectures organised by the UCWS in 1895 were delivered by the Fabian trio, with Champion taking as his subject 'The Claim of Woman', Besant-Scott 'The Advanced Woman in Recent Fiction' and Strong 'Woman, Her Place and Power'. It is indicative of the distance which even advanced opinion within the colony had still to travel that male dominance of the proceedings seems to have been seen by the Fabians neither as incompatible with their principles nor even incongruous.[108]

THE NEW LIBERALS

Champion's initial assessment of his new political stamping ground in Victoria was formed following his nomination as one of five candidates for the heavily working-class Legislative Assembly electorate of Albert Park at the 1894 general elections. The circumstances of his candidacy suggest that any hopes he may have entertained of entering parliament with the blessing of the labour movement - or without its active opposition - had already been abandoned. His mind was already at work on alternative sources of support, which before long led him to court the New Liberals who had dominated Victorian politics intellectually since the middle 1880s and were to continue to do so until well into the second decade of the new century. The interventionist outlook and intense Empire loyalties of their principal spokesman, Deakin, in key respects closely resembled Champion's Tory socialism. The Victorian New Liberals - like their counterparts in Britain - were influenced profoundly by teachings such as those of the ethical idealist philosophers T.H. Green at Oxford and Edward Caird and Henry Jones at Edinburgh.[109]

Green largely provided the over-arching framework which enabled the New Liberals to reconcile a fullblooded disregard of the *laissez-faire* view of the state, which had been dear to the hearts of their Cobdenite predecessors, with adherence to the traditional liberal emphasis on individualism. A robust discussion of the concept of the state by his Australian disciple Francis Anderson reads in part:

> The state is society organised for the common good, for the protection of individuals against groups, associations, unions of masters, unions of men, who, without such common state action, would make freedom of the individual impossible. To reduce state functions to a minimum would be to reduce the possibility of individualism to a minimum.[110]

'The State,' Jones told a Sydney audience during his 1908 lecture tour of Australia, was 'nothing else but the coming of the Kingdom of God on Earth'. Jones was welcomed to Australia with encomium from Deakin's close associate and biographer-to-be, Walter Murdoch: 'no philosopher that ever lived had been more keenly intent . . . [on] applying philosophy to the problems of modern life'.[111] He was Deakin's guest at lunch and dinner, and Deakin took time off from his duties as prime minister to attend his Sydney lecture. 'The description of colonial state activity as "state socialism"' had been for Deakin's mentor, Syme, 'neither blasphemous nor inaccurate, rather it simply reflected the way the world worked in the colonies'.[112] Any reservations about the state that Deakin himself may have entertained had long since been stilled. 'My scruples as to state interference easily vanished', he recalled, 'and gradually I became satisfied that fiscal interference in the interests of the working classes and their interests was justified and necessary'.[113] 'Instead of the State being regarded any longer as the object of hostility to the labourer', he declared on a further occasion, 'it should now become identified with an interest in his work, and in all workers, extending them its sympathy and protection, and watching over their welfare and prosperity'.[114]

A second notable New Liberal was Deakin's former fellow law student at Melbourne University, Henry Bournes Higgins, whose turbulent career on the back bench of the Victorian parliament was followed by a term as Attorney-General in the commonwealth government formed by the Labor Party under J.C. Watson in 1904. Higgins was founder president of the Arbitration Court; and – through his judgement in the Harvester Case – the father of the Basic

Wage. As a small child, Higgins' niece Nettie Higgins is said to have confused her uncle with God. Describing a comment passed by Higgins in conversation with her father, Nettie wrote, 'It didn't sound as if you or I had said it. He seemed to have two judge's wigs on, and the air stood still to listen'.[115] A third New Liberal was Samuel Mauger, the felt hat manufacturer, sometime Trades Hall Council delegate for the Hatters' Union, and honorary minister and later Postmaster-General in Deakin's 1906 Liberal federal government, of whom it was written following his death in 1936 that 'scarcely a movement of any importance in Victoria to improve the average lot and secure a greater measure of social justice did not gain in coherence and strength from his influence'.[116] The New Liberal agenda shared with its Labor counterpart measures such as anti-sweating legislation, income tax and old age pensions, in the pursuit of what Deakin saw as 'a far wider and more advanced liberalism than had been acclimatised before the gold era'.[117]

Further links between Deakin and Champion stemmed from their deep loyalty to the Empire and support for the strengthening of imperial ties through measures such as imperial preference. The new flowering of the imperial ideal to which both subscribed is memorably encapsulated in a passage from the introduction to the diaries of Leo Amery, the erstwhile London Fabian whose long and exceptionally distinguished career as a Tory MP and minister climaxed in the House of Commons on 7 November 1940, when he flung at Neville Chamberlain the words used by Cromwell to dismiss the Long Parliament: 'You have sat here too long for any good you have been doing. Depart, I say, and let us have done with you. In the name of God, go!'. The introduction describes Amery as having returned from service in South Africa with a sense of mission:

> He would devote his life to helping to weld the self-governing colonies and dependencies which made up the rather ramshackle Victorian Empire into an effective Imperial Union; united for defence, for foreign affairs, and for trade, investment and migration. Here was a civilising mission to which the British people could dedicate themselves; one from which they could derive a sense of purpose and a source of pride. This concept was more than a political programme. It was an ideology which constituted a coherent system of thought to which every issue, political and economic, social, cultural and even moral could be related. This faith would sustain him throughout his life.[118]

Exceptions such as the Irish-born Higgins apart, Amery's vision was generally shared by both Deakin's New Liberal contemporaries and the highly talented younger men and women who looked to Deakin for leadership and inspiration. Deakin was a long-serving president of the Melbourne chapter of the Imperial Federation League, which outlived the demise of the London parent body in the late 1890s and gave rise to a Melbourne offshoot of the Round Table, which former members of Alfred Milner's South African 'kindergarten' founded in 1909 to raise Empire consciousness and strengthen imperial ties. The trigger for the transition was a visit to Melbourne by Leo Curtis, known to his Round Table associates as 'The Prophet'.[119] The aim, in Deakin's view, was to achieve 'a central imperial body, on which all the self-governing Dominions are represented and have an effective voice'. It was his further hope that the binding decisions of such a body 'being arrived at, not by the counting of votes, but through the unanimity reached by inquiry, argument and mutual concessions' would be assured of endorsement by the parliaments of the participants.[120] The spaciousness of his thinking commended him to rising young imperial statesmen of the stamp of Amery, and prompted invitations to enter British politics which were no less flattering for being wildly unrealistic.

There were reasonable grounds for Champion's belief that overtures to the New Liberals might be reciprocated. There was, for a start, a good deal of confusion in all electorates as to which candidates were labour nominees, reflecting the no less confused state of a parliament where faction politics remained more influential than party politics, and the allegiances of individual members were subject to change at short notice. In 1894, as Peter Kellock points out:

> The United Labour and Liberal Party urged supporters to vote for twenty-one 'social-democrats', which included Alfred Deakin, Sir Graham Berry and Hume Cook. Yet only seven of these candidates were directly connected with Trades Hall, the base of labour power. The *Argus* list of successful labour candidates numbered ten, and did not include either Deakin or Berry. Champion himself was inconsistent, sometimes referring to the twenty-one 'social-democrats' in the House, at other times conceiving of labour as the narrow Trades Hall representation in parliament, numbering only six until Barrett's election in 1895. Labour members also were ambivalent in their allegiance, Sangster and Trenwith both numbering the Party at twenty-one, and in 1895 refused to receive a T.H.C. deputation on the grounds that they should not be interviewed as a body of people would think that the T.H.C. controlled the Party.[121]

Not only were some key New Liberals associated with the labour movement in the United Labor and Liberal Party, but the trade unionists, Prendergast and Trenwith, had also offered themselves to the voters as Liberals, as had the socialist MP, Dr Maloney. Deakin and the labour men, J.A. La Nauze writes, regarded one another 'not merely as useful temporary allies, but as actually engaged in the same cause as themselves'.[122] In response to an invitation to join the PLC prior to the 1892 elections, Deakin replied cordially that 'Pending a determination of the course to be pursued at the coming general election by those with whom I have always acted in the interests of Liberal principles, such as you too support, I hesitate to accept an invitation which were I an elector only I should probably already have embraced'.[123] 'The rise of the labour party', he declared on an earlier occasion, 'is more significant and cosmic than the Crusades'.[124] The New Liberals of the day leaned generally far more to the labour side of politics than to the conservatives, whom they regarded as being automatically and adamantly opposed to progress. At the same time, they were increasingly fearful of the demands of the pledge of adherence to caucus decisions which the labour movement seemed likely to require its representatives to undertake – an attitude which Champion might reasonably have interpreted as indicating that they would be receptive to another suitor.

An article published over Champion's name in the *Australian Herald* now argued that – in the absence of a party for the colony's 'able men and women' to support, or a leader round whom they could rally – 'the self-seeker and the wind-bag, the wire-puller and the local politician, have their way . . . [which] leads to the ruin of the country'. It was his intention, the article declared, to form 'a permanent political organisation' in Albert Park and the surrounding districts, once the elections were over. If others saw the advisability of following his example, he and his friends were prepared to help. Those who joined, the article continued, should be 'democrats who understand that, with all its disadvantages, that form of government which most nearly represents the people is best' and that 'the business of the State is not confined to the defence of the property of the few citizens who have any, but includes the organisation of the affairs of the people for the common good'. The new group would endeavour, it stated finally, 'to bring into public life some of the very large number of men who are now unwilling to face all the disagreeable and degrading experiences before any one who tries to force his way into a representative position'.[125]

The prospects for success seemed bright, with thousands attending his meetings, and the *Bulletin* commenting that 'Champion says nothing without giving a reason for his doctrine and at answering every question from both sides of it at once he is much smarter than Deakin . . . He has been a revelation in fluent democratic argument to the denizens of Albert Park'.[126] Ultimately, however, he withdrew from the contest when it seemed that a split vote among the progressive candidates might enable a conservative to be elected. The episode marked a further milestone in the deterioration of his already strained relationship with the THC.

Victoria, Champion's candidacy clearly implied, was in need of an independent labour party, for which he was able and willing to provide leadership. Having thrown down the gauntlet to the THC over the Maritime Strike, he was now ready to do so again in the political arena. The result, unsurprisingly, was that allegations about his Maritime Strike role were used against him in the campaign, in a way which showed plainly that the antagonism of the trade union movement towards him was unabated. Such initiatives as he took subsequently, and such causes as he espoused, inevitably attracted far greater suspicion and hostility than otherwise might have been the case. The victims, as will be seen, included the Melbourne Fabian Society project, on which he embarked in the final months of 1894, the 1895 May Day Committee, where he was a delegate for the MFS, the Social Democratic Federation of Victoria, which shortly supplanted the MFS in his affections, and, perhaps, the National Anti-Sweating League, in whose establishment he played a leading part.

CALLS FOR ACTION

The social and economic factors which prompted Archer to join the London Fabian Society had, by the time of Champion's return to Victoria in 1894, begun to inspire calls for an indigenous Fabian organisation. A front page article in a July 1894 issue of the *Worker* is a case in point.[127] While Sam Merrifield attributes the piece to the local journalist George Andrews,[128] the style and content are consistent with its having been inspired and perhaps largely written by Champion. All the able men in the British labour movement had been produced, according to the article, by the Fabian Society and the Social Democratic Federation. The success of the Fabian approach resulted, it was further argued, from the fact that the Society's principal essays and lectures were issued as pamphlets, and so became 'so many revolutionary seeds'. Melbourne, in the author's view, was 'utterly devoid of anything of a like character', and it followed, he believed, that a 'Melbourne Fabian Society only required a determined start to demonstrate its great utility as a leading factor in the education not only of the masses of the workers, but also of the so-called middle section of society which is essential to bring about a correct line of thought, but who now hold aloof simply from lack of knowledge of those true principles of social progression'. 'There are all the elements of success', the conclusion read, 'if such can be taught to realise the illimitable benefits that such a society would confer on the community as a whole'.[129] Similar sentiments are said to have been expressed privately by Annie Besant, when she lectured for the Theosophical Society in Victoria in September 1894 – and this despite her recent defection from the Fabians in Britain.[130]

Champion was quick to respond. Noting in the December 1894 issue of the *Australian Herald* that 'A proposal has been made to put on foot in Melbourne a society for the discussion of social problems, and some of its promoters wish to follow the example of the Fabian Society in London', he proceeded to extol the London Society as 'a small band of hard workers who have done much to instruct the public'. The Society's strength, he wrote, stemmed from 'the energy of a number of its members who have delivered innumerable lectures and addresses, and circulated pamphlets and leaflets by the hundred thousand'. The attitude of the Fabian Society towards the Liberal Party might be ambiguous, he acknowledged, and the merits of its permeation approach open to debate, but he believed the issue was irrelevant in Victoria, where 'there is no definite party organisation to be permeated or opposed'.[131] Victorians, in his view, had no need 'to be instructed in the possible advantages of State ownership and control', since, as he saw it, 'There is in Victoria plenty of the crude kind of Socialism that consists in throwing all burdens on the State, but there seems to be little informed and intelligent opinions upon the real difficulties about these matters': 'Clearly State Socialism as here conducted is impossible'. 'A Society which would find out and explain whether it is the principles, or the way in which they are put into practice, that is at fault', he rounded off, 'might do a great deal of good if it displayed as much ability and industry as the Fabian Society'.[132]

THE FOUNDATION OF THE MELBOURNE
FABIAN SOCIETY

Radical opinion was quick to take Champion at his word. The *Australian Herald* reported in February 1895 that 'As the outcome of several semi-private meetings of ladies and gentlemen interested in the Social Question, a Fabian Society has been formed in Melbourne'. It would not have been lost on Champion that this account would have applied with equal accuracy to the process followed by Pease a decade earlier in bringing to birth the London Fabian Society and the Fellowship of the New Life. Mr Thomas Palmer MA, LLB, the report stated, had delivered the new society's first lecture the previous month, dealing 'from a moral point of view' with the topic of 'What Socialism Would Do for Victoria'. The Society's aim, it was said, was 'the promotion and study of social-democratic principles in their application to Australia' and arrangements were foreshadowed for 'a course of lectures in socio-economic subjects' and the distribution of literature 'with a view to encourage people to study the social problem for themselves'.

Further details of the lecture series were provided in April, when the Society's sole pamphlet – *Manifesto of the Social-Democratic Party in the German Empire as Adopted at the Erfurt Congress 1891* – appeared with the rider that 'The following manifesto is now published, not as affording an example of servile imitation in the different circumstances of Victoria, but as showing the basic principles of the most powerful and best-organised working-class party in the world'.[133] A list of lectures incorporated in the pamphlet read in part:

April 22   H.H. Champion 'European Socialism'
May 6   Rev. Charles Strong 'Socialism and Christianity'
May 20   W. Hamilton, MLA 'Socialism and Co-operation'
June 3   E. Besant-Scott 'Recent Socialist Fiction'
June 17   T. Palmer, MA 'Socialism in Victoria'

Meanwhile, Ross became the Society's first secretary, with authority to collect the two shilling annual subscription; donations for a Literature Fund were also solicited, so that the lectures could be published. The Society advertised in the Erfurt manifesto pamphlet that it was willing to provide lecturers for other organisations.

The Melbourne Fabian Society acquired a meeting place in Champion's office at 7 Queen's Walk, 'for conversational discussion of social questions, and occasional readings from the works of well-known writers on social subjects', where access could be had to 'the latest papers and pamphlets'.[134] The rooms themselves were inhospitable, but their location – close to the corner of Swanston and Collins Streets, and in the same building as the feminist Warrawee Club's discussion centre and tearooms, as well as the women's employment agency and town shopping service operated by the journalist Alice Henry – was ideal for the energetic networking in which Champion was engaged. In 1896, he and Elsie Goldstein chose premises in Queen's Walk for the Book Lovers' Library, which they operated in part as a means of enabling 'the comparatively small number of persons who wish to study works which do not appeal to the general reader to do so at a trifling cost'.[135] The Society also offered pamphlets for sale at larger venues, such as the hall of Dr Bevan's church in Russell Street, where some of its public lectures were delivered. The stock included a full range of London Fabian Society publications, on which the *Champion* commented, 'Some of these apply to British politics only, but the majority may well be studied by any Victorian who wants to qualify himself to express an opinion upon modern political thought'.[136]

The *Australian Herald* reported in May, 1895, that, in introducing Champion to 'a good audience' in Garroway's Rooms prior to his address on 'European Socialism', the chairman, Strong, had commented that 'Whatever might be people's prejudices for or against Socialism, it was desirable that all should understand what Socialism really meant, and that whether the audience sympathised with Mr Champion's views or not, they would all agree that Mr Champion was well able to expound to them the aims of Socialism, that he was a man of honour, and one who had made sacrifices for what he believed to be in the best interests of his fellow men'. Champion, the report continued, 'spoke for an hour and a half, giving glimpses of the Socialist parties in the different countries of Europe, and reminiscences of his experiences as a Socialist leader'. 'The great principle of Socialism', he was quoted as pointing out, 'was the abolition of all monopolies of the means of production'. Socialism, in his view, did not mean legislation for any one class, but 'recognised only one class – those who laboured by hand or brain, and did useful work for the world'.

THE *CHAMPION*

In June 1895 Champion launched a new weekly which, characteristically, he named after himself. While the *Champion* was never formally an MFS publication, it clearly figured in its proprietor's mind as relating to the Society in the same way that *Justice* had related to the Social Democratic Federation in Britain, and his *Labour Elector* had related to the Independent Labour Party. The paper is belittled by some as having read 'more like a society than a socialist weekly, with its lengthy features on theatre, writers and artists, business and high finance and, on occasions, up to three of its eight pages devoted to cycling'.[137] It is also possible to take the more charitable view that, in the course of its two-year lifespan, the *Champion* injected a welcome note of wit, irreverence and crusading spirit into the drab conformity which had so largely overtaken Melbourne journalism – in part, perhaps, as a reaction to the excesses of the previous decade. An open letter on the front page of the first issue taxed David Syme with having failed to rise to the level of the responsibilities conferred on him by the power of the *Age*: 'It should be gall and wormwood to you to be told what is one of the truths that are never recognised till someone voices them loudly and insistently, namely, that you are the most conservative force in this country'. 'For yourself', a second open letter reminded the Reverend Dr Bevan of the Independent Church, 'you are better here than in London or New York, if only because the Melbourne public is the most gullible and long-suffering'. 'History', the visiting Irish nationalist, Michael Davitt was informed in a further contribution to the series, 'will record, as your lifework, the destruction of Ireland's only possible saviour'.[138]

Prison reform featured prominently in the pages of the *Champion*, as did more humane treatment for victims of psychiatric illness and intellectual disability, action against sweated labour, women's suffrage, child protection, the Single Tax, Legislative Council reform and anti-sweating legislation. The paper reported hard political news from Britain which would not otherwise have been available to readers in Victoria, and foreshadowed, through its coverage of the arts in all their forms, the formula which would be adopted subsequently with triumphant success by the Webbs in Britain for the *New Statesman*. Nor was the attention devoted to bicycles in its columns necessarily inappropriate. Cycling was a major form of recreation both for the founder Fabians in Britain and socialists generally. 'On wheels', according to Shaw's biographer, Michael Holroyd,

> the Fabians appeared to become schoolboys and girls again. Beatrice, who (until Sidney had one smash too many) rigorously prescribed it during the long Fabian summer afternoons, reckoned that the bicycle added a dimension of 'fun' or 'sport' to their desk-anchored lives; and Shaw hygienically explained: 'Unless I seize every opportunity of bicycling off into the country, if only for a couple of hours, I get beaten by the evil atmosphere in which I have to pass so much of my time'.[139]

Amy Strachey, whose husband, St Loe Strachey, edited the *Spectator*, recalled Beatrice 'scudding on before me down one of the back streets of Pimlico'. 'She was', Mrs Strachey noted, 'a graceful and intrepid rider'.[140]

THE CO-OPERATIVE MOVEMENT

Hamilton's lecture on socialism and co-operation provided an instructive illustration of the capacity of Fabian Societies for advancing their goals through the creation of specialist offshoots, and also of Champion's use of his journal to promote constructive projects. How Champion was able to bring co-operation to the fore with the help of Hamilton and the successful demonstration of co-operation in practice which followed are worth closer inspection. Hamilton was reported in the *Champion* on 22 June 1895 as describing for his audience how, four years earlier, he and a friend had conceived the idea of starting co-operative production in Bendigo. Only eight people, he said, had attended the first meeting they called, and these pioneers had gone on to establish a co-operative bakery, in the teeth of united opposition from the wider baking industry. In the last three years, he continued, no less than £800 had been earned as net profit on an average capital of £400, representing a 66 per cent return on members' funds. The co-operative, in his view, had become the best equipped bakehouse in Australia, and was now able to exercise a fair measure of control over the bakery trade in the Bendigo area.

According to the *Champion*, Hamilton's remarks resulted in twenty or more people from his audience coming forward to register their interest in the establishment of a Melbourne co-operative bakery. The *Champion*, in its turn, called for public support for such a venture, on the grounds that a bakery along the lines proposed could be expected to achieve a rapid success, and, perhaps, 'grow into a very big thing indeed'. In the Bootmakers' Union alone, the *Champion* asserted, there had to be enough breadwinners within a half mile of Collingwood whose involvement as co-operators would enable the bakery to flourish. Hamilton's help in getting the ball rolling was available, the paper argued, and 'any who are disposed to take this plain and simple step towards social amelioration' were invited to leave their names at the Queen's Walk office 'for transmission to those who have the matter in hand'.[141]

All this was in close conformity with the commitment of Champion's fledgling Social Democratic Federation of Victoria, whose platform read in part: 'To found co-operative associations, bakeries, stores, etc., under socialistic management, a percentage of the profits from which shall go to the Federation'. It was therefore not wholly surprising that those who 'had the matter in hand' turned out to be Champion and his Fabian associates. The *Champion* for 6 July 1895 carried a report that proposed rules for a Melbourne co-operative bakery had been drawn up and were available for study by interested readers. It was also suggested that Port Melbourne and Collingwood were the locations most conducive for the co-operative's success. This was followed two weeks later by an announcement in the *Champion* that the Social Democratic Federation of Victoria was about to establish a co-operative bakery, inviting 'all who wish to replace production for private profit, with all its attendant horrors, by production for the public welfare' to communicate with the Federation secretary at 7 Queen's Walk. A 'well-attended' meeting at the same address on 12 August saw the Australian Co-operative Society formed to operate a Carlton or Fitzroy bakery, where the workers could 'by co-operation produce and distribute the necessities of life without the interference of the capitalist, and retain the profits to be shared among themselves'.[142]

Strong was elected as the new co-operative's president. A campaign to recruit members was launched, with the slogan: 'Co-operation is a Cure for Sweating! Union Wages! Profits to the Customers and Workers! Honest Materials and Work!'.[143] Production at a weekly rate of 1,913 loaves began in September 1896, in premises at 16 Elizabeth Street, Richmond, and within two weeks demand became so great that a third delivery cart had to be obtained. Hamilton became manager in December and, by the following April, a weekly output of 4,235 loaves was achieved. The success of the venture further emboldened Champion to undertake the establishment of a Co-operative Medical Attendance Society, again in conjunction with his fellow Fabians, Strong and Palmer. There is a sense in which his involvement with the co-operative movement exemplifies his more positive, constructive and attractive qualities, and, in so doing, accentuates the sense of loss for what might have been achieved on behalf of the Fabian cause in Victoria if these qualities had been more generally applied.

In immediate terms, Champion came to see the bakery project as a model for ultimately bringing the bread industry as a whole under public ownership, 'by voluntary co-operation in open competition with the private employer who pays sweating wages, makes bad bread and gives you short weight of it'. It was his belief, more generally, that to 'obtain control of a whole trade and run it on human and not profit-grinding principles would be an immense feat, and the finest object lesson in practical Socialism which could possibly be given'.[144] The bakery and the Co-operative Medical Attendance Society – together with the co-operative store, the co-operative savings bank and the proposed co-operative farm, in which the Social Questions Committee and the Victorian Socialist Party later involved themselves – were all means to a clearly envisaged socialist goal, for which Champion worked consistently and constructively throughout his political career. They were not, however, sufficient to break down the hostility and wounded *amour propre* on the part of the trade union movement which he was now about to further exacerbate.

DISTRACTIONS

A seventh Melbourne Fabian Society lecture was delivered by Ross in the hall of Strong's Australian Church on 29 July 1895. Its title was 'State Banking'. The series then went into recess, in order to avoid clashing with the Monday night talks on social issues – including 'Sweating', 'Land and Landlords', 'Newer Methods of Charity', 'Competition', 'The Ethics of Investment' and 'The Ethics of Charity' – held by the Church of England in its Cathedral Chapter House. These, perhaps, were seen by the Fabians as their chance to convert the preachers rather than preach to the converted. The Society's aim, as the *Champion* expressed it, was 'To encourage the various Bishops, Deans and Canons by their presence, and, if necessary, to stimulate them by sensible and kindly criticism'.[145] However, the unlikely targets for this attempt at permeation in the classic Fabian tradition responded to the Society's attentions with a notable lack of enthusiasm, and Champion in particular drew down on himself the lightning of clerical disapproval. The Reverend Charles E. Perry fulminated in the *Church of England Messenger* for 11 October 1895 that:

> To use a vulgar expression, Mr Champion appears to be 'having a loan of' the clergy. An extreme socialist, he wants support. His case needs some dignity, and he obtains the assistance of the Church. No one can object to his speaking at the meetings in the Chapter House, nor his remarks in his own paper; but it seems most necessary to remember that he is wedded to one expedient for the amelioration of society, namely, Socialism. In his own words, this means national co-operation. If anyone knows the opinions of the best thinkers in England, they know that this doctrine, if put into practice, would involve bondage to the individual and stagnation to the community – stagnation industrial and otherwise.

THE MAY DAY COMMITTEE

A more far-reaching reason for the suspension of the Society's lectures may well have been that Champion's notoriously inconstant attention was beginning to shift from the MFS to a venture which held out the promise of faster and larger political returns. What began as an attempt on his part to invest Victoria's observance of the May Day festival of international worker solidarity with the significance attached to it in Europe shortly gave rise to a new Social Democratic Federation of Victoria. This, in turn, engendered what was probably Champion's most significant single involvement in Victoria's industrial and political life: the National Anti-Sweating League. Such positive results as these projects may have achieved were, however, eclipsed in the eyes of the trade union movement by the affronts and challenges – real or imagined – which Champion's methods inevitably presented to them.

Celebrating May Day – which had been introduced into Victoria as recently as 1890, and taken the form of a march since 1893 – was scarcely more popular with the THC than Champion himself. The THC remained wedded to the observance of Eight Hours Day in April. Champion allied himself with the May Day camp by having himself accredited to the 1895 May Day Convening Committee as a delegate of the Melbourne Fabian Society and the Women's Suffrage

League. The convening committee then elected a demonstration committee, on which Champion served as joint honorary secretary with the THC delegate and Labor senator-to-be Ted Findley. A series of disputes and schisms between the committee and the THC followed, leading finally to the THC's withdrawal from the committee on the grounds of Champion's involvement in it. The THC's action was prompted in part by its receipt of letters from Keir Hardie and the SDF, which were interpreted as having 'shown that Mr H.H. Champion's English career was discreditable, and that he had been expelled from the Social Democratic Federation for conduct unbecoming a professed Trades Unionist'. A request by the committee's chairman, the socialist Labor MLA, Dr W.D. Maloney, that the THC should invite Champion to put his side of the story was refused.[146] When Champion announced his intention to retire from his committee secretaryship the following year, the THC's delegates were reappointed, but when he became president instead, the rift reopened. Majority thinking within the THC was encapsulated in the *Argus'* report of a speech by the Labor MLA for South Carlton, the future Senator J.G. Barrett: 'The Trades Hall Council could not tolerate the existence of a rival' and 'If a wise and beneficent Creator removed Mr Champion from the face of the earth the May Day Committee would cease to exist'.[147] All told, the episode was clear confirmation that any group with which his name became associated would automatically forfeit any sympathy or support from the THC.

THE SOCIAL DEMOCRATIC FEDERATION OF VICTORIA

However, well before Champion and the May Day Convening Committee went their separate ways, an offshoot better suited in every way to Champion's purposes had emerged. In the early months of his committee membership, he was able to secure the appointment of a subcommittee to determine how effect could best be given to the 'general objectives' of May Day's 'international promoters'. Copies of the MFS's Erfurt manifesto pamphlet were made available to the subcommittee members, whose work began on 12 May 1895 and was completed three days later. As was inevitable with any project involving Champion, its charter was interpreted in the broadest possible terms. The subcommittee's report concluded that the affiliates of the demonstration committee were 'in general accord, but that separately they are deficient in numerical, financial and political strength to obtain their separate objects, which, however, are ardently desired by that large majority of Victorians that is anxious for political and social advance, and ready to support any body which will attack these problems with wisdom, courage and ability'.[148]

It followed, in the subcommittee's view, that a new association should be formed, adhering to the social democratic principles set out in the MFS pamphlet, and known as the Social Democratic Federation of Victoria (SDFV). The SDFV, the subcommittee argued, should have a governing council, consisting of 'not less than one and not more than five members of each affiliated society', supported by seven subcommittees, whose individual areas of responsibility would be political, industrial, educational, international, financial, co-operative and organisational.[149] The report's principal recommendations were given effect on 19 May 1895, when the Social Democratic Federation of Victoria was formed, and effectively eclipsed the MFS as Champion's preferred mechanism for the pursuit of his political goals.

The obdurate hostility and incomprehension of the Trades Hall Council had refined and strengthened Champion's commitment to the establishment of a labour party independent of the labour movement, along the lines he had adopted from Parnell. The new party in its colonial setting, he now saw clearly, should seek to combine those socialist and more politically conscious labour MPs and grassroots activists who might be prepared to exercise some independence from the THC with the more radical of the New Liberals whose outlook in Victoria paralleled in so many key respects his distinctive Tory socialism. The SDFV, he hoped, would in due course merge with the ULLP to form the independent labour party of which he had so long dreamed, which might realistically aspire to hold the balance of power within the legislature, as it had been held in Britain by Parnell. In as much as the THC continued to block his overtures to its adherents, the necessary support would have to come preponderantly from the New Liberal camp, with whose members he had already begun to foster friendly working relationships through bodies such as the Australian Church and the Australasian Section of the Theosophical Society. A shopping list for immediate political action which he presented in July 1895 indicates the thrust of his thinking. 'The things that are wanted', he wrote in the *Champion*, 'are obvious enough; "one adult, one vote" to give us a real instead of a sham Democracy; "a tax on land values without exemptions" to throw the resources of this unpopulated country open and allow the remission of revenue taxes on the food of the people; "a Factories Act" to protect the neediest from the worst results of competition'.[150] Significantly, none of the items on the list would in any way have given difficulty to New Liberals of the stamp of Deakin. The SDFV Chairman, W.J. Lormer (whom the *Age* identified as a liberal), was a longtime associate of the Liberal and Protectionist League, and so too were the Treasurer, J. Cook, and another notable adherent, Samuel Mauger. 'Is it impossible', Champion asked rhetorically in a leading article for the *Champion*, 'that all who are not afraid to claim the name of Democrat and mean by it that they desire to further the common weal, should sink the little personal jealousies evoked by past squabbles and try to find out whether they do not agree on a great deal and cannot prefer to differ on the remote and less pressing reforms, rather than stand convicted of deferring all reforms by acting as foolish children rather than as sensible men and women?'.[151] In the meantime, he set about maximising his opportunities for cultivating the New Liberals on a day-to-day basis, by throwing his formidable energies and skill as an organiser behind the establishment of further reformist groups, such as the Australian Criminology Society and the National Anti-Sweating League.

The effect of establishing the SDFV was, however, to confirm the worst fears of Champion's detractors within the THC, namely that his betrayal of the council's trust and hospitality at the time of the Maritime Strike would now be compounded by challenging its exercise of proprietorial rights over such labour members as might secure election to parliament, in the context of an on-going alliance with the parliamentary Liberals. The executive of the ULLP complained formally to the THC about the May Day Committee's presumption in establishing an organisation whose political subcommittee was entrusted specifically with considering political strategy and activity, and the SDFV's proposals for co-operation with the ULLP were turned down: 'We decline to have anything to do with them, the S.D.F., because in our opinion their intention is to try and split up the Labour and Liberal Party in Victoria'.[152] In the face of this inhospitable reception, and its implicit message that nothing but suspicion and hostility could be expected from the labour establishment, adequate support for the SDFV from the New Liberals remained elusive, and Champion's aspirations for the project were disappointed.

THE ANTI-SWEATING LEAGUE

Frustrated politically, and unwilling to write off the SDFV prematurely, Champion opted for the new tack of associating it with the anti-sweating movement, through an involvement in the establishment of the National Anti-Sweating League which was probably greater than has generally been supposed. As with the women's suffrage movement the previous year, it was now a case of instigating the adoption of an appropriate organisational structure for a cause which others before him had originated. Concern over sweating – a treatment of workers such 'as would deprive them of a proper reward for their labour, such reward being filched to augment the already inflated income of the sweater' – dated back at least to the middle 1880s, but the cut-throat tactics adopted by manufacturing industries struggling for survival in the intensely competitive environment of the 1890s had caused the problem to become 'more urgently pressing and the object of inescapable attention'.[153] Extensive anti-sweating agitation in 1893 had centred around the leadership of the Wesley Church, and a further wave was touched off in 1895 by discontent among members of the Tailors Trade Protection Society and the dismissal of thirty employees of a boot factory in Richmond on the grounds that their output could be obtained at a lower cost through the use of outworkers. The result was a strike by the unionists who had retained their jobs and a series of public meetings culminating in a 'monster demonstration' chaired by Samuel Mauger in the Melbourne Town Hall on 8 July, at which sweating practices and perpetrators were exposed and denounced and amendments to toughen the Factory Act were demanded. The National Anti-Sweating League was launched at a public meeting on 29 July, which elected the Reverend Professor A. Gosman of the Congregational Church as president, Mauger as secretary and Deakin as treasurer.

It is suggested by Cutler that a small group of people, perhaps arising from the Wesley Church agitation two years earlier, had 'decided about mid-'ninety-five to make their effort against sweating "into one of a national character", by extending an invitation to "all who are in sympathy with such an object" particularly the clergy and the trade unions who were already making an effort independently'.[154] The existence and antecedents of such a group are in no way incompatible with Champion's having played a major role in prompting and assisting its members to upgrade their activities with a formal structure and a public face. In his capacity as SDFV secretary Champion sent letters to unions offering co-operation in a united effort to suppress sweating. This was prior to the invitations to the meeting on 29 July, which were issued over the signature of Mauger. The meeting was chaired by Champion, and he and the Chairman of the SDFV, Lormer, were elected to vice-presidencies of the League, in circumstances where for Champion to have become president would have been unacceptable to the THC. A rejection of the presidency by Champion on the grounds of the likely THC reaction would have been consistent with the approach he adopted later in the naming of the Social Questions Committee. The League adopted the tactic of urging ratepayers to vote for candidates for municipal office who supported legislation against sweating which had been initiated weeks earlier by Champion, at the South Melbourne municipal elections. It shamed sweaters through public exposure in the same way as Champion had done in Britain in the columns of the *Labour Elector*. An investigatory committee established by the League to inquire into wages and conditions in various firms used the *Champion* to promote those which survived its scrutiny, and Champion became a member of the large committee which drafted provisions for the Factory Act at meetings above Mauger's shop. Champion's guiding hand was constantly evident, shaping the League's tactics from behind the scenes and, on occasion, publicly putting them into effect.

The Anti-Sweating League was successful in securing the passage of the Factory Act in 1896 – and its renewal and reinforcement four years later, in 1900 – and continued in an investigative and fact-finding capacity until 1912. Even so, such hopes of mending his relationship with the labour movement as Champion may have invested in it were thwarted, as always, through no fault but his own. Before long, he was again giving full rein to a savage baiting of the THC establishment, whose senior members he largely held in contempt. A trustee of the Trades Hall and erstwhile THC president, George Sangster, the *Champion* reported on 24 August 1895, had 'graciously intimated that he would transfer his custom to a "union" baker if he could get his bread as cheap as at a non-union house'. Sangster, the report continued, had refused to buy his bread at a union house 'preferring to deal with a sweater in Port Melbourne (the constituency he represents in Parliament) to patronising an honest employer in South Melbourne'. 'All the Federations of employers which ever existed, with all the Banks, Blacklegs and Brigadier-Generals thrown-in', the writer concluded, 'would not do so much harm to trade unionism as the above utterances of its alleged friends, who rant about "sweating" while they are encouraging the practice to save a few pence or to get a vote'.

While Sangster complained to the THC that 'the Bakers' Society were allowing themselves to be used as a tool by the proprietor of the *Champion*' by supplying the list of union bakeries which appeared in its columns, the fracas continued to the point where he was obliged to announce publicly that, at his insistence, the sweater in his constituency had adopted union rules. 'We venture to congratulate the M.L.A. on his escape from a ridiculously inconsistent position', the *Champion's* final comment on the matter rejoined, 'and ourselves on our own contribution to such a satisfactory result'.[155] Irrespective of the justification for Champion's outrage, his strictures did nothing for the advancement of the League, his own rehabilitation in the eyes of the labour movement, or the good name of the Fabian cause with which he was now inextricably linked. It may well have been due to his presence that the involvement of unionists in the League's affairs remained minimal. The episode provides a further instance of his unfailing aptitude for snatching defeat from the jaws of victory, by turning even the most promising situations to his own disadvantage, and alienating those he most needed as allies and friends.

THE WALLABY CLUB

The shift of Champion's search for allies from the labour movement to the New Liberals was exemplified finally by his involvement in the Wallaby Club – 'a fundamentally upper-middle class group of professional men with cultural interests and a liking for bush-walking' – for which he was put up in 1896, perhaps by Thomas Palmer, who had been a foundation member two years earlier.[156] While the club was in no sense political, nor made up exclusively of members from liberal circles, it provided a further opportunity to meet and work regularly with influential liberals – including, for a time, Deakin – in circumstances which were conducive to the development of friendships and mutual respect. Champion's contemporaries in the Club included Higgins, Geoffrey Syme, Frank Gavan Duffy, Fred McCubbin, Sir Henry Wrixon, Frank Tate, Theodore Fink and Martin Peter Hansen. Gavan Duffy and Wrixon were barristers who became, respectively, Chief Justice of the High Court of Australia and President of the Victorian Legislative Council. Syme was the son of the founder of the *Age*, David Syme, and succeeded his father as the paper's editor; McCubbin became one of Australia's leading painters. Fink was a Member of the Legislative Assembly and the author of an influential Royal Commission report on technical education, and Tate and Hansen became Directors of Education.

The Wallaby Club had been going through a crisis in the months immediately prior to Champion's admission, possibly arising from the difficult personality of its founder and president, Dr Louis Henry, who also founded the Victorian Branch of the British Medical Association. Champion – described by the club historian, Alfred Hart, as 'a very able, popular, and well-known newcomer to Melbourne'[157] – promptly became the secretary, and proceeded to put its affairs in order with a characteristic vigour which was rewarded with a vote of thanks at the 1897 annual general meeting. If any falling out between Champion and Henry was involved at the time it was later reconciled, and they are credited with having jointly brought about a further revitalisation of the Club in 1899, when an influx of new members – including Deakin and a further notable New Liberal, Donald Mackinnon – took place.[158] Champion continued to serve on the committee until 1902, when his membership of the club was resigned, perhaps, in part, as a result of the ill health which had obliged him to resign his position as parliamentary secretary of the United Council for Women's Suffrage a year earlier, but more likely because his hopes for the labour movement had been revived by the arrival in Victoria of his friend and erstwhile comrade-in-arms, Tom Mann.

LAND TAX

In the event, there was no resumption of the Fabian Society's public lectures when the Chapter House series concluded. Instead, MFS members continued to meet informally on Friday evenings at their

Queen's Walk headquarters. The *Champion* reported on 21 September 1895 that these gatherings were 'attracting increased attendance'. 'It is evident', the report continued, 'that if they go on increasing a larger room will have to be secured'. At the same time, a subcommittee of the Society was preparing a report whose subject – 'the land system in Victoria, the effect of railway construction upon the unearned increment, and the probable result of a tax on unimproved land values' – recalled Champion's roots, and those of the London Society, in the Land Reform Union and the teachings of Henry George.

The subcommittee's report, in the *Champion's* eyes, was 'a most important addition to the available knowledge on the subjects', which the paper published in four instalments between 26 October and 16 November. The series provides a useful insight into the MFS's thinking. Victoria, the report stated, suffered from 'glaring social evils', which included:

1. An unjust monopoly of land;
2. An unjust incidence of taxation;
3. An unjust extortion of interest;
4. An unjust system of suicidal competition;
5. An unjust distribution of the proceeds of labour; and
6. An unjust franchise.[159]

Land tax, in the view of the report's authors, would provide a practical remedy for the first two of these evils. A land tax was necessary, the argument continued, because of a situation where, between 1876 and 1892, Victoria's population increased from 840,300 to 1,167,373, its public debt from £13,996,822 to £46,711,287 and the unimproved value of its land from £48,715,230 to £131,577,287. As the report pointed out, the enormous increase in land values was due entirely to government borrowings, on which the colony's citizens were paying interest. One striking example, the authors believed, was the construction of the Kew railway line, at a cost to the taxpayers of £72,061:

> In 1865 the population of Kew was 5,800, in 1888 it was 6,500. In 1885 the unimproved land value was £327,998, which had increased to £864,032 in 1888, after the opening of the railway. So the surprising result of this little State enterprise was that £536,034 went into the pockets of the land owners. Before the line was made the unimproved value of land in Kew was £92-6-6 per acre, which jumped after the line was opened to £243-3-8. Every £1 spent by the State on this mile and a furlong of

railway that ends in a hill made a present of £7-7-3 to some private individual.

It was the report's conclusion that the only available and just remedy for the evils on which it had dwelled was a land tax 'which would be a burden to no one and an injustice to no one, but a benefit to everyone'.[160]

CONCLUSION

The appearance of the subcommittee's conclusions in the pages of the *Champion* marked an end to the MFS's short-lived phase of public activity. Invitations to the Queen's Walk Friday evenings continued to appear in the *Champion's* 'Notes' column, but the hopes the paper's proprietor had invested in them were not fulfilled. This was not altogether surprising. Despite the visibility and accessibility of their location, Champion's rooms were an inauspicious setting for welcoming potential middle-class recruits. He himself described them as 'just an office with a counter and other adjuncts of a business department, just an ordinary editorial room, within which Intellect sat immersed in one Damnation Grind for the education and delectation of the public'.[161] This was in marked contrast to the London Fabian Society, where venues for meetings 'if not specifically "aristocratic" in the way Shaw suggested in his report in 1892, tended always to have a self-consciously aesthetic quality about them, whether highly refined or slightly bohemian in nature'.[162]

Ross, moreover, turned out to be an ineffectual secretary, who lost the MFS's membership records and resigned his position within a few months of having assumed it. Besant-Scott, as will be seen, was distracted by the breakup of his marriage, as was Palmer by his financial difficulties. Strong and Hamilton alone of Champion's five partners in instigating the MFS seem likely to have been able to give its affairs anything like their wholehearted attention and, in the face of Champion's notorious capacity for distraction and the hostility of the labour movement, this clearly was not enough. May 1896 saw the MFS mentioned for the last time by the *Champion*, in a list of May Day Committee affiliates; then it vanished from sight.

Verity Burgmann points out that had 'Champion behaved himself in Australia, he might well have continued to his dying day to enjoy the lionising of the locals'.[163] He seemed, when he arrived in Victoria

1. *William Archer, the first Australian member of the London Fabian Society.*

2. *The Reverend Charles Marson, founder of the South Australian Fabian Society.*

3. *Lucy Morice, South Australian Fabian Society member and a founding member of the Women's League, the all-women South Australian Co-operative Clothing Company, the Kindergarten Union, the School for Mothers Institute and the Women's Political Association.*

4. *David Charleston, South Australian Fabian Society member, president of the South Australian United Trades and Labour Council and one of the first three Labor representatives elected to an Australian parliament.*

5. *The Reverend Charles Strong, founding member of the Melbourne Fabian Society and the first minister of the Australian Church.*

6. John Howlett Ross, founding secretary of the Melbourne Fabian Society, journalist, author and theosophist.

7. *Ernest Besant-Scott, founding member of the Melbourne Fabian Society, journalist and theosophist.*

8. *Henry Hyde Champion, founding member of the Melbourne Fabian Society, the Social Democratic foundation of Victoria, the Victorian Socialist League, the Social Democratic Party of Victoria and the Social Questions Committee.*

9. *Nettie Higgins (later Palmer), member of the Fabian Society of Victoria, writer and critic.*

10. The first interstate conference of the Australian Peace Alliance, September 23 1916. Frederick Sinclaire (chairman) is third on the right, Vida Goldstein is third on the left. Both were founding members of the Fabian Society of Victoria.

11. Elizabeth Lothian, the first Australian woman to join the Cambridge Fabian Society and a founding member of the Fabian Society of Victoria.

12. Bernard O'Dowd, poet, journalist, orator and a member of the Victorian Socialist League, the Social Democratic Party of Victoria, the Social Questions Committee and the Fabian Society of Victoria.

13. Thomas Mann,
organiser for the Melbourne
Trades Hall Council and
Political Labour Council,
and a founding member of
the Social Democratic Party
of Victoria and the Social
Questions Committee.

14. John Percy Jones, a former butcher and
drover who made his fortune from the
establishment of Melbourne's first pay-as-you-
wear tailoring business. A socialist and
admirer of Ruskin, he was a founding
member of the Social Questions Committee.

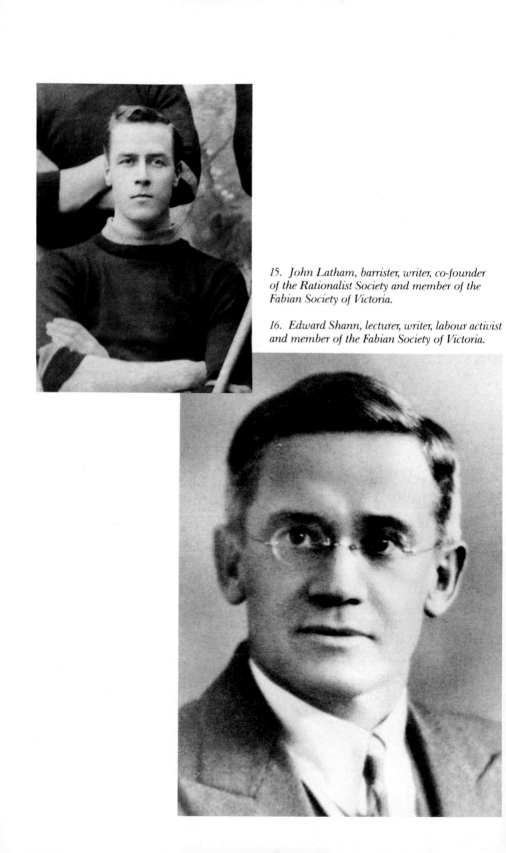

15. *John Latham, barrister, writer, co-founder of the Rationalist Society and member of the Fabian Society of Victoria.*

16. *Edward Shann, lecturer, writer, labour activist and member of the Fabian Society of Victoria.*

in 1890, to have all the qualities of a leader who, had it been his intention to stay, might have enabled labour activists and middle-class radicals to work together harmoniously, as happened in South Australia at Marson's instigation. He had been a leading participant from the outset in the socialist resurgence of the 1880s and, as Pelling rightly recognises, was 'a pioneer of labour representation'. His friends or associates included all the leading labour identities of the day. His standing following the London Dock Strike – in the eyes of the public, if not necessarily of his closest associates – was at its peak. Unlike Marson and some other London Fabians, he was unabashed about soliciting the involvement of the colonial New Liberals, whose differences from the Cobdenite liberals in Britain he clearly recognised. His Tory socialism and the New Liberalism of Deakin and his associates closely resembled one another in key respects, including their protectionism and aspirations for the Empire.

Champion's open opposition to the 1890 Maritime Strike deprived him, then, of most of his advantages in both Australia and Britain, so that it was a much diminished figure who returned to Victoria to re-establish himself four years later in 1894. His candidature for the Legislative Assembly seat of Albert Park five months after his arrival suggests, in some respects, that he would have preferred to work within the mainstream of the colonial labour movement and its nascent parliamentary arm, the ULLP, but he was denied the opportunity to do so because earlier indiscretions had made him the target of enduring trade union distrust and hostility. The choice of 'European Socialism' as the theme for his first Melbourne Fabian Society lecture, and of the Erfurt manifesto for its first pamphlet, were his way of installing on Victoria's agenda a new theme whose character owed more by far to the Independent Labour Party phase of his career in Britain than to permeation in the Fabian mould. This was not to be taken, however, as necessarily indicating that Champion himself was more of a social-democrat in the Marxist sense than a Fabian. The importance of the Erfurt manifesto in the annals of socialism stems in part from its division into two sections which formalise the distinction between the maximum and mini-mum programs. The first section is by Kautsky, and the second by the arch-revisionist Bernstein, who became notorious in Marxist circles as a Fabian.

The prospect that beckoned Champion was that labour activists, middle-class Fabian socialists and New Liberal radicals might be induced to come together as a new party which, at the least, would hold the balance of power in the Legislative Assembly in the same way as he had seen it held in the House of Commons by Parnell and his followers. In Strong, Ross, Hamilton and Palmer, he and Besant-Scott chose lieutenants who were linked intimately with key sections of a broad social-democratic constituency which encompassed both socialist and New Liberal elements. Collectively, the networks at the command of his associates represented a toehold for the venture in 'advanced' Christian circles, the women's suffrage movement, the co-operative movement and numerous reformist organisations, such as the Australian Criminology Society, to which single-issue enthusiasts could look for the advancement of their aims.

The *Champion*, in this model, constituted a mechanism through which both the broad-brush social-democratic ideology and the single-issue causes which Champion associated with it could be amplified. It is not surprising that such a blueprint should have been conceived. Champion was simply applying the lessons of his long political experience. The bravura political style which had made possible his London Dock Strike triumphs was again evident in the aplomb with which he thumbed his nose not only at critics within the labour movement but also at key opinion makers in the wider circles of colonial society, such as the proprietors of the *Age* and the *Argus*, and the public figures he excoriated in classic muck-raking style, for bench packing, jury squaring and secret compositions.[164]

It was a corollary to these matters, however, that the existence of the Melbourne Fabian Society and the activities it undertook had little significance in themselves for Champion beyond their contribution to his broader design. The Society's brief flowering produced no prompt sheets for grassroots electoral involvement, such as the *Questions for Candidates* tracts which the South Australian Fabians issued. Nor were there any studies of specific policy issues other than the report of its land tax subcommittee. There was no reason, once the Social Democratic Federation of Victoria had been established, for Champion to interest himself further in the Melbourne Fabian Society's continuation. The place of the MFS as a modest beach-head for his entry into colonial politics was taken by the SDFV as, in effect, the grandiose launching pad for the new social-democratic party which he hoped might capture the loyalties of key sections of colonial opinion, enable him to out-manoeuvre his THC adversaries, and become for all practical purposes the independent labour party which had so tantalisingly slipped through his fingers in Britain.

All this would have mattered less if, in the course of Champion's machinations, both the Melbourne Fabian Society and Fabian socialism generally had not been stripped of much of their credibility in the eyes of the labour movement. A number of the initiatives Champion launched were seen as usurping labour movement prerogatives or aspirations, and so compounded his original offences. So much was this the case that the Fabian Society idea was brought into some disrepute by his association with it, and the attitude of trade unionists to middle-class intellectuals was in part soured. Marson's South Australian Fabian Society had attracted active support from the cream of that colony's trade union leadership, and the establishment of the Melbourne Society had arisen in part from a call published in a union journal, but – Hamilton apart – unionist members of the MFS were conspicuous by their absence (as they were in the Anti-Sweating League). In as much as suppositions about a more benign attitude to socialism on the part of the Melbourne THC, cited earlier, are soundly-based, the advantages for Fabians and the Fabian cause were dissipated, and antagonism to intellectual and middle-class influences was fortified. Failing the good will of the opinion makers within the labour movement, or any effective access to the rank and file of the movement, Champion's fertile imagination and restless energies were for all practical purposes ineffectual.

That the responsibility was his own is plain from the fact that the warmth of the reception the unions accorded to such other expatriate Londoners as Ben Tillett was retained (and in Tillett's case enhanced). It was not only Champion who became the victim of the union anathemas his ill-advised actions and utterances attracted, but also all the causes with which his incessant networking led him to be associated. The harm so caused was now about to be exacerbated by another newcomer to Melbourne, Tom Mann, whose origins could hardly have been more different from those of Champion, but whose ultimate impact was no less damaging. Meanwhile, the years when Champion in effect had been sent to Coventry by the labour movement were invested by him and Besant-Scott in further cultivation of the New Liberals. They were rewarded in due course with some conversions to the Fabian outlook which were no less notable for in some instances being short-lived.

CHAPTER 4

Tom Mann and the Fabian-In-All-But-Name Social Questions Committee

Once the Melbourne Fabian Society had finally faded away, the political activism of most of the members of its inner circle diminished sharply. Even so, the efflorescence of socialist sentiment elsewhere within colonial society continued. The places of those who dropped out were taken by newcomers such as Jones and the cigar manufacturer, George Carter; O'Dowd and his fellow public servants, Hugh Corbett from the Mint and Jack Castrieau from the Chief Secretary's Office; the poet Marie Pitt, for whom O'Dowd left his wife and family; the Trades Hall Councillors Ted Findley, Martin Hannah and Robert Solly; Harry Scott Bennett, who was regarded by Mann as 'Australia's ablest socialist orator';[1] and the exotic Chris Casimir, who conducted a private school and was of French and Mauritian parentage.

In addition, the identities of more senior stalwarts – including the socialist medical practitioner and MLA, W.D. Maloney; Tom Tunnecliffe, who inherited Maloney's West Melbourne state seat when Maloney was elected to the House of Representatives; George Prendergast, who became leader of the state parliamentary Labor Party; George Elmslie, who was Victoria's first Labor premier; and Frank Anstey, the firebrand orator and prophet of revolution who became a Labor federal minister – took on sharper focus with the unfolding of their parliamentary aspirations and careers. There was no immediate reappearance of a body in the Fabian mould, which followed later in the form of Mann's Fabian-in-all-but-name Social Questions Committee (SQC) in 1905, hard on the heels of four intervening socialist organisations – the Victorian Socialist League (1897), the Tocsin Clubs (1897), the Victorian Labour Federation (1898) and the Social Democratic Party of Victoria (1902). These had either failed or faltered, but nonetheless constituted a necessary prelude to the emergence of the SQC, introducing and testing many of the features which it adopted and refined.

The SQC was – despite its relatively short lifespan – a paradigm of Fabian organisation and among the most successful Fabian bodies which have ever existed. Its activities in most respects paralleled those of the London Fabian Society, and in some ways were more enterprising and imaginative. It was probably better at providing a satisfying, self-sufficient way of life for its members and, in proportion to population, it was larger by far than the London Society. Although the SQC changed its name to the Socialist Party in 1906, it did not then cease to be a Fabian body but continued to develop along Fabian lines until the end of 1907. The subsequent erosion of its Fabian character – and the consequent development of an adversarial and mutually antagonistic relationship with the Political Labour Council – were sources of frustration to a number of its leading members, and led to the formation of the Fabian Society of Victoria in 1908 in an attempt to repair the breach and revive Fabian aims and activities which they saw as having been neglected or discarded.

CAUSES OF THE NEW SOCIALIST UPSURGE

Poverty apart, the dynamism behind the new socialist upsurge was fuelled from three sources. In the first instance, socialist outrage was exacerbated by the absence of effective action to combat unemployment and poverty on the part of the liberals and conservatives who governed Victoria immediately before and after the turn of the century. The Turner government was more concerned with balancing its budgets than creating jobs. Characteristically, it initiated no major public works and ruthlessly eliminated all but the most essential public expenditures.[2] The refusal of the liberals to respond to pleas for relief from their labour parliamentary allies has been seen by some as evidence that they

> shared one common assumption with their conservative 'foes': the middle classes were the rightful and principal shareholders in the vast enterprise of economic liberalism, which the State had so bountifully assisted. Once this assumption was questioned seriously, the Liberals stopped playing politics, and forsook the Labor party which they had previously wooed with such persistence.[3]

Irvine and Bent, in their turn, maintained the inactivity of their predecessors, in the face of the indisputable evidence from the SQC of the problem's extent and gravity. Mann recalled years later that:

> The chairman of the Committee, Mr J.P. Jones, now the Hon. J.P. Jones, Member of the Legislative Council, spent much time in the endeavour

to get responsible statesmen to accompany him to the homes of the destitute. At length, after months of effort on our part, several statesmen paid a few visits, and admitted that the evidence of their own eyes alone could have convinced them of the reality of what they saw.[4]

Secondly, the conservative forces compounded their neglect of unemployment and poverty with an extravagant anti-union rhetoric and savage repression of strikes. The effect, for many, was to confirm that working men and their families could expect no justice from those who identified themselves in so blatant a fashion as the class enemy and that redress could be expected only from the alternative social order that socialism was seen to represent. The 1903 Railways Strike was a case in point. Anti-strike legislation introduced by the Irvine government provided that railway employees who left the service without fourteen days' notice could be deemed to be strikers and subjected to a £100 fine or a twelve months' prison sentence. Strike meetings – defined as discussion of the strike by groups of more than six people – were banned, as were picketing, the distribution of strike notices and the collection of strike funds. Strikers were deprived of their pensions and blacklisted from further public sector employment.

While, as has been seen, 'Melbourne paid homage to the Iceberg' when the strike collapsed, the fact that the legislation was passed with the support of Liberals such as John Murray, Alexander Peacock and W.A. Watt could scarcely have failed to make socialists of some whose hopes of ameliorative reform had previously been pinned to the 'Lib-Lab' parliamentary alliance. It was no coincidence that the railway unions subsequently became a citadel of socialist support within the labour movement, nor that the leaders to whom they turned were high-profile socialist activists of the stamp of Frank Hyett. It was to Hyett, along with associates such as the young John Curtin, that O'Dowd referred when he commented that Mann had created tigercubs, who would be as dangerous and ferocious as himself.[5]

Finally, in ideological terms, Victoria's socialists had no shortage of guidance or encouragement in interpreting the events they saw unfolding around them. Over and above empirical observation and the work of local theoreticians such as Anstey, socialist books, pamphlets and periodicals from other countries were imported widely by successive socialist groups and through other outlets, and circulated on loan by Champion and his wife Elsie through their

Book Lovers' Library. As well, the colony was visited by a stream of overseas socialist luminaries, which included – in addition to Mann – his former Dock Strike colleague and fellow London Fabian Society Executive member, Ben Tillett; Sidney and Beatrice Webb; Keir Hardie; and Margaret and Ramsay MacDonald. Each of these either belonged to the London Fabian Society or was a former Society member. The Webbs apart, they gave their hosts no reason to regret the heroes' welcomes which were extended to them; passed on such insights and experience as they had to offer in ways which respected local sensitivities; and in some instances formed lasting local friendships.[6] All told, there was good reason for debate within the colonial socialist ranks to be wide ranging, vigorous and well informed.

THE VICTORIAN SOCIALIST LEAGUE

The immediate effect of the economic, industrial, ideological and moral ferment was to give rise to a succession of socialist organisations which paved the way for Mann's foundation of the SQC in 1905 by providing figures who were later prominent in the SQC with their introduction to socialist activism, and by pioneering the practice of socialist community which gave the SQC and its successor, the Victorian Socialist Party, much of their unique flavour and appeal. The Victorian Socialist League – established in June 1897 by, among others, Prendergast, Bennett, Tunnecliffe and the Reverend Archibald of Melbourne's Labor Church – had Casimir as its founding secretary,[7] and formed branches at Richmond, Carlton, South Melbourne, Brunswick, Footscray, West Melbourne and Mitcham.[8] Crowds gathered for the VSL's Sunday afternoon meetings at Studley Park, Clifton Hill, Port Melbourne, Hawthorn Bridge and Merri Creek, and for its rallies on Sunday evenings in the city. There were VSL social nights with 'first-class bands', VSL progressive euchre parties and VSL monster socialist picnics – Tillett's arrival in Victoria in 1898 was marked by a dinner for 100 VSL members at the Victoria Coffee Palace. A VSL quadrille club and a VSL band were available to provide entertainment at its functions, and provision for the education of members was made through a Saturday afternoon economics class, which studied texts such as J.S. Mills' *Political Economy* and Hyndman's *Economics of Socialism* under the guidance of O'Dowd.[9]

A VSL weekly, the *Socialist*, was launched in September 1898, and a VSL industrial department marketed 'Liberty Tea'. The League's objective was stated to be 'the establishment of a system of co-operative production, distribution and exchange, through the restoration to the people of all the means of production, distribution and exchange to be administered by organised society in the interests of the whole people, and the complete emancipation of society from the domination of capital'. The view was taken that 'the same economic forces which have produced and now intensify the capitalist system will compel the adoption of socialism – the collective ownership of production, distribution and exchange for common good and welfare, or result in the destruction of civilisation'.[10]

It was through the VSL that Champion began his rehabilitation when he was admitted to membership in July 1898. Eight months earlier, the *Tocsin* had made contemptuous reference to him as 'Gussie' – an 'exquisite bescented popinjay' who had been 'kicked to the rightabout as worthless' by 'the real representatives of the workers'.[11] The *Tocsin* was a socialist weekly, many of whose backers were prominent in the ranks of the organisation which now extended Champion its welcome. The explanation for the paradox was Tillett's arrival in the colony; his warm embrace of his erstwhile London Dock Strike comrade-in-arms and fellow member of the London Fabian Society prompted the colonial socialists – and some THC identities – to sit up and pay renewed attention to the perplexing figure whom they had resigned themselves to treating as beyond the Pale.

Three other factors which led to Champion being seen in a new light included, in due course, the success of the National Anti-Sweating League with whose establishment he and his SDFV had been prominently associated; his acceptance into the highly-regarded Goldstein family through his marriage to Elsie Goldstein in December 1898; and, above all, the imprimatur of his acknowledgement as friend, proven comrade and trusted lieutenant by Mann. The change in his standing was reflected dramatically in the fact that his candidature for the Legislative Assembly at the 1900 elections was endorsed explicitly by fourteen union secretaries in a letter to the *Age* which read, in part: 'if a vote of members of the Trades Hall Council were taken an overwhelming majority would decide in favour of Champion'.[12] While his parliamentary aspirations were never fulfilled, his acceptance as a member in good standing of the colonial socialist mainstream enabled him to serve subsequently as a vice-president of the Social Democratic Party of Victoria, the SQC and the VSP, in addition to being a VSP trustee, treasurer and president and, briefly, editor of the VSP journal, the *Socialist*.[13]

THE TOCSIN CLUBS

Views of a less apocalyptic stamp than those of the VSL characterised the socialist weekly, the *Tocsin*. The new journal was established in October 1897 under the editorship of O'Dowd, together with Corbett and Castrieau, by a *Tocsin* Printing and Publishing Co-operative Society, whose members included Prendergast, Anstey, Tunnecliffe, Findley, Carter and Jones.[14] *Tocsin* readers – the 'Tocsinners', as they became known – formed themselves into Tocsin Clubs, whose public meetings on Saturday evenings near the corner of Johnson and Smith Streets in Collingwood, and on Sundays at Studley Park, Merri Creek, Footscray and Yarra Bank, attracted crowds on a similar scale to those of the VSL. Among the figures associated with the *Tocsin* were a number of Fabians who will be the subject of further examination in the context of their involvement in the SQC and the Fabian Society of Victoria. These included the paper's principal editor, O'Dowd, who is also credited with having inspired the Tocsin Clubs,[15] and Jones, who insisted, in regard to its massive 74-point program of social, economic, legal, literary and artistic reform, that 'we must bombard the workers with appeals and keep it before them every day for six months and if they won't support it then they ought to be kicked'.[16] Initially of the belief that 'the Labor Party will go straight ahead, working for the good of the people, without the ulterior motives of place-hunters and place-holders', the *Tocsin* was warning before long of the danger that 'Rip Van Winkelism' would lead to the Party's demise and absorption by the Liberals.[17] At the same time, its approach is seen to have remained 'cautious, pragmatic and empiricist', with respect emphasised for the 'scientific' methods of investigation, 'data-hunting' and 'precise observation of the actual facts' as practised by the Webbs, and the path to socialism defined in gradual steps as 'Licence, Inspect, Regulate and Swallow'.[18]

THE VICTORIAN LABOUR FEDERATION

No such caution or gradualism constrained the Victorian Labour Federation (VLF), whose foundation by Anstey, Tunnecliffe and

Elmslie followed in 1898. More oriented by far to the trade union movement than to parliament, the VLF foreshadowed the Industrial Workers of the World of another place and a later era by adopting as its objective 'the unification of the workers in one all comprehensive and extensive union', whose 'all-embracing combination' and 'unity of power, numerically and politically' would enable socialism to triumph over capitalism 'so that the people may own and control the industrial appliances by which they live – upon which their real liberty, independence and comfort depend'. Parliamentary action figured in this model as being second best to industrial action, and VLF officers were forbidden to stand as candidates for parliament, on penalty of forfeiting their positions and being debarred from future appointments. In addition to catering for the social needs of its members, through picnics, 'nights of song and speech' and lantern lectures, the VLF operated a Co-operative Commonwealth and Tailoring Department for the supply of tea, coffee, clothing and boots. There were VLF senior and junior cricket clubs, a VLF choir, a VLF orchestra, a VLF boys' fife and drum band and a VLF Christmas Goose Club.[19]

The VSL, the Tocsin Clubs and the VLF marked a considerable advance on earlier organisations in satisfying the appetites of the colonial socialists for self-education and in proselytising in the wider community through what was effectively soap-box oratory and propaganda. In addition, they enabled socialists to give mutual support to one another through social and co-operative structures which they saw as involving them in living socialist lives and giving effect to socialist values as they worked for the reconstruction of the social order. However, maintaining three separate organisations was more than the leadership and administrative resources of the movement could sustain and, by 1902, all of them were either defunct or in difficulties. The VSL absorbed the Tocsin Clubs, with which its membership substantially overlapped,[20] only to falter itself at the turn of the century, when the *Socialist* had to cease publication, and plans to send a delegate to the Paris Congress of the International were abandoned. The VLF was weakened in the same year by the resignation of Elmslie as secretary, and the exclusion of Anstey as president on the grounds of his unsuccessful candidature for parliament.[21] A financial crisis overtook it in 1901, and within a further twelve months it had ceased to exist.[22] At that point, the socialist ranks – and the labour movement generally – were galvanised by a new arrival from Britain, in the person of Mann.

TOM MANN IN BRITAIN

Mann was born at Foleshill on 15 April 1856 to the wife of a clerk at the Victoria Colliery, and put to work underground at the age of ten, dragging heavy boxes of coal or dirt through 'Egyptian darkness' on all fours, so that 'Many a time did I actually lie groaning as a consequence of the heavy strain on the loins'.[23] At the same time, he was aware of erstwhile playmates, younger even than himself, turning the drive wheels of bar-looms from 6 am until 8 pm in local weaving rooms, so that numbers of them dropped in their places from giddiness and exhaustion. Others succumbed to the neurological toll of the 'peculiar motion which kept their heads and bodies in a whirl'. It was at this point, as he later recalled, that 'the iron entered into my soul'.[24]

Mann's political consciousness was able to develop further when the Victoria Colliery was destroyed by fire in 1870 and he became an engineering apprentice in Birmingham. Birmingham's rich resources – and the advent of the nine-hour day for engineering workers – enabled him to begin making good the shortcomings of such education as he had contrived to acquire between his sixth and ninth birthdays, at the Foleshill 'Old Church' School and the Little Heath Congregational Church School. He read widely in the city's public library, visited its theatres and heard speeches in its great public halls from orators of the calibre of its MPs, John Bright and Joseph Chamberlain, the secularist Charles Bradlaugh, the co-operator George Jacob Holyoake, and Annie Besant. Three nights each week were devoted to classes in machine construction in the Severn Street Institute's Department of Science and Art, and a fourth to a Bible Class conducted by the Society of Friends.

On Saturday evenings Mann attended meetings of a Temperance Society, and on Sundays two sessions of Sunday School and an Anglican service at St Thomas' Church in Holloway Road, followed by a further evening service in the church, chapel or chapter house of some other denomination. The profound Christian faith he absorbed from his mentors prompted him to take an active part in the food reform and temperance movements, with the result that, when he left Birmingham for London in 1877, at the age of

twenty-one, it was with the intention of becoming a Christian missionary, and eliminating 'the evils in the community, the existence
of which I deplored' by 'urging individuals of every class and station
to live "godly, righteous and sober lives" '.[25] His situation may have
been unusual by Fabian standards, but was far from unique. As has
been seen, the tradition of Christian motives giving rise to Fabian
principles was exemplified by the Reverend Stewart Headlam, who
was followed into the London Society by his fellow members of the
Anglican Guild of St Matthew.[26]

It remained for London to complete the radicalising process
which Mann's Foleshill experiences had initiated. His life there
began inauspiciously, with 'two grey, blank, lonely years'[27] when he
was unable to find work in the trade for which he had laboured so
long to prepare himself. Instead, he was unemployed for a lengthy
period, and then forced to accept stop-gap jobs as a warehouse clerk
for the Swan and Edgar drapery in Piccadilly and a porter for a
Hampstead Road tailor. In the process, 'it was not the missionary
in him which was tested, but the missionary's belief in his faith'.[28]
His Anglican links were put aside in favour of the social doctrine
of Swedenborg's New Church, that 'the life of religion is to do
good',[29] and remained quiescent until the middle 1890s, when he
considered entering the Anglican clergy. Meanwhile, as a turner in
the engineering workshops of firms such as Cubitt's in Gray's Inn
Road and Westinghouse at King's Cross, he became a member of
the Marylebone Branch of the Amalgamated Society of Engineers,
heard socialism preached on Saturday mornings outside the south-
east gates of Battersea Park and joined the Battersea Branch of the
SDF: 'I was now entirely devoted to the advocacy of socialism . . .
for the curing of social distress. I found in socialism a more complete
satisfaction than I had ever before experienced'.[30]

The turning point in Mann's life had been reached. The settled
status as a skilled aristocrat of labour which his tireless self-
improvement had gained for him – 'He was a husband and father,
a trade unionist and co-operator, interested in his trade and
delighting in the Shakespeare Mutual Improvement Society, in
music, poetry and astronomy; he used his telescope and played his
violin' – was now exchanged for the uncertainties and exigencies
of militant agitation, to the point where it is noted that 'eighteen
months after he joined the S.D.F., no engineering shop in London
will give work to the Socialist Tom Mann; about six months later

the same story is repeated at Tyneside'.[31] He addressed the Fabian Society on the subject of the 'The Eight Hour Working Day' as early as 1886; became a member through the affiliation of the East London Group in 1889; and served on the Society's Executive in the early 1890s.[32] The London Reform Group, which made him its secretary at about the same time, was a predominantly Fabian organisation, and the Fabians were heavily represented in the Independent Labour Party, where he was secretary from 1894 to 1897. In that capacity, he moved for the establishment of a national socialist party which would have brought together the Fabian Society, ILP and SDF.[33] So much was his membership of the 1891 Royal Commission on Labour a Fabian undertaking that his minority report is seen by some as having been written for him by Sidney Webb.[34] He and his fellow SDF member Champion were closely associated in crucial ventures such as the London Dock Strike and the struggle for an independent socialist party. Mann was a candidate for parliament at elections in Colne Valley in 1895, North Aberdeen in 1896 and Halifax in 1897; president of the International Federation of Ship, Dock and River Workers from 1896 to 1898; and the instigator and moving force behind the Workers' Union from 1898 to 1901.

However, behind the facade of his successes, Mann was troubled by a deep-seated ambivalence about whether it was through industrial or parliamentary action that the well-being of his fellow workers, the overthrow of the social order which was exemplified for him by his Foleshill experiences and its replacement by socialism could best be achieved. The Fabian phases of his career were characterised by the gradualist view that the workers, in true reformist style, 'might legitimately make use of Parliament and thus secure, by legislation, all the advantages that might accrue from a strike without its accompanying disadvantages'; while the Ideal State would be 'the outcome of successive steps in advance by the mass of the people'.[35] These phases both followed on and preceded other periods – notably in the early 1890s in Britain and in Broken Hill during the following decade – when the industrial emphasis was predominant.

Mann's inner turmoil moved to a climax towards the turn of the century, when the abortive Workers' Union, into which he had poured his energies and life's savings, exposed the gulf between his version of the 'new unionism' thinking and the larger labour movement orthodoxy and self-interest. It may well have seemed to him at the time that the objectives to which he had given his heart when he was admitted to the SDF had eluded him, and that any clear vision of the way forward had been lost. An offer of the position of secretary of a new Department of Labour by the Liberal government's President of the Board of Trade, A.J. Mundella, was refused. He considered – and rejected – the possibility of becoming deacon of a large Anglican parish in industrial London, which would have provided him with a more productive platform for his advocacy of socialism;[36] he renewed the links with the SDF which he had allowed to lapse;[37] and he was, briefly, secretary of the National Democratic League, which had the reform-minded editor of *Reynold's Newspaper*, W.M. Thompson, as its founder and president, and Lloyd George as vice-president.[38]

To these upheavals in his public life were added others of a private nature. His marriage with Ellen Edwards in 1878 had broken down, and it seems probable that he was already living with his future second wife, Elsie Harker, whose talents, as will be seen, made a significant contribution to his Australian successes. He obtained the licence of the Enterprise Hotel in the Covent Garden area of London, and experienced the exquisite humiliation of being convicted on charges – which he strenuously denied – of having watered its beer. Other factors exacerbating his distress may well have included Boer War jingoism, the return of the Tories to power in 1900 with a large majority and the Taff Vale decision in July, 1901.[39] Overall, the appearance of disorder created in the minds of his associates and the labour movement generally was interpreted as confirmation of an erratic, impatient and perhaps even reckless streak in his makeup. The announcement in 1901 of his decision to emigrate to New Zealand prompted the comment from the *Yorkshire Factory News* that a new country might be the remaking of him into 'such a man as he was ten years ago'.[40] When New Zealand, in turn, fell short of his hopes for it, he moved on to Australia, where he had been offered a lecture tour by the Melbourne impresario R.S. Smythe.[41]

TOM MANN IN VICTORIA

The reputation which preceded Mann to Victoria was such that he was importuned for support by 'a deputation in a small boat' even before his steamer had landed. The state was on the eve of its 1902 elections, and he addressed as many as a dozen meetings for PLC candidates in the brief period before Irvine's victory.[42] A VSL deputation comprising the president William Roth, together with Prendergast, Hannah and Bennett – put proposals for a 'straight out Socialist Party'[43] to him, which he endorsed. When lecturing for Smythe failed to provide him with an adequate income, and the Social Democratic Party of Victoria which the VSL proceeded to establish was unable to afford his services as an organiser, he went to work for a joint committee of the THC and the PLC.[44] These interventions defined the scope of his activities throughout the remainder of his stay in Victoria. The period was coloured throughout by the redirection of the ambivalence he had hitherto reserved for the relative merits of industrial and parliamentary action, to the crucial issue of whether it was through the agency of the Labor Party or an alternative party (actually or potentially in electoral competition with Labor) that a socialist future for the colony could most usefully be pursued. The upshot, as some have seen it, was that 'Though he worked relentlessly for the Labor Party, Mann remained, in his heart of hearts, with the SDP'.[45]

The need for a livelihood apart, Mann's acceptance of the position of paid organiser for the THC/PLC can therefore be seen as an attempt to hedge his bets. While continuing to support the 'straightout Socialist Party' which the VSL had now created, he would also work from within the heart of the PLC, in an effort to have socialism adopted as the party's policy and philosophy. The fact that he was unsuccessful in no way detracts from the great benefits the party derived from his services. His presence, in the aftermath of the crushing defeat of the Liberals and the PLC by Irvine's conservatives, came as a proverbial 'breath of fresh air' for a body whose attention to its organisational obligations – particularly in country Victoria – had hitherto been sporadic and half-hearted. Organising began in earnest in April 1903, with a series of meetings in workplaces around Melbourne, culminating in a week-long 'Organising Mission' at the Trades Hall, where overflow audiences and the use of music and singing created the atmosphere of a crusade. At the same time Mann undertook country tours, so that meetings were held and PLC branches established at centres such as Bendigo, Castlemaine, Ballarat and Echuca. In all, eighty-two new branches were formed in the nine months following Mann's appointment (as opposed to ten in the two years preceding it), and it was said that fifty-three of them were due solely to his personal efforts.[46] It was his estimate that, all told, he addressed no fewer than 200 meetings and made direct contact with more than 90,000 people.[47] His overt advocacy of socialism was initially restrained, but its intensity increased with his confidence that he was carrying a message which many in country areas were eager to hear.

Elmslie, who accompanied Mann on one of his tours, lauded the number of occasions on which he was able to record 'another branch formed, secretary appointed and night of meeting fixed'. A further travelling companion, Anstey, took admiring note of Mann's 'dauntless courage and mode of handling hostile audiences'.[48] However, in the midst of his successes, Mann was depressed by the refusal of the PLC or the rest of the labour movement to commit themselves to socialism. Even so, his efforts were largely responsible for the PLC's standing additional candidates at the federal elections in December 1903, where its support more than doubled, from 12.82 per cent to 25.98 per cent.

Well before the counting of votes was completed, Mann's link with the PLC had loosened. Notice of his resignation over the socialism issue was given in October and took effect in the first week of December. However, such was the warmth of feeling that he and the PLC members had for one another, and the lack of rancour over their differences, that in January he agreed to return for a further round of organising until the state elections were held in May or June. Once again, the project was an outstanding success: the number of electorates had been cut back from ninety-five to sixty-five, but the number of PLC MPs rose by half, from twelve to eighteen. Five of the additional Labor seats – Ballarat West, Bendigo West, Geelong, Grenville and Maryborough – were in country areas.[49] An extension of Mann's appointment was negotiated, but the combination of reservations about the likelihood of his employers ever committing themselves seriously to socialism and the desire to devote himself exclusively to socialist advocacy brought about a final parting of the ways in January 1905.[50] At the same time, however, when his need for the alternative platform of the SDPV was most acute, his hopes for it were dashed.

The SDPV, in whose inception Mann's imprimatur played so seminal a part, successfully brought together the colony's hitherto disparate threads of socialist activity, and also synthesised the organisational ideas and aspirations their adherents had developed over the thirty-year period since the establishment of the original Democratic Association of Victoria in 1872. In formal terms, the new group was a merger between the VSL and what remained of Champion's SDFV. The presidency and one vice-presidency were taken by the last two presidents of the VSL, Bennett and Roth, and the other vice-presidency by Champion, while Bennett became general secretary when the more senior positions were abolished because they were considered incompatible with socialist principles.[51]

These arrangements reflected both the positive effect that Mann's friendship had on Champion's standing in the eyes of his associates and the importance attached by Mann to unity among socialists. They ensured, moreover, that the SDPV had a clear playing field on which to operate, free of competitors other, perhaps, than the PLC. The objective adopted by the SDPV was the 'socialisation of the means of production, distribution and exchange to be controlled by a Democratic State in the interest of the entire community, and the complete emancipation of Labour from the domination of Capitalism and Landlordism, with the establishment of social and economic equality between the sexes'. Its stated methods were 'the education of the community in the principles of socialism; the independent and political organisation of the workers; and independent representation of socialist principles in all elective bodies'.[52]

More than 1,000 people regularly attended SDPV meetings on Sunday evenings, where entertainments such as 'violin and piano solos, funny recitations, Herr Arnold's Zither Club, the stirring performances of the S.D.P. Orchestra, the splendid "glees" of the S.D.P. Choir and, above all, the operatic voice of Elsie Mann, licentiate of the Academy of Music' were joined with addresses from a star cast of the movement's most notable orators. Singing was also prominent at the SDPV's Wednesday meetings, where lecturettes were delivered and discussed. Like the VSL and the VLF before it, the SDPV had its picnics and other social functions, and there was an SDPV Socialist Sunday School for members' children. SDPV pamphlets, including P.Z. Conurbian's *Capitalism Exposed* and Mann's *Socialism*, were published and the SDPV Literature Department distributed around 1,000 copies a month of books and periodicals from socialist sources overseas. The 105 members who belonged to the SDPV at the time of its first half-yearly meeting in May 1903 eventually rose to more than 600.[53]

Mann was the driving force behind much of this progress, buoying up SDPV members with his belief that it was the duty of socialists 'to enjoy the gayer and brighter things in life', and providing support for Bennett in his untiring organisational efforts to maximise the organisation's following.[54] It may well be that his model – in addition to the London Fabian Society – was such British SDF branches as Bow and Bromley, where, as the Labour Party leader, George Lansbury recalled:

> Our branch meetings were like revivalist gatherings. We opened with a song and closed with one, and often read together some extracts from economic and historical writings . . . Every Saturday we ran dances – humorously telling our critics we were going to dance into socialism . . . We ran an economics study class under Comrade Hazell and weekly struggled with *Das Kapital* and Engels' *Socialism Utopian and Scientific*.[55]

However, at the peak of its success, the SDPV was overtaken by a series of major setbacks. Attendances at the Sunday evening meetings fell away when complaints on sabbatarian grounds resulted in the dropping of the entertainment features which had contributed so markedly to their drawing power.[56] Elsie Mann became ill, and was unable to provide the choir with her customary leadership and focus.[57] The gap in the affairs of the SDPV brought about by Bennett's election to parliament in 1904 remained unfilled, and the social democratic credentials of the group were brought into question by a delay in the expression of its support for the 1905 Russian Revolution. When Mann returned from a three-month speaking tour in Queensland in May the same year, it was to find that 'the S.D.P.'s activities were lack-lustre at best'.[58] For all this, the relatively short lifespan of the SDPV saved its members from the need to make a decision on whether or not candidates for parliament should be run in opposition to the PLC, a decision which otherwise would inevitably have arisen, and – as has been foreshadowed – overtook the VSP later, with devastating effect.

Mann's initial response to the failure of the PLC and SDPV to live up to his hopes was another of the abrupt changes of course whose habitual nature was becoming plain. His disappointment with parliamentary politics and the SDF in the middle 1890s had precipitated his flirtation with joining the Church of England ministry. His disappointment with trade unionism at the turn of the century had influenced his decision to become a publican. Now, disappointed with political organisation in Australia, he seriously considered making a new life for himself as a pig and poultry farmer.[59] Land for the project actually seems to have been purchased, but other counsels ultimately prevailed, and he embarked instead on a series of Sunday evening appearances at the Gaiety Theatre, where he lectured to capacity crowds on topics of major social and political significance. Earning a living apart, the motive for the move may well have owed something to the Fabian strategy which he set out in pamphlet form in May 1905, under the title *Socialism*.

A socialist or co-operative society, Mann's pamphlet argued, was one where raw materials and the means of production would be owned by the people as a whole, and the regulation of industry would be entrusted to experts and rewarded in proportion to the work performed. While its achievement would require 'the complete supersession of the present capitalist system and private owner-ship',[60] that process would occur gradually, in conformity with Darwin's model of the evolution of the species. The PLC was to be encouraged in such support for socialism as it might exhibit, but there was a need for affiliation with the International Workers' Congress and the Second International, as well as for the establish-ment of a new organisation which would influence the PLC in the direction of socialism. It may well have been implicit in this formulation that the proposed new organisation should not be a self-styled 'party' like the SDPV, but by conforming to the Fabian model should avoid giving offence to even the more sensitive elements of the PLC.

Be this as it may, an opportunity for Mann's thinking to be given effect shortly presented itself. It came in the form of a suggestion from the floor of one of his lectures that a new committee to research and publicise social issues and their socialist solutions should be formed. The originator was J.P. Jones, who has been characterised by the writer most closely familiar with his life and career as 'a pragmatic Fabian socialist, enthusiastic for genuine social reform'.[61] Jones and his close friend O'Dowd typified the clearest sighted of the Fabian element among the indigenous socialists to whom Mann now turned, in a triumphant, if all too brief, implementation of the Fabian approach in an antipodean political environment.

Once again, in Jones and O'Dowd as in their expatriate mentors, the archetypal Fabian traits exemplified by Archer were evident. Both were lapsed Catholics,[62] of whom it can be said in the most literal sense that 'the service of God was transferred to the service of humanity'. Both were upwardly socially mobile, with the coachman's son, Jones, rising to wealth and influence as a successful businessman and cabinet minister, and the country policeman's son, O'Dowd, to literary fame and the prestigious position of Chief Parliamentary Draftsman. As a career politician and a senior public servant, both were functionaries of good standing in the ranks of Webb and Shaw's *nouvelle couche sociale*. Both exhibited the 'growing unease' among 'men of intellect and men of property' over poverty, as detected earlier in Britain by Beatrice Webb. O'Dowd was squarely in the mould of those Fabians who loved beauty for its own sake and were repelled by capitalism because it was beauty's antithesis, while Jones was squarely in the Benthamite stream of those who rejected capitalism's wastefulness, inertia and inefficiency.

MANN'S VICTORIAN COLLEAGUES

J.P. JONES

John Percy Jones was born to Irish Catholic parents on 22 October 1872 at Hobart Town, where his mother died before his third birthday. Raised by his father, he worked from the age of eight as an out-of-school-hours stable hand and chemist's delivery boy, and then, at eleven, graduated to the position of rouseabout and boundary rider on R.Q. Kermode's 'Mona Vale' sheep station near Ross. Further jobs followed in Victoria: as a butcher, a drover and the purveyor of a brand of brass polish of his own invention, and in 1893 the foundations for his fortune were laid with the establishment of Melbourne's first pay-as-you-wear tailoring business. This is said to have reflected his recognition that a working man's suit was often needed before it could be afforded. A team of men on bicycles was recruited to collect the weekly instalments, and ultimately the services of the cloth middlemen in Melbourne were eliminated by dealing directly with the British manufacturers. Jones was able to harness nationalist sentiment to commercial advantage by his use of the business slogan 'Be true to the Southern Cross', and sales of his suits also benefited from his links with the Melbourne sporting fraternity. He was enough of a boxer to find himself in the practice ring with the redoubtable Bill Squires, who knocked him out. He also matched himself in the Austral Wheel Race against cycling notables such as Charles Kellow and 'Plugger' Martin. Jones' commercial involvements were systematically diversified. He acquired rural property and tenement housing, and was elected chairman for the 1907 Australian Manufacturing Exhibition.[63]

While Jones was making himself rich, he was also acquiring industrial and political interests and acumen. His brief sojourn as a butcher led him to become an early member of the Butchers' Union, and he attended classes at the Working Men's College. His imagination was fired initially by the teachings of Henry George, whom he met and questioned during George's 1890 Australian tour. John Ruskin, Edward Bellamy and the early Fabians also influenced him powerfully, and his special regard for Ruskin was marked by naming his Croydon home 'Ruskin Park', his Kew home 'Ruskin Hall' and the Victorian Socialist Party football team which he served as vice-president the 'Ruskin Football Club'. The result, inevitably, was that Jones found himself irresistibly drawn to the socialist cause. In 1897 he became secretary of the North Melbourne Branch of the Political Labour Council and of the *Tocsin* Printing and Publishing Co-operative Society. His Tocsin Group membership involved him in providing financial support for Ben Tillett's 1897 Australian visit. Jones and Tillett struck up a close friendship, and when Jones in his turn visited Britain on a number of occasions dating from 1901, he was introduced by Tillett to a range of socialist luminaries, including Bernard Shaw, H.G. Wells, Keir Hardie and John Burns. He was also accorded life membership of Tillett's dockers' union. When the Jones family's 1926 visit to Britain coincided with the general strike, they were the only passengers whose luggage could be unloaded from the ship.

BERNARD O'DOWD

Like Jones, Bernard Patrick O'Dowd was of humble origins. His mother presented her police constable husband with their first son at Beaufort on 11 April 1866. The boy's obvious intelligence encouraged the devout Ulster Catholic family to hope that he might come to qualify for a three-year secondary education, followed by three years of university, on one of the eight exhibitions (scholarships) which were awarded annually to the most outstanding students of the colony's non-denominational schools. Accordingly, instead of the Catholic schools his brother and sisters attended, he was sent to Mr Pennell's Beaufort Private School, Snake Valley State School and the Soldiers' Hill and Mount Pleasant State Schools in Ballarat. Meanwhile, he absorbed elements of geography and Irish history and mythology from his father's well stocked and inquiring mind, avidly borrowing books from sources such as the Snake Valley Mechanics Institute and haunting the exotic world of Ballarat's China Town. It is said that he had read ' "Paradise Lost" at eight, Hume at nine and Virgil at ten years of age'.[64] 'Even at school', by a second account, 'he had an encyclopaedic mind. He was interested in everything'.[65] His matriculation examination was passed in 1880, when he was fourteen, and the following year he entered Grenville College on the coveted exhibition.

His studies there were cut short when his father was invalided out of the police force with a back injury and the family moved to a small farm at Beaufort. O'Dowd remained behind as the seventeen-year-old head teacher of the St Alpius' boys' school in Ballarat East, but his Catholic faith was giving way to an open advocacy of free thought doctrines which were unacceptable to the school authorities and ultimately made his position untenable. Claims that he was a corrupter of young minds followed him to the school he opened in the family home in Beaufort and, at the end of 1885, he sat the public service examination with several of his Beaufort students and was appointed to a Crown Solicitor's Office position in Melbourne. The arts degree studies he had commenced in Ballarat were completed in 1891, as was a law degree four years later, when he was working as an assistant librarian in the Supreme Court.

O'Dowd's student days in Ballarat and his teaching sojourns at Ballarat and Beaufort also saw the start of his life's work as a poet. His first poems appeared in the *Ballarat Evening Post* when he was sixteen, as did later pieces in the *Ballarat Courier*. By 1894 he was being published in the *Bulletin*. A number of collections of his work were issued, including *Dawnward?* in 1903 and *The Silent Land* in 1906. In the view of Dame Mary Gilmore, writing in 1953:

> No one knows now, except a few of us who are left, how his *Dawnward?* burst open the doors of narrowness when he wrote it. Today because liberty is abroad, and theirs, writers refer chiefly to his later verse. They did not know of the need of his early times for the reformer, and (hackneyed though the word be) standard-bearer.[66]

His 1909 delivery of an address on 'Poetry Militant' to the Literature Society was remembered by his fellow writer Katherine Susannah Prichard, as an occasion when:

He made such an impression on those of us who were beginning to think seriously that, upon leaving the meeting, we were almost too exalted and exhilarated to speak. I felt that my eyes had been opened to what I could do, as a writer, to help relieve the woes of the world.[67]

As O'Dowd grew older, and his creative powers waned, he increasingly assumed the mantle of a literary elder statesman, lecturing on aesthetic issues and giving public poetry readings. 'He exerted', his principal biographers note, 'a mesmeric power over those who heard him and it was easy to imagine him as a tribal bard standing on some outcrop of rock and exciting his fellows assembled in the hollow below with the passion of his verse'.[68] 'Bernard O'Dowd', it was said by A.G. Stephens, 'is a priest without a frock, devoted not to the service of a creed, but to the service of humanity'. He looked, according to Walter Murdoch, 'like an Irish Messiah'.[69]

Ballarat also provided O'Dowd with his introduction to politics. He gained a reputation as a 'boy orator' in Home Rule debates at the Catholic Young Men's Society, and was selected as one of the city's three delegates for the 1882 convention which welcomed to Melbourne the Irish leaders John and William Redmond. Subsequently, the agnostic preoccupations of his period as a teacher caused him to be dropped by his former Catholic associates. In Melbourne his allegiance was captured for the radical and Australian nationalist causes, through friends such as the anarchist J.A. Andrews and by reading and corresponding with the American poet Walt Whitman. He also joined organisations such as the Progressive Lyceum at Carlton – characterised by J.A. La Nauze as 'the Spiritualist Sunday school' – Charles Strong's Collingwood Workingmen's Club and the Australian Natives' Association, with which he later fell out over federation.[70] His Fabian affiliations were seen by him in some moods as stemming from necessity rather than preference. In a letter to the young Nettie Higgins he said: 'I'm not a socialist myself: I accept evolution doctrines sufficiently to compel me to see that my own ideal anarchistic communism can only come – after a long time – along the socialistic disciplinary road – and that's why I work with socialists'.[71] Even the disavowal, however, had Fabian overtones, as witness its counterpart in the final passage of Shaw's discussion of 'Transition' in his *Fabian Essays in Socialism*: 'Let me, in conclusion, disavow all admiration for this inevitable, but sordid, slow, reluctant, cowardly path to justice'.[72] O'Dowd met his future wife, Evangeline Fryer, at the Progressive Lyceum. The five sons born to them between 1890 and 1904 had names reflecting his recondite learning: Montaigne Eric Whitman, Rudel Arion, Auster Bernard, Amergin Oison and Vondel Kevin. 'Feeling that "father" had a too authoritarian ring', it is said, 'O'Dowd had them call him "mate" '.[73]

O'Dowd's contribution as editor of the *Tocsin* included writing the paper's column of general comment – 'The Forge' – over the signature of 'Gavah the Blacksmith'. The topics which attracted his scrutiny in 'The Forge' included land tenure laws, the relationship between tenants and landlords, women's rights, Sunday observance, consumer protection and gambling, while the column's most passionate opposition was deployed against federation legislation, which O'Dowd saw as making any real improvement in the social system impossible for years to come. An estrangement from his fellow members of the *Tocsin* Printing and Publishing Co-operative Society led him to sever his links with the co-operative shortly after the turn of the century, but he continued his work for the socialist cause through the VSL, the SDPV and ultimately through the SQC, the VSP and the Fabian Society of Victoria. Meanwhile, his feelings towards his associates and his friends were recorded in his verse. Champion, for example, was extolled on 15 June 1896 with the lines:

> And I who whirl the storms of pain
> To purge the skies of wrong
> Demand a niche in Freedom's fame
> A verse in Freedom's song[74]

Tillett, who paid frequent visits on his bicycle to the O'Dowd family home in Pascoe Vale Road during his stay in Victoria in 1898, was farewelled on his departure for England with verses which read in part:

> You came when Faith was heart-sick
> And Hope began to nod,
> A Mercury to Labour
> With messages from God[75]

THE FABIAN CHARACTER OF THE SQC

The Social Questions Committee (SQC) which Mann initiated at Jones' suggestion shared most of the objectives and character of the London Fabian Society and engaged in most of the London Society's activities.[76] The SQC's initial commitment to collect 'reliable data concerning the number of underfed children in Victoria, and to ascertain to what extent this is due to the unemployment of the parents or other causes'[77] stemmed from the same preoccupation with poverty and statistical evidence which prompted the London Society to make the subject of its first Tract, *Why Are the Many Poor?*, and *Facts for Socialists* the subject of Tract 5. The same revulsion over unemployment which led the London Fabians to participate in the 'Black Monday' and 'Bloody Sunday' street marches side by side with members of the SDF and other radical clubs also prompted protests from members of the SQC. The opening words of the London Society's Basis – 'the Society consists of Socialists' – were echoed by the declaration of the SQC's executive that 'All members shall realise that our chief work is the persistent advocacy of Socialism'.[78]

Detailed and painstaking research into specific economic and social problems figured prominently among the activities of both organisations. Both carried out programs of socialist education and consciousness raising by means of public lectures, while the propaganda functions of the London Society's pamphlets and its periodical, *Fabian News*, were fulfilled in the case of the SQC, by its more ambitious weekly, the *Socialist*. The SQC also published pamphlets of its own, such as Mann's *The War of the Classes*. The Hampstead Historic Society meetings through which the London Fabians clarified their understanding of socialism had their parallel in the SQC's economics classes and its classes for speakers. Entertainments with a political message, such as Marson's presentation of Somerset folk songs to the London Fabians, were paralleled on a much more expansive and robust scale by the musical performances staged for the SQC by Elsie Mann.

Both organisations assumed for many of their members a significance above and beyond conventional party political loyalties. The London Society has been described by the son of Rebecca West and H.G. Wells, Anthony West, as a 'play-thing', which members of its 'Old Gang' valued so highly that they maliciously misrepresented Wells in order to stop him taking it away from them.[79] A perhaps more objective view ascribes the treatment of the Society as a toy to Wells, and sees the 'Old Gang' as having been maliciously misrepresented by him. What the accounts have in common is the passionately proprietorial feelings the Society so plainly evoked. For many of its adherents, Fabian socialism could even more aptly be described as work and play combined in a totally self-sufficient way of life. SQC members, for their part, were ultimately able to sing in a choir of their own; mix socially at their own dances and entertainments; play football in a team of their own; keep abreast of events by reading their own weekly newspaper; satisfy their household needs through their own co-operative trading society, with Mann and Champion among its directors; and have their spiritual needs catered for by 'socialist sermons' preached regularly from SQC platforms, while those of their children were met through the SQC Socialist Sunday School. The inescapable conclusion is that Mann initially wanted – and was supported in this by Jones – a Fabian Society on the model with which he was familiar. The name it went by was immaterial. Calling it the Social Questions Committee at Champion's suggestion, as in fact transpired, was simply a commonsense way to avoid the kind of animosity associated with Champion's earlier affronts to the labour movement and other indiscretions that a premature re-use of the Fabian label might otherwise have revived.

SQC RESEARCH ACTIVITIES

The Gaiety Theatre lecture at which Jones made his proposal was delivered on 20 August 1905. A report to the following Sunday's gathering confirmed the need for information on underfed children, unemployment and 'various other matters', and emphasised, presciently, that any body formed for the purpose should adopt an attitude of 'friendliness and helpfulness' to other socialist and labour organisations. Mann's response was positive and prompt. Within less than a week – on Friday, 1 September – a meeting of seventy-six people, chaired by Jones in Furlong's Rooms in Royal Arcade, inaugurated the new group. It was agreed that the aim of the SQC should be 'the collection, tabulation and dissemination of information relating to the Social welfare of the community'.[80] Jones was elected president, Champion and the militant trade unionist Charles Gray were made vice-presidents, and Mann was secretary and Carter treasurer. A threepenny monthly subscription rate was adopted.[81]

A meeting on 4 October agreed that Mann's lectures should be taken over by the SQC, and transferred to the Queen's Hall in Bourke Street. Mann was appointed to the paid position of organising secretary, and a 'purely voluntary' propaganda fund was established.

The SQC's mission statement was effectively rounded off in November, with a ringing declaration from the executive that:

All members shall realise that our chief work is the persistent advocacy of Socialism. All other work is incidental to this, but to enable this to be done effectively a variety of educational activities are really necessary.[82]

Meanwhile, the SQC was proceeding to give effect to its brief, through avenues including research, the provision of a congenial environment for its members, lecturing, and defence of the right of assembly, where comparisons with London Society counterparts can usefully be drawn.

The London Fabians had the advantage over the SQC, in as much as the hard-slog, door-to-door inquiries required to establish the extent and nature of poverty in Britain and provide the basis for an appropriate policy response had been carried out for them by Charles and Mary Booth. The Booths were not Fabians or socialists of any kind, but it was while working for their London survey that Beatrice Webb embarked on her lifelong vocation as a social investigator, and that the seeds of her socialism were sown. The outcome, in part, was the proposal for a 'National Minimum' standard for wages, health and industrial conditions which were put forward by the Webbs in 1897 in their book *Industrial Democracy* and, earlier on, by such radical liberals as John Hobson and Beatrice's brother-in-law Leonard Hobhouse.[83] Elements of the 'National Minimum' were implemented for the first time in the Factory Act adopted in Victoria in 1896 at the instigation of Champion and such colonial counterparts of Hobson and Hobhouse as Deakin and Mauger. The Victorian legislation was a model, in part, for the Trades Boards legislation adopted in Britain in 1909 following further agitation by the Fabians and their allies.[84] It was also a precursor for the Commonwealth Arbitration Court, where, as has been seen, yet another of Hobson and Hobhouse's colonial counterparts, Mr Justice Higgins, was able to achieve what may well have been the most triumphant of all applications of the 'National Minimum' philosophy, in the 1907 Harvester judgement which gave rise to the Basic Wage.[85]

In the case of the SQC, data about the incidence of poverty and unemployment in Melbourne were unavailable, and its work had to be started from scratch. Throughout the preceding winter, groups of unemployed people had demonstrated daily on a vacant block in Swanston Street. Deputations had been received by the lands minister and the premier, and parliament's attention had been focussed by Solly on the number of state school pupils who were underfed, but with no result other than a promise by the premier to refer the matter to a commission of inquiry into education, which was not kept. It followed, in the view of Mann and his associates, that the problem would have to be quantified before action would be taken. Plans were therefore developed for a house-to-house survey of Richmond, South Melbourne, Port Melbourne, Prahran, Carlton and Collingwood, on the model of the Booths' work in London. A team of seventy volunteer interviewers was recruited under Jones' leadership, and given the task of administering a questionnaire: '(1) In work or out? (2) How long out during the last twelve months? (3) What is the weekly wage when in work? (4) What number in the family? (5) How many working? (6) Are the children well fed? (7) How many rooms are occupied? and (8) What rent is paid?' A single interviewer in Richmond is reported to have recorded thirty-four quarto pages of notes – 'every one of which is a vivid reflection of the conditions that prevail' – in the course of visits to 596 households.[86]

The SQC concluded that, in the areas covered, 2,800 workers or 15 per cent of the workforce were unemployed. The first of many examples from the survey quoted in the *Socialist* read:

> There is a family of five in three rooms, for which five shillings a week is paid as rent. The mother says the children rarely have enough to eat, and her husband does not work more than three months in a year.

According to another: 'Mother, six children, rented four rooms for 6/-; husband in W.A., remitted only £4 in twelve months due to unemployment there; mother earns 10/- weekly cleaning and scrubbing; owed fortnight's rent; no food in house, little clothing or blankets'.[87]

Further damning evidence was obtained as the result of Mann and Solly's request to the Medical Board of Health for 'a medical investigation in representative industrial and residential areas, to ascertain the anthropometric differences in the children living under different conditions'. The Board's report confirmed that – as the SQC had anticipated – 'the children of the poorer districts were considerably below those of other districts in regards physique and general fitness'. Armed with this body of facts, a meeting on 13 March 1906 resolved that: 'A deputation be arranged to wait upon the Hon.

Thos. Bent, the Premier, to urge upon him the desirability of carrying out his promise regarding the Commission of Enquiry'.

When the deputation was refused, Jones was able to enlist the backing of the Australian Natives' Association, through a resolution from its conference at Shepparton that: 'This Conference instructs the in-coming Board of Directors to bring the matter under the notice of the Government, and to urge them to take immediate action to at least provide food for such children of school age whose parents are unable to provide' [it].[88] Even so, Bent and his colleagues remained adamant. Looking back, eighteen years later, Mann concluded 'No cure of unemployment was achieved, for the outlook of those in authority was as completely bourgeois as that of the Coalition Government in Britain today'.[89]

Mann's comments require qualification. The credibility of his proposals to the Bent government on state farms and workshops[90] was compromised by the failure of two earlier such movements: the village settlement scheme which Strong and the Vicar of Christ Church South Yarra, the Reverend Horace Finn Tucker, had seen collapse around their ears a decade before,[91] and the state-funded Labour Colony which operated under the direction of Champion's father-in-law Colonel Jacob Goldstein at Leongatha from 1893 to 1905.[92] Demands for a major program of public works flew in the face of the conventional economic wisdom, for which no rebuttal or replacement was offered. Far from the SQC's setting out to influence Bent's massively entrenched conservatives as the London Fabians attempted to influence the similarly entrenched Liberals in Britain, it opted instead for a confrontationist policy of demonstrations in the Melbourne churches, which were among the key symbols and citadels of the city's conservative establishment.

No policy development process along the lines which gave rise to the London Society's 'National Minimum' package was undertaken, and efforts by Jones to have the survey data published in a single volume were unsuccessful.[93] All told, the SQC, no less than the 'bourgeois' conservatives Mann criticised, was bereft of practical ideas. It may well be that this shortcoming on the part of the SQC reflected no more than the fact that, with a fall in unemployment to 9.2 per cent in 1905 (as against 11.9 per cent in 1904 and 13.1 per cent in 1903)[94] the steam had begun to go out of the issue at about the time the data from the interviewers were beginning to arrive. Alternatively, it may be seen as early evidence that the group was already being seduced from its Fabian resolve by the siren songs of more adventurous or millennial alternatives.

THE COMMUNITY OF SOCIALISTS

It has been said of the London Fabian Society that 'However debatable its wider influence on public affairs may have been, there can be no debating its value as a focus for the extraordinary energies and enthusiasms of an alienated section of the late-Victorian and Edwardian middle classes, nor its effectiveness as an agency of pleasure and recreation for the same group'.[95] A Stage Society was formed in 1889 and Fabian Society 'Subject Groups' – including an Arts Group, a Philosophy Group, a Biology Group, a Local Government Group, an Education Group and a Women's Group – through which the Society was linked subsequently to bodies such as the Standing Joint Committee of Labour Women's Organisations and the Women's International League, were formed in the first decade of the new century.

The Women's Group promptly involved itself in the great women's suffrage demonstrations. Group members were gaoled for their parts in the campaign, and the Society passed 'urgent resolutions on the treatment of suffragettes in prison'. Activities of a more typically Fabian character included the preparation of publications such as the Group's first book, *Women Workers in Seven Professions*, and Tracts which appeared under the Group's own imprint, as well as the holding of classes and conferences. An annual dinner was instituted and, in the 1920s, the Group gave birth to a Poor Persons' Legal Advice Bureau. Evidence on behalf of the Group was presented to the 1946 Royal Commission on Equal Pay, and 'Only gradually did it sink into oblivion, as it became apparent that the newest generation of Fabian males was even less interested than their predecessors in women's problems, and that those Fabian females who were, preferred to pursue their causes along more sympathetic channels'.[96] In the view of the Society's centenary historian Patricia Pugh: 'The unique role of the Group in the fight to gain recognition of a woman's right to be treated by the state as the equal to a man had been to seek the truth about her existing status, dispel many false illusions about her incapacity to fulfil a position equal – though not necessarily identical – to a man's, investigate her true economic, physical and intellectual needs and those of her family, educate her about these and give her the confidence to claim them'.[97]

The introduction of the Fabian Summer Schools in July 1907 enabled members to enjoy a collective working holiday which, while being 'relaxing as well as stimulating, not only broke down regional barriers; it also nurtured an ease of intercourse between the disparate sensibilities attracted to the Fabian Society'. The Society also offered 'Entertainments', 'At Homes' and 'Soirees', and evening meetings of its branches in provincial areas were sometimes organised as moonlight rambles, picnics or whist drives. An 'inexpensive club', operated by the Society in Tothill Street, Westminster, around the time of the First World War, featured a smoking-room and games-room in addition to a 'considerable library' and reading room, which mixed 'fiction and the drama' with 'Socialist and Labour journals of the whole world', and a Fabian Nursery was created in April 1906 for the Society's younger members. Even so, the 'club-like comforts and securities'[98] enjoyed by the London Fabians could hardly match the richly comprehensive quality of those provided by their counterparts in far-off Victoria.

While Jones and his fellow interviewers were refining the capacities of the SQC as a data-gathering and research organisation, Mann was lifting its public profile, expanding its membership and strengthening the solidarity and camaraderie which were among its most notable features. A choir on the model pioneered with such triumphant success by its predecessors was formed, as was an orchestra. There was also a dramatic society 'to bring members together under educationally helpful conditions, enabling members to get rid of nervousness, and developing the power to read and think clearly, and to enunciate correctly'. This was in line with the London Fabians' concerns for oratory, as were the economic and speakers' classes under Tunnecliffe's direction, where about forty-five students attended, 'half the evening being devoted to text-book work and half to reading and discussion of papers written by the students'.[99]

Ultimately, there were also a history class, an English class, an Esperanto class and a library, while current socialist publications from Britain, Europe and America were offered by the Socialist Institute – as the SQC's headquarters at 117 Collins Street was known to members – through its reading room and information bureau.[100] The opening of the Institute, on 26 November 1905, attracted a capacity crowd of 250, who sat down to 'a cold collation, and songs and speeches' at tables headed by the SQC officers.[101] A bicycle club was formed, together with cricket and football teams, a calisthenics club and a Cosmopolitan Committee to foster links with Melbourne's ethnic communities. Sales of 'Red Flag' tea for 1/6 a pound gave rise to a Socialist Co-operative Trading Society which supplied general household goods, groceries, boots, clothing and books, and a Socialist Savings Bank was opened. The establishment of a Socialist Co-operative Farm was discussed – and attracted a £100 donation – but failed to proceed in the light of further, perhaps wiser, counsels.

The *Socialist* was revived in April 1906,[102] to provide reports of the 'diverse committees' which had been set to work by the first half-yearly meeting of the SQC the previous month, together with 'reports from other quarters of the world on the Party's growth and activities', which were seen as being 'systematically concealed by all the newspapers controlled by the capitalist class' and 'far more important than the rubbish with which the Press is crammed'.[103] A further revival was the Socialist Sunday School – an affiliate of the International Young Comrades Movement, which, at its peak, had an enrolment of around 200. The scholars studied ethics, calisthenics and socialist principles, and were encouraged to observe the Socialist Ten Commandments. The Sunday School's spectacular growth resulted in a spin-off: a Young Comrades Contingent of the Socialist Army, whose members – including, early on, names as richly evocative of labour associations as Ida Mabel Pitt, Evaline Marie Pitt, Tom Mann, Bob Mann, Jennie Bruce, Yatala Bruce and Beryl Bruce[104] – affirmed 'I am very sorry that there is suffering through poverty. I believe socialism will cure this evil and make it possible for all to be happy'.[105] The religious flavour which characterised so many of the SQC's activities – and the pervasive belief of its members that socialism was a sacred cause – were reflected in references to Mann's Sunday lectures as 'socialist sermons', and the performing of 'socialist christening' ceremonies.

The Sunday gatherings at Queen's Hall touched new heights on occasions such as the 'magnificent meeting' in celebration of the Paris Commune on 18 March 1906, when:

> The inception and development of the International was detailed and its work set forth. The machinations of M. Thiers and the rest of the reactionaries were detailed, and the truly noble behaviour of our Parisian exemplars cited. The audience completely filled the hall, and was

gloriously enthusiastic. Frank Hyett was chairman. The choir sang splendidly, and the orchestra, under the direction of Comrade Green, contributed much to the success of the evening. The Socialist song, 'The Red Flag', was on a sheet in type large enough to be seen by the audience, and the heartiness with which it was sung was delightful, and those who were present are not likely to forget for a very long time the truly successful gathering of 18th March, 1906.[106]

There were annual balls, picnics, party socials, theatre trips, bay cruises and celebrations of special events such as the 1906 May Day observance, where the *Socialist* advertised:

> We shall have a social in the fine new Cathedral Hall, Brunswick Street. Dancing till 12 o'clock. No singing during the evening except 'The Red Flag', which Mrs Mann will sing as a solo and all present will join in the chorus, and at interval Tom Mann will give a ten minutes address on 'The Day We Celebrate'.[107]

The demands and rewards of SQC and VSP membership have been summarised eloquently by Lloyd Ross, who grew up in the movement as a son of the leading VSP identity and editor of the *Socialist*, R.S. Ross. In his biography of John Curtin, the prime minister and wartime leader who became the most famous of their number, he said:

> What a world! What an all-rounded life was demanded of these men and women. They were expected to distribute leaflets, read and listen to poetry; attend Bernard O'Dowd's class in history and listen to John Curtin or Scott Bennett or R.S. Ross on public speaking; read Marx, Swinburne, Shelley, and Jack London, Robert Blatchford, Eugene Sue and Upton Sinclair, Robert Ingersoll, Shakespeare and Omar Khayyam; that their interests should be as wide as the world that they would conquer for socialism and as intense as the activities they followed in the streets or in the study classes; that they would donate a shilling a week to a sustenation fund, take up a collection, sing in the choir, run a bazaar; all this was part of the training of a Prime Minister who said, 'I got my education on the Yarra Bank'.[108]

It was Mann's considered view that 'The Socialist Party aimed at fulfilling the requirements of its members in every phase of life's activities, and was more successful in this respect than have been any of the other organisations I have belonged to'.[109] Its achievement, all told, was to provide a foretaste of what the feel of life might be like in the socialist society of its members' dreams that was more richly all-encompassing than their London counterparts ever enjoyed – or than possibly harder-headed members of the London Society

'Old Gang' would have thought appropriate. It may well be that the less austere outlook it adopted was reflected in the fact that in late 1907 it attracted roughly the same number of members as the London Society, from a far smaller population.[110]

LECTURING AND FREE SPEECH AGITATION IN THE SQC

Research apart, the activity to which the London Fabians attached greatest importance was lecturing. Lecturing was undertaken by the SQC with no less vigour or seriousness of purpose, if necessarily on a smaller scale. The fledgling group was able to report, within six months of its inception, that thirty lecturers had taken part in a total of 113 propagandist meetings at venues which included Port Melbourne pier, South Melbourne, Northcote, Richmond, Fitzroy, Collingwood, Carlton and Brunswick, and that it was now able to run 'eight meetings simultaneously, with five speakers for each meeting'.[111] By August 1906, sixty-one lecturers were available, including the Labor MPs Solly, Bamford and Maloney, together with their future federal parliamentary colleague whose qualities so comprehensively eclipsed those of his contemporaries, Curtin.

Saturday nights, as Curtin later recalled, 'would see fifteen street corner meetings held simultaneously', while on the Yarra Bank 'Each Sunday afternoon a roster of six to eight speakers – practised and unpractised, of all ages and both sexes – would trumpet the slogan of the new dispensation'. The meetings figured in his memory as occasions when 'There was a borrowing of boxes, gathering in of money, literature selling, and there was always a dependable group of valiants to make the nucleus of a crowd'. SQC lecturing was not restricted to Melbourne. Bennett, for example, toured Gippsland in 1907, while Curtin and Hyett were among the lecturers who appeared on platforms in country towns such as Longwood, and regional centres such as Maryborough, Geelong, Bendigo and Ballarat. A VSP member who heard Curtin at Ballarat in 1908 – and was surprised by 'the fire and ability of the address' – reported that 'When Jack had been speaking for a few minutes, a large crowd gathered'.[112]

Curtin, however, was only one among the many clergymen, Labor MPs, academics and public servants who featured in the various streams of the lecture program. It was Mann, above all, who carried the brunt of the program earlier on, speaking as he did at seventy-three of the 124 Sunday evening gatherings which took place between April 1906 and January 1908[113] as well as the Wednesday evening meetings and innumerable other SQC and VSP functions. Mann's belief that the scope of the program should not be limited to political ideology, but should range broadly over art, science, religion and the whole range of human experiences was reflected in a series of Sunday evening lectures on 'Sociology, History, Ethology, Mythology', which he delivered in Melbourne in 1906 under the titles: 'Confucius, the Great Chinese Teacher', 'Life and Work of Joseph Dietzger', 'Socialism in Germany and Switzerland – the Recent Elections', 'The Development of Japan: Its Effect on Western Nations', 'Recent Developments in Machinery and Science', 'The Class Struggle: the Churches and the Socialist Party', 'Lessons from Shelley, the Poet of Revolution', 'The Great Buddha – Indian Mythology' and 'Swedenborgism'.[114] A Wednesday evening lecture which he delivered in September the same year was advertised as:

A MENTAL PILGRIMAGE
To Europe, the East, Ancient Rome, Greece, Egypt and Babylonia.
Prehistoric Man. The Monsters of the Pre-human Age.
Children of the Earth –
The Earth's Child – the Moon.
The Earth's Father – Old Sol.
The Earth's Brothers and Sisters.
How They Were Born, and When.
Meteorites, and How They Are Caught.
Comets and Suns, Live Suns, Double Suns.
The Nebular Hypothesis.
The Mind of Man Soaring Onward and Upward
Ever Travelling Towards Perfection[115]

A member of one of Mann's Sunday night audiences in 1906 wrote enthusiastically in the *Socialist*:

Oh, what a lecture Tom Mann had up his sleeve! Why didn't you give us this before, Tom? . . . your adventures in Belgium, Holland, Germany, France, Spain, Denmark, Norway and Sweden. It did make us think. We seemed to be in touch with revolutionary Europe, like scratching a tiger's back, all alive, electric, vibrating, pulsing.[116]

The wider significance of the Sunday gatherings for antipodean socialism was captured in an article written by Curtin on the occasion of the tenth anniversary of the VSP. Curtin mused:

There are men mustering stock in North Queensland, laying rails on the North-West track, and yarning, when the day is done, in an unkempt humpy, lost in the tall timber, who know of this meeting, and who speculate on Sunday nights as to who is the speaker and what is the subject. And on each succeeding Sunday there returns some one wanderer who was familiar in days now dead, and who once again feels the spirit of fraternity, and dreams anew the old wonderful dreams, which are but anticipation of the world as it will be.[117]

Mann himself later reminisced in a letter to a friend: 'The Sunday afternoon meetings at Elizabeth Street we shall always remember, and the lectures in the week, and the Sunday nights, are all engraved on our memories indelibly'.[118] All told, it seems unlikely that any lectures organised by the London Fabians ever equalled – much less exceeded – the size and fervour of the Sunday evening SQC and VSP gatherings. While the number of lectures held under SQC and VSP auspices was clearly fewer by far than those under London Society auspices, the discrepancy is less marked in proportion to the populations for which they respectively catered. The members of the SQC were no less dedicated to lecturing than their London counterparts, nor was the response from their audiences less enthusiastic. The defence of freedom of speech and assembly which the London Fabians and other radical groups mounted in Trafalgar Square on 'Black Monday', 8 February 1886, and 'Bloody Sunday', 13 November 1887, were paralleled in the case of the SQC by the Prahran Free Speech Fight of 1906.

VSP meetings in Prahran in 1906 were opposed by the Prahran Council and harassed by the local police. This resulted, early on, in the imposition of a fine on a VSP member, Joe Swabjeses, for addressing a meeting which the police had prohibited. He was imprisoned when he refused to pay. The VSP vigorously resisted what the failure of the authorities to impose similar restrictions on Salvation Army meetings showed to be a blatant and discriminatory attack on the right of free speech and assembly. Another seventeen members, including Mann, had themselves arrested and imprisoned for periods of up to five weeks in sympathy with Swabjeses. Funds for the conduct of a defence were raised by a defence committee, in part from the sale of 5,000 postcards showing those already convicted in their prison dress. Denunciations of the Prahran Council and the police thundered from the pages of the *Socialist*. Messages of support were received from PLC branches; Prendergast raised the situation in the Legislative Assembly on behalf of the PLC; and protest meetings were addressed by other PLC MPs including Bennett and

Anstey, who also offered to take Mann's place on platforms which would otherwise have been left empty by his imprisonment. The campaign was briefly a *cause celebre* which attracted attention within the broad socialist movement as far afield as Britain, and prompted calls for a nationwide unification of all Australia's socialist organisations.[119]

Even so, the image which some VSP members held of their organisation, as 'a lonely standard bearer of working class hopes', capable of facing down the massed forces of reaction, was ultimately unsustainable. Following Mann's release from gaol, the free speech fight was rapidly wound down. Instructions were given for speakers to transfer their meetings to vacant blocks when moved on by police and, at Hyett's suggestion, the funds collected by the defence committee were donated to striking building workers. The real significance of the episode was less in any concrete gains than in the further indications it afforded of the existence of elements within the organisation who were anxious to place it on a collision course with the PLC. At the height of the furore, a *Socialist* editorial carried 'the thinly-veiled threat that the VSP, "the vanguard of the Victorian political advance, and the teacher of ideas, as yet but dimly apprehended by the masses" would soon have to supplant the Labor Party electorally, if socialism was to be achieved'.[120] The PLC was criticised in some quarters for having failed to give adequate support to the protest, in the face of clear evidence that such was not the case.

FABIAN-STYLE PERMEATION

These early instances of mischief making were incompatible with the policy of permeation which was supported – albeit in forms adapted to their radically different political environments – both by Mann in Victoria and by majority opinion among his erstwhile London Society associates. Permeation as it was originally understood by the London Fabians proceeded from the belief that, as the 1892 conference was reminded by Shaw: 'In 1885 there was not the slightest excuse for regarding the Tory party as any more hostile to Socialism than the Liberal Party'.[121] It has been defined by the Society's former secretary and longtime activist, Margaret Cole, as 'primarily honey-combing' or 'converting either to Socialism or to parts of the immediate Fabian programme, as set out in the continuous stream of Tracts and lectures, key persons, or groups of persons, who were in a position to take action themselves or influence others, not merely in getting a resolution passed, or (say) inducing a Town Council to accept one of the clauses of the Adoptive Acts, but in "following up", in making sure that the resolution or whatever it was did not remain on paper but was put into effect'. It was Shaw's claim – since disputed by some historians – that, thanks to permeation, 'We gained the solid advantage of a Progressive majority, full of ideas that would never have come into their heads if the Fabian had not put them there, on the first London County Council', while 'It is only necessary to compare the Nottingham program of the National Liberal Federation for 1887 with the Newcastle program for 1891, or to study the Liberal and Radical Union program for the 1892 London County Council election, to appreciate the extent to which the policy of permeating the party organisations with Socialism had succeeded'.[122]

Education was another case in point. In Britain, as earlier on in the Australian colonies, rivalry between denominational and non-denominational school interests was a massive obstacle to educational reform. The issue was discussed for the first time by the London Society in 1896, and a set of six general principles was adopted at the instigation of Sidney Webb in 1899. Education Acts introduced by Balfour's Conservative government in 1902 and 1903 were heavily influenced by Webb, to the point where they have been characterised by some as 'very nearly the dream of Fabian "permeators" come to life – proposals drafted by intelligent and hard-working Fabians conveyed to puzzled or sympathetic administrators, and carried into effect by a Conservative Government'. Webb, it is said, 'was so aware of the need for modernisation that he was prepared to compromise with the bishops on points that his nonconformist colleagues considered matters of principle, and he was equally prepared to risk his reputation in a long drawn out campaign to get these critics of the Bills to accept and work them'.[123] The episode marked the high water mark of the Society's permeation approach, but some Society members, including Wallas and Headlam, were as passionately opposed to the conservatives' measures as Webb was supportive of them, and Wallas resigned when the legislation was finally enacted. 'One wonders', Beatrice Webb confided to her diary in one of her many moments of self-doubt, 'whether all this manipulating activity is worthwhile'.[124] Even so, efforts to permeate the Liberals continued until focussing exclusively on the Labour Party was seen belatedly to be a more rewarding proposition.

Mann's model in establishing the SQC was clearly the relationship of the London Fabians with the newly born Labour Party. Earlier on, in the 1880s and 1890s, he had been contemptuous of permeation as a means of planting socialist policies, cuckoo-like, in the anti-socialist nests of unsuspecting conservatives and liberals. His energies were directed instead to bringing about the socialist working-class party which emerged finally as the Independent Labour Party. It seems certain that, had he been in the country to do so, he would have supported the association of the ILP with the trade union movement, the SDF and the Fabian Society in the Labour Representation Committee; the subsequent status of the ILP as an affiliate of the Labour Party; and the decision by the Fabians to pursue persuading the Labour Party to socialism through the permeation tactics whose application to the conservatives and liberals he had previously rejected. In Victoria, as has been seen, he argued the case for the PLC's becoming a socialist organisation from his vantage point as a paid PLC organiser. At the same time he ensured that additional pressure for the PLC to comply was applied from outside its ranks, through his involvement with the SDPV.

When both were ineffectual, he turned once more for inspiration to the British labour movement, where his greatest triumphs had been achieved and his reputation established. His Fabian-in-all-but-name SQC lacked the advantage of being a direct affiliate of the PLC, but most of its members also belonged to PLC branches, often as office-holders on branch executives. Even during the formative stages of the SQC - when Mann's PLC position had finally been resigned, in exasperation if not overt anger - emphasis continued to be given to the need for any new body to be friendly and helpful to other socialist and labour organisations. Two of the PLC Senate candidates for the 1906 elections - Tunnecliffe and E.J. Russell - were prominent VSP members whose deposits were provided for them by Jones.[125] The first issue of the *Socialist* carried an explicit declaration from the VSP: 'We are Labor men politically, but we shall at all times urge the necessity for all Labor men and women being straight-out socialists'.[126]

INTERNAL DISSENSION IN THE SQC

Before the London Fabians could proceed towards the 'broad sunny uplands' of Webb's compact with Henderson, an internal upheaval of formidable dimensions had to be surmounted: what has been described as 'The Episode of Mr Wells'. H.G. Wells' evanescent presence burst on the Fabian scene in 1903 at a point when, in the view of some, the London Society had become excessively staid, unadventurous and self-satisfied. As a protégé of such 'Old Gang' Society members as Sidney and Beatrice Webb – who are said to have recruited him in the course of an unannounced descent by bicycle on his Sandgate home[127] – and Wallas and Shaw, who were the proposers of his nomination, Wells originated a scheme for a reorganisation of local government along 'scientific' lines. This became the centrepiece of the Society's 'New Heptarchy' series of pamphlets, and was eventually (in 1920) incorporated by the Webbs in their *Constitution for the Socialist Commonwealth of Great Britain*. Wells had originally dazzled the Society at large with the virtuosity of his lecture – later a best-selling pamphlet – on *The Misery of Boots*. The substance of the address rather than its delivery made the impression. Wells was a poor public speaker, who described himself at a key juncture as 'speaking haltingly on the verge of the inaudible, addressing my tie through a cascade of moustache that was no help at all, making ill-judged departures into parenthesis, correcting myself as though I were a manuscript under treatment'.[128]

At the same time, however, he installed himself at the head of elements who were seeking – as they saw it – to bring about a reinvigoration of the Society, and in so doing placed himself at odds with his former patrons and friends in a bitter struggle for the control of the Society. The highly personalised character of the struggle did neither side credit. The task, in Wells' own perception, was 'to turn the little Fabian Society, wizened already though not old, into the beginnings of an order, akin to those Samurai in *A Modern Utopia*, which should embody for mankind a sense of the State'.[129] His paper, 'The Faults of the Fabian', delivered to a crowded meeting of Society members on 9 February 1906, resulted in the appointment of a special committee on how increases might be brought about in 'the scope, influence, income and activities of the Society'.[130] Far-reaching recommendations were brought forward by the committee in a report prior to the great meetings of Society members at Essex Hall on 7 and 14 December 1906. The Society was to be renamed the British Socialist Party. A fund was to be established to run Fabian candidates for parliament.

In the event, however, Wells overplayed his hand in the vehemence of his attacks against the Old Gang members whose removal from their positions of influence within the Society he had come to see as necessary for the Society's good. As Beatrice Webb recorded in her diary, 'His accusations were so preposterous, his innuendoes so unsavoury and his little fibs so transparent, that even his own followers refused to support him and the 80 per cent of undecided numbers swayed round to the old leaders'.[131] The writer Ford Maddox Ford, a Wells supporter, interpreted the occasion differently:

> It was all I could do, much as I deprecated Mr Wells' desertion of Litera-
> ture for Public Affairs, to prevent myself from shouting: 'Oh, H.G. There's
> the lecturer's bottle behind you. Smash them on the head with it. For
> Heaven's sake!' So much affection did H.G. inspire even in his enemies
> and so much did one dislike to see the Old Gang, as they were even then
> called – Mr Shaw and the Sidney Webbs, now Lord and Lady Something
> or Other – combine with grim coldness to get the better of that beloved
> general of young things and causes that were then also young.[132]

The Reform Committee's principal recommendations were rejected, and Wells ultimately resigned from the Society on 16 September 1908, on the grounds that he had lost any hope of it 'contributing effectively to the education of the movement'.[133] As he himself saw the situation, his intervention in the affairs of the Society had been 'confused, tedious, ill-conceived and ineffectual'.[134] It was Shaw's view that 'the Old Guard did not extinguish Mr Wells, he annihilated himself'.[135] Even so, the Old Gang had reason to congratulate itself on the fact that the Society had been turned away from what, as is clear in hindsight, would almost certainly have proved to be a blind alley, isolating it from the labour movement and exchanging the real achievements of the years immediately ahead of it for impotence and ineffectuality. Wells subsequently satirised the Webbs in two of his novels. The literary editor of the *New Statesman*, Desmond MacCarthy, recalled Beatrice saying cheerfully on the second occasion: 'I'm in this one too; I'm the woman whose voice is described as a strangulated contralto; but you're not in it, Sidney'. 'Oh, yes, I am', said Webb, speaking from a sofa on which his legs and feet looked absurdly small in comparison with his broad brow and head, 'Oh, yes, I am, I'm the man who is described as one of those supplementary males often found among the lower crustacea'.[136]

The VSP had in Walter Mizon a counterpart of sorts for Wells' unbridled tongue and disruptive influence. Mizon was an engineer by trade, a Marxist by conviction, and a former socialist candidate for municipal and Legislative Council office in South Australia. The sensational charges he levelled against Mann and such of his closest associates as O'Dowd, Champion and Hyett convulsed the VSP in 1907 and 1908, damaging the sense of socialist community which had been among the party's most notable assets and paving the way for the end of the Fabian phase in its affairs. The episode stemmed from bruised feelings on the part of Mizon, who believed that his contribution to the socialist cause over a nineteen-year period had been belittled by 'a clique in our party in connection with our paper the *Socialist*'. He associated the clique with Mann – who was plump – and described it as 'the fatman's friends'.[137]

Mann – according to a letter published over Mizon's signature in the *Labor Call*, and subsequently circulated as a handbill under the title *A Correction* – had incorrectly attributed to another VSP member, E.F. Russell, a status as 'the first Socialist candidate in Australia for municipal office', which properly belonged to Mizon. Champion, it was alleged, had tried to deprive Mizon of 'the credit or honour of being the first depositor' in the VSP's Socialist Savings Bank, together with recognition as a generous donor to the party's Premises Fund, the trading co-operative and a proposed party bakery. The complaint was made, Mizon argued, 'believing that he is the greatest coward who, knowing he is right, allows himself to be beaten', and on the principled basis that 'Ye shall know the Truth, and the Truth shall make you free!'.[138]

A second handbill – headed *The Supplementary Socialist*, and 'Issued by Walter Mizon' – featured the further claim that the pages of the *Socialist* had been filled 'with the rhapsodical ravings of the fat man's friends', to the point where 'whole-souled, genuine Socialists were directing their time and intellect writing genuine Socialistic articles, letters, verse, etc., for insertion in our paper, only to be REPRESSED TIME AND TIME AGAIN, ALMOST WITHOUT NUMBER'. In his own case, Mizon continued, there was 'AN ACCUMULATION OF NO LESS THAN NINE LETTERS, ARTICLES OR VERSES FROM ME NOT ONE OF WHICH HAS BEEN INSERTED'. An 'ode' – quoted, perhaps to counter-productive effect, as having been 'SUPPRESSED (as were eight other contributions of mine) by H.H. Champion and Bernard O'Dowd' – opened with the lines:

> Why should the money-bags sit at their ease
> While Smith, Brown and Jones are busy as bees,
> Working, and slaving, and gathering honey
> For OTHERS, whose souls are centred in money?

The 'ode' concluded:

And to workers, and strikers one and all, I would say,
STAND SHOULDER TO SHOULDER, AND YOU'LL SURE WIN THE DAY.
Present a brave front, don't waver or falter
Is the advice of a worker who signs himself

WALTER[139]

What had begun as a petty, slightly absurd storm in a teacup assumed a graver character when Mizon refused either to account for his outbursts before a VSP meeting or to discontinue them. The result was his expulsion from the party. The *Supplementary Socialist* then became a periodical, 'printed and published by Walter Mizon' as 'the Searchlight of the Vigilance Committee of the Victorian Socialist Party', and any restraint that might have been exercised in the earlier attacks on Mann and his friends was discarded. Mann – according to a 'Special Issue' of the new paper, priced at one penny, and purportedly with a print run of 10,000 – had left Hyndman's Social-Democratic Federation 'and joined the milk-and-water, wishy-washy, side-tracking organisation known as the Independent Labour Party, or I.L.P., becoming a paid officer of this body, which was a schismatic movement, detrimental to the growth of Revolutionary Socialism'. 'Our pseudo-Socialist "Leader" ', the paper continued, had, on this basis, 'ACCEPTED PAID OFFICES TO HELP DIVIDE THE MOVEMENT', only to have his appointment terminated 'owing to the determination of the leading members (chiefly the women), who were determined not to be identified with T.M., owing to his views on the Marriage Question'.[140]

The VSP in turn, it was argued, had been harmed by a situation where 'the Satellites or quasi-"leaders" "follow their Leader" and live in open adultery'. Those concerned, as the paper saw it, should 'form themselves into a "Free Love" Society, so that the husband who allows his wife to join, or the wife who agrees to her husband joining knows what to expect', but 'For common decency's sake, do not fasten yourselves on a decent Cause, that has no sympathy with such views, and thus bring the said Cause into disrepute'. The 'fornicating and dishonest, peculating members' were not numerous, it was concluded, and 'the clean, strong men of the Movement should not resign, but remain in, and purge out these few reactionaries, so that the name of the Socialist cause shall not stink in the nostrils of the general public'.[141]

This was not all. Champion, Mizon stated, was a 'hopelessly insolvent person', who 'if he had any sense of honour' would resign from his position as treasurer of the trading co-operative. Hyett was charged 'with falsifying the accounts of the Socialist Co-operative Society, with misappropriation of its funds, with issuing a false balance-sheet, with illegally passing the aforesaid balance-sheet'. Mann, it was said, was a 'PROFESSIONAL EXPERT AT LIVING OFF THE GAME' whose 'SERVICES HAVE BEEN TO THE HIGHEST BIDDER IRRESPECTIVE OF PRINCIPLE', and he, Hyett and Champion had presided over the VSP's affairs as a point where 'Trust funds were absorbed or misappropriated without the slightest compunction'. 'B.O'D and Co', finally, were 'rhapsodical dreamers', who 'in their zeal to swamp Australia with every race, creed or colour, NO MATTER WHAT THEIR STATE OR PROGRESS', entirely forgot that 'they have WHITE BROTHERS AND SISTERS HERE ACTUALLY STARVING'.[142]

While in no sense Wells' intellectual equal, Mizon at least matched Wells in his capacity for bringing about turmoil in the affairs of the organisation whose advancement he purported to champion, and, perhaps, he improved upon Wells' rancour and vituperation. Like Wells, he did not scruple to use personal recrimination against his fellow socialists to further his objectives, although, in this regard he had the advantage over Wells of being in a position to originate charges of sexual misconduct rather than having to dodge them. As in the case of Wells, his activities were the more effective for being motivated, in part, by profound personal insecurities. Unlike Wells, however, he was also used by others of like mind within the organisation, whose agendas were more sophisticated and specific than his own, and to whose manipulations as much as his own obduracy his expulsion was owed.[143] Unlike Wells, he had the consolation of seeing the largely Fabian elements whom he held responsible for his misfortunes having their own hopes disappointed in their turn.

For all their extravagant and unsavoury flavour, Mizon's strictures and sallies against Mann and his largely Fabian circle – like Wells' against the London Fabian Old Gang – stemmed from an openly acknowledged political standpoint and were geared to explicit objectives. Wells' plans for the London Society were paralleled by Mizon's conviction that it was his Marxist duty to return the VSP to the revolutionary socialist orthodoxy from which self-seeking opportunists such as Mann had been allowed to divert it. The VSP, he believed, should be guided by the 'One Big Union' philosophy of the Industrial Workers of the World, recognising that when 'Marx urged the "workers of the world to unite" he did not mean the workers of one country or the workers in one trade or the workers in any of the numerous sections of any trade, but he meant just what he said, workers of the world'. The implications, as it seemed to him, were plain:

> The adoption of I.W.W.ism would be so beneficial to the employee that a strike would not last 24 hours. Exit all the pain and anguish of hungry children wanting food, when by I.W.W. the workers have only to ask for anything and it would be forthcoming. Should the 'Old Adam' refuse them, all you would have to do is simply fold your arms, one and all, and heigh, presto, the thing desired is accomplished.[144]

Mizon's advocacy of the IWW approach was in no way unique or even unusual among Melbourne socialists. An IWW Club was formed in January 1908, in part by O'Dowd's firebrand son Montaigne – better known as Monty – and joined by other VSP members. The Interstate Socialist Conference which met in Melbourne in 1907 unanimously adopted the IWW Preamble, and resolved that 'the time has arrived for the re-organisation of the Australian working class on the lines of the "Industrial Workers of the World" '.[145] In the event, however, this frail consensus was short-lived. 'The moderates', in the view of some, 'were not necessarily interested in I.W.W. aims and Party members of the I.W.W. were disinclined to see its activities absorbed by the moderate-dominated Party'. The IWW thus figured briefly as a rallying point for those within the VSP who rejected the permeation tactics of Mann and his fellow Fabians in favour of a radical separation of the party from the PLC. Mizon, for his part, returned to the obscurity from which he had come. His credibility was gravely compromised when court proceedings for misappropriation which he and W.H. Emmett – a VSP executive member, press committee member and trustee, and a director of the Socialist Savings Bank – initiated against Hyett resulted in Hyett's exoneration, with damages which ultimately amounted to £420, and again when Mizon was obliged to defend proceedings against himself for having assaulted his wife.[146] The episode demonstrates, *inter alia*, that Fabian groups are not immune from fratricide, for all their conviviality and eschewal of dogmatism. Their very lack of extremism tends to exasperate those more restless socialists who from time to time enter their orbit.[147]

HIGH TIDE AND AFTER

Earlier on, as has been seen, a deep-seated separatist or 'go-it-alone' sentiment on the part of some Victorian socialists had been evidenced by episodes such as the hostility of the VLF to its members standing for parliament; the unwillingness of majority opinion within the VSL to settle for anything less that the 'straight out Socialist party' for which Mann's imprimatur was asked and given in 1902; and the rapid development of the SDPV as a freestanding political force, independent of the PLC and potentially its electoral rival. While separatism seems to have remained largely dormant in the six-month period between the inaugural meeting of the SQC on 1 September 1905 and the first half-yearly meeting of its members in the following February, intimations of its revival were apparent in the aftermath of the SQC's change of name to the Socialist Party.

The Political Labour Council's alleged failure to provide sufficiently zealous backing for the Prahran Free Speech Fight drew criticism from within the VSP, as did the failure of the Federal Labor Congress in March 1907 to alter along socialist lines an objective which was attributed by Mann to a 'smug Parliamentary respectability that helps to kill the movement' and condemned by the *Socialist* as 'so vague as to be acceptable to capitalists'; and the rejection by the PLC Annual Conference in April 1907 of the motion that 'The State and Federal Platform be altered to provide for the socialisation of the means of production, distribution and exchange'.[148] The motion was criticised by PLC members as an attempted takeover of their organisation by Mann and the VSP, and the organisation's secretary, Heagney, stated publicly that what the electors wanted was not vague socialist objectives, but the creation of small property holders and the encouragement of individualism, both of which were PLC policy.[149]

Further minor irritants included the refusal of the PLC leader, Prendergast, to move a resolution for a shorter working day from the VSP platform at the 1907 Eight Hour Day celebrations, or to support the repeal of bans on the sale of literature on Sundays; and PLC endorsement of a wages board system which, in the eyes of the VSP, 'only deepened the workers' plight'. The deterioration of relations between the groups was exemplified by an exchange of recriminations over the 1907 May Day celebrations, where the PLC claimed that VSP speakers 'looked as if they were playing some drama intended to portray the conditions and troubles of some by-gone society of which they had not very extensive knowledge', and Bennett volleyed back for the VSP that the PLC was 'virtually indistinguishable from the Liberals or even the Conservatives'.[150] An article in the *Socialist* warned capitalists to make friends with the PLC, on the grounds that 'there won't be a million-in-one chance to make friends with us'.[151] The upshot was that when the 1907 conference convened, 'relations between the Political Labour Council and the Victorian Socialist Party were strained by mutual suspicion, and conflict about basic principles'.[152]

Strained relations with the conservative New South Wales Labor Party were a fact of life which socialists in that state had long since come to take for granted, and now expressed forcibly in their agendas for both the 1907 and 1908 conferences. After establishing the Socialist Federation of Australasia, the 1907 conference resolved on the motion of the Sydney International Socialists – and in the face of opposition from VSP delegates such as the redoubtable R.S. Ross – that 'no member of the Socialist Federation of Australasia shall seek election as a candidate of either the Australian Labor Party or any other non-socialist party, for either Parliamentary or municipal positions'. The 1908 conference resolved that SFA affiliates should not 'retain membership in the Labor Party or any other non-socialist political party' or support Labor candidates, but rather should field candidates of their own, who, once elected, would 'devote their time and talents to harassing the Parliamentary machine and institutions of the ruling class in the spirit of Revolutionary Socialism'.[153] The VSP endorsed contesting parliamentary elections in competition with the PLC at a referendum instigated by Mann in 1908 and, at the 1908 state elections, Angus McDonnell gained eighty-five votes as a VSP candidate for Collingwood, while Percy Laidler won eighty-two votes as its candidate for Melbourne – an episode which Champion may have recognised wryly as replicating the SDF's fielding of candidates for two London seats for similarly small returns at the 1885 elections. The only difference was the absence of Maltman Barry.

The impact on the VSP's fortunes of the whole unhappy sequence of events - from the SQC's change of name to the state election humiliation – was disastrous. Having first been needlessly alienated, the PLC was now disabused of any fears that the VSP had potential electoral support, as a number of conciliatory overtures suggest were entertained, and henceforth had no reason to treat its self-appointed rival as other than a paper tiger.[154] The majority within the party who previously had also belonged to the PLC were forced to take sides, with the result that, as the party's principal historian has observed, 'Many abjured V.S.P. membership to remain with the P.L.C., while others stayed with the V.S.P. either because they regarded the P.L.C. as worthless or because their commitment to the V.S.P., *per se*, overrode qualms about the consequences'.[155] Irrespective of which choice was made, the overall effect was to destroy the tie of overlapping memberships which hitherto had been among the VSP's greatest strengths, and to deprive it of a number of the prominent labour movement figures on whose presence its credibility so largely depended. In the event, the VSP succeeded in fulfilling neither its potential as an agency for social research and political education in the Fabian mould, nor the dream of an electorally viable socialist alternative to the Labor Party. The camaraderie, solidarity and sense of shared participation in a perceived community of socialists, to which the unique character of the VSP was so largely owed, fell victim to a bitter internecine warfare, which saw former friends and associates who previously had been united in their common opposition to the class enemy preoccupied instead with mutual recrimination. The future of the Fabian approach and the influence of 'academics' and 'intellectuals' within the Labor Party were prejudiced irrevocably for decades to come. Wells, by comparison, had nowhere near so damaging an impact in London.

The fracas provided glimpses of a moderate, predominantly Fabian camp forming within the party around Mann and his associates, while members of a separatist, more radical and in some instances consciously Marxist turn of mind identified themselves less with the erratic Mizon than with those like Emmett, who, from time to time, found it expedient to take up Mizon's accusations for reasons of their own. Champion found himself the subject of claims by Emmett and a visiting Broken Hill International Socialist Group member, H.J. Hawkins, that he had mishandled his editorship of the *Socialist*, and an Investigating Committee had to exonerate Will Thom of charges laid against him by Swableses.[156] Such was the preoccupation with the accusations and counter accusations – Hyett's life, for example, being 'totally disrupted for many months' by the court proceedings in which he was involved with Mizon and Emmett[157] – that the day-to-day administration of the VSP and its financial well-being were neglected. By January 1908, expenses exceeded income by £5 per week, and debts totalling £72 had been accumulated, which were not paid off by the party for another three years.[158]

The withdrawal of the last of the separatists and other dissidents – Monty O'Dowd prominent among them – in October 1908 effectively marked the end of the era of great turbulence in the VSP's affairs.[159] Inevitably, and ironically, it also resulted in the party's being alienated as deeply from the SFA as from the PLC. Most of all, it came too late. Although the VSP was able to recover something of its former cohesion, and subsequently involved itself in a number of fruitful campaigns, its distinctively Fabian characteristics were not recovered, and it never again touched the heights to which it had been able to rise briefly in the heady months of late 1905, 1906 and 1907, when Australia's first Fabians enjoyed what was truly their Golden Age.

MANN'S ROLE

Mann's role in the debacle requires a final comment. Clearly the outcome was not as he wished, and caused him considerable disappointment. The question therefore arises: why at two crucial junctures – when the issue of the name of the SQC was raised for the first time, and when it first became apparent that the Interstate Socialist Conferences and the Australasian Socialist Federation would be dominated by strongly separatist forces from New South Wales – did he act (or did he fail to act) in ways which were incompatible with his declared objective of permeating the PLC with his socialist approach and philosophy? As has been seen, within six months of the SQC being established, it was fulfilling all that he and fellow Fabians like Jones and O'Dowd could have hoped from it. It follows that Mann's failing to oppose a change of name which, in its turn, could hardly fail to be taken as an affront by the PLC – or, as is possible, actually conniving with or acquiescing in the change – may well have been the expression less of some anticipation of specific and positive gain than of the fact that he was a man of less strong character than has sometimes been supposed, and a victim once again of the infirmity of purpose which marked earlier stages of his life, and which was a subject of comment among associates in Britain when he left to go to Australia. The episode also exemplified an element of hubris which evokes, in some respects, the well known occasion when, on the eve of Beatrice and Sidney Webb's departure for Australia, she noted in her diary that 'We now feel assured that with the School as a teacher body, the Fabian Society as a propagandist organisation, the L.C.C. Progressives as an object lesson in electoral success, our books as the only elaborate and original work in economic fact and theory, no young man or woman who is anxious to study or work in public affairs can fail to come under our influence'.[160] Rereading the entry years later, Beatrice Webb commented 'An hubristic passage',[161] as Mann might well have done of the SQC's rechristening.

The same absence of any explanation in pragmatic terms also characterises Mann's agreement to the VSP's participating in the proceedings of an Interstate Socialist Conference – where he knew that, by the nature of the rules, the decisions would be taken by groups antipathetic to his permeation objectives – and his failure, once the inevitably disastrous outcomes emerged, to declare that the VSP would have no part in them. Since it cannot be argued that Mann lacked the influence over the Victorian socialists which would have enabled him to have his way over both matters, it is at least probable that the demise of the SQC, like that of the Melbourne Fabian Society before it, owed something to the human frailties of its mentor.

CHAPTER 5

Frederick Sinclaire and the Fabian Society of Victoria

The point at which the VSP could no longer be regarded as an organisation in the Fabian mould, even by the Fabians among its members, had clearly been reached by August 1908, when Jones, O'Dowd and Champion associated themselves with another London Society expatriate, the Reverend Frederick Sinclaire, in establishing the Fabian Society of Victoria. The FSV in no sense marked a return to the halcyon Fabian days of the SQC and the VSP, between 1905 and 1907. The investigation into the living wage which its members launched at their inaugural meeting seems to have petered out early on, with no record of such data as may have been gathered on the forms generously donated for the project by Champion. The London-style series of autumn lectures on the principles of socialism which it envisaged holding in 1909 seems to have been abandoned. Its meetings took place in the homes of members, who heard papers and readings from one another or listened to the occasional guest speaker – a regression, in effect, to the infancy of English Fabianism, before the London Society outgrew Pease's rooms in Osnaburgh Street.

The Fabians' sense of loss over the changed character of the VSP was acute. Even so, many remained in the party, and they encouraged others to join it. As the *Socialist* was careful to point out, 'Needless to say, there will be no clashing of functions between the Fabians and any other Socialist bodies'.[1] The mood of the group can be characterised, perhaps, as autumnal, and its role as an epilogue to the brief golden time which preceded it. Its disappearance around the middle of 1909 marked the departure of organised Fabian activity from the Victorian political scene, virtually for a forty-year period. Only the capacities and subsequent careers of some of those involved – and those like Shann, Latham and Vance Palmer, whose lives briefly brushed its orbit – evoke once again the familiar, haunting

questions about what might have been the result if events had
followed a different course, rather more akin to that of the Society
in Britain.

KEY FIGURES IN THE FSV

Frederick Sinclaire

Sinclaire was born on 10 July 1881 in New Zealand's Papakura Valley,
where his Irish-born parents had their farm. Scholarships enabled
him to attend Auckland Grammar School and then Auckland
University, where he was awarded a Bachelor of Arts in 1902 and
a Master of Arts the following year. His inability to accept the thirty-
nine articles of the Church of England led him to abandon the
Anglican faith in which he was raised – along with an ambition,
early on, to join the Anglican ministry – and to embrace Uni-
tarianism. Further study at Manchester College, Oxford, under the
auspices of the British and Foreign Unitarian Association, gained
him the Williams Theological Scholarship in 1907, and he graduated
in divinity in 1908 as a prize-winning essayist with First Class
Honours for his college examinations. He joined the Fabians in
Oxford, and his admiration for Shaw and advocacy of Shavian
thought was a subject of comment by his fellow students in their
magazine *Poz*, as was his reputation for having 'an eye for the ladies'.[2]
Like Shaw before him, he was influenced deeply by the Reverend
Philip Wicksteed, to whom he attributed, *inter alia*, a lifelong
enthusiasm for Dante.[3] The upshot was that Melbourne's Unitarian
congregation acquired an idealistic, intellectually adventurous young
minister 'with a liberal leaning in religion and a left-of-liberal
leaning in politics'.[4]

People, as Sinclaire saw them, were religious beings in the same
sense that they were artistic or social beings, so that 'to reject or ignore
religion meant denying part of ourselves and was on the same
footings as rejecting or damaging the rational part'.[5] The duty of
humankind, in Sinclaire's eyes, was to substitute Christ's universal
law of love for the Mosaic Laws of the 'lesser God' or 'artificer of
God' to whom he attributed the world's creation. This required
'agitators, reformers, poets and martyrs for humanity's sake' (Shaw
was a clear example of the type), to whose ranks, by implication,
he himself aspired.[6] It was, in his view, 'part of his personal mission

and religious purpose to combat boredom, lack of purpose and deadening routine, particularly in a society in which the religious spirit was often censorious, prurient, conservative and narrowly religious'. In repeated clashes with the wowser element among his fellow clergymen, he championed the view that criminal and immoral acts were often attributable to social injustices, which, in their turn, 'were not merely unfortunate aberrations, but were based on self-perpetuating inadequacies in the social system'.[7] It may well be that his model here – at least in part – was the Anti-Puritan League which had been formed in the early years of the new century by such London Fabians as Headlam and Bland. Churchmen, he argued, had to recognise 'that changes in the structure and moral assumptions of their society were essential if the immoral and brutalised were to be changed into upright citizens'.[8] It was time, as he saw it, that 'We heard the last of this Pecksniffian cant about honest poverty, and began to face the plain fact that poverty is the mother of every kind of sin'.[9]

Sinclaire's Melbourne appointment did not in any way inhibit him from continuing the outspoken socialist advocacy of his student days. Mann's delivery of one of his 'socialist sermons' – on the theme of 'A Challenge to the Ungodly Religious' – enabled Sinclaire to demand the opportunity for a rebuttal, which was given from the stage of the Bijou Theatre in April 1908, under the title 'Socialism and the Churches'. His entry into the meeting was greeted by 'a round of hearty cheers', from a capacity audience which included members of his Eastern Hill congregation, along with others who had come to heckle what they anticipated would be an apologia for orthodox Christianity. His speech turned out, however, to be notable for his explicit identification of himself as a socialist, his scathing denunciation of the *Argus* as 'the Bible of the Rich', and his persuasive vision of religion and socialism combining forces in a socially progressive common cause.

The churches, Sinclaire argued, were in the process of abandoning 'superstitions' such as the literal truth of the Bible. In their place, as he saw it, there was a new awareness of the importance of having detailed information about the living conditions of ordinary people, so that 'a knowledge of correct economics and the inspiration of the church . . . might combine to the general good of mankind'. At the same time, he held, there was a need for the churches to receive more charitable treatment than they had been given in Mann's sermon, in order to avoid 'a widening of the breach between the churches and the people'. The audience is reported to have responded with delight to this evidence of 'a community of thought and desire for the general welfare'. One likely result, the *Socialist* foresaw, was 'a quickening in the Valley of Dry Bones where the Unitarian Church has been residing'. Within a few weeks, the VSP had welcomed Sinclaire as its first clergyman member.[10]

The extent to which the strife-torn VSP had strayed from its Fabian origins was already plain to Sinclaire. Prior to his Bijou Theatre appearance, he had suggested the establishment of a Fabian Society to O'Dowd, who agreed that it was 'badly needed'.[11] O'Dowd proceeded to canvass his friends – including the young Nettie Higgins – for the names of likely recruits, and on 5 June 1908 the *Socialist* carried the news that 'the names of several Oxford and Cambridge Fabians are mentioned as desiring to continue their old work here'.[12] Cambridge was represented by Elizabeth Lothian, a sister of O'Dowd's publisher Thomas Lothian, who had joined the Society while Sinclaire was a member at Oxford. She was almost certainly the first Australian woman to be admitted to Cambridge or belong to its Fabian Society, and her University of Melbourne MA and Cambridge Tripos (in classics) placed her among the most accomplished women scholars of her generation. Lothian's Fabian contemporaries at Cambridge included Amber Reeves, whose child by Wells was born after her marriage to Rivers Blanco White, to the great scandal of some older members of the Society; Ben Keeling, whose brilliant political promise was cut short by his death in the First World War; the poet Rupert Brook, another war victim; and Hugh Dalton, who preceded Stafford Cripps and Hugh Gaitskell as Chancellor of the Exchequer in the Attlee government.[13] By late July, O'Dowd was able to report to Nettie Higgins that – 'thanks I fancy in good measure to you' – the prospects for the project were 'distinctly good',[14] and on 14 August a circular letter over the signatures of Jones, Champion and Sinclaire announced a meeting on 22 August, when 'men and women who believe that land and industrial capital should be emancipated from private ownership and vested in the community for the general benefit' would establish 'a Society of Socialists' which, 'while abstaining from direct political action, would undertake work similar to that which is being done in England by the Fabian Society'.[15]

The *Socialist* duly reported on 11 September that 'The contemplated Fabian Society, composed of Socialists, accepting the principles of Socialisation of the means of production, distribution and exchange, but taking no part as a society in party politics, was ushered into being towards the end of August at Mr H.H. Champion's rooms in Bank Place, and its members are already actively at work collecting facts as to housing, wages. living expenses, sanitation, rent, and unemployment by house to house visits in various parts of Melbourne and suburbs'. The report continued, 'Friends, with time on their hands, during which they might be able to conduct inquiries into the actual social conditions of the people in town and country, would be especially welcome as members of the Society, and of its working sub-committees'.

A Mr Funston apologised for his inability to be present at the meeting, as did the rising young barrister, Latham. Agreement was reached that a subcommittee should be established to undertake what was summarised as 'an investigation of the living wage', and that a series of public lectures on the principles of socialism should be conducted in the autumn of 1909.[16] Champion was made the Society's chairman, and Sinclaire its secretary. Jones became an executive member, as did Elizabeth Lothian, Dr Thompson, and Champion's sister-in-law, Vida Goldstein.

VIDA GOLDSTEIN

Vida Goldstein was born on 13 April 1869 the first of the four children of a Warrnambool storekeeper and his wife, Jacob and Isabella Goldstein, who later established notable reputations in Victoria's welfare and reformist circles.[17] Her sparkling intelligence enabled her to gain a solid education from the family governess, the artistically and literarily talented Julia Sutherland, and her matriculation, with honours in French and English, was gained in 1886 at Melbourne's Presbyterian Ladies' College, where she was a predecessor of Elizabeth Lothian and Nettie Higgins.[18] As a young woman she shone at sports such as tennis, horse-riding and clay pigeon shooting, and enjoyed a hectic social whirl of parties and dances. She and her sisters, Elsie and Lina, became proprietors of a small co-educational school which operated at their Alma Road home from 1892 until Elsie's marriage to Champion in 1898.[19] At this time the Goldsteins were being introduced to the suffrage and social causes which were to dominate Vida's career, in part through the influence of Strong and Champion.

The family were strong supporters of the social gospel which Strong preached from his Scots Church pulpit, and followed him into his Australian Church.[20] Isabella and Vida were members of Champion's Anti-Sweating League and Strong's Criminology Society, and supporters of Strong's slum clearance campaigns and the 1897 'Willing Shilling' Queen's Jubilee Appeal to fund building extensions for the Queen Victoria Hospital. Inspections undertaken by Vida as a National Anti-Sweating League member enabled her to see for herself the extent of poverty in homes such as one where, she later recalled, a child suffering from pneumonia had 'just enough strength in it to sit up and hold a pair of scissors finishing off the corners of buttonholes sewn by her mother'. She and Isabella also joined the Prahran Women's Franchise League, and were introduced to a sister member, Annette Bear-Crawford, who became Vida's political mentor and close personal friend. Vida was associated with Bear-Crawford and Champion in the establishment of the United Council for Women's Suffrage in 1894, and developed outstanding skills as an organiser and public speaker under Bear-Crawford's tutelage.[21] On the occasion of her first political speech, 'feeling decidedly nervous, she stipulated that she should not have to answer questions afterwards. But on finishing her speech she found herself jumping up and eagerly answering whatever questions were asked'.[22] An incident at a meeting in the Fitzroy Town Hall in 1903 exemplifies her eventual mastery of platform skills:

> At the end of her speech, she asked for questions and was handed an obscene note. Miss Goldstein told her audience of the insult she had received and her supporters angrily rose to her defence, threatening to attack the man. But Vida lightly remarked that, as he had been sensitive enough to put his indecent suggestion in writing, his delicacy should be rewarded by sparing him a thrashing. The mood of the crowd cooled instantly and Vida managed to avoid an ugly incident and at the same time gain a few more supporters.[23]

When Bear-Crawford died from pneumonia while attending the Women's International Conference in England in 1899, the leadership of the Council gravitated naturally to Vida. Two years later she began drawing a salary of thirty shillings a week as the suffrage movement's first full-time organiser. The office from which the Council serviced its thirty-two affiliate organisations was moved to the Goldsteins' city apartment, where it operated alongside Champion's literary journal, the *Book Lover*, and Vida's penny-a-month feminist monthly, the *Australian Women's Sphere*. As Australia's delegate to the International Womanhood Suffrage Conference in Washington in 1902, Vida was elected conference secretary, testified before a committee of the US Congress and talked with President Theodore Roosevelt, who, she reported, 'seemed to be in favour of women's suffrage'.[24] She was also able to represent Australia at the 1902 International Council of Women Conference.

In her absence, the new Commonwealth parliament gave women the right to vote and stand at federal elections. Vida was an independent woman candidate on five occasions – for the Senate in 1903, 1910 and 1917, and for the House of Representatives in 1913 and 1914. Her election meetings attracted capacity crowds and, at her first attempt, 51,497 votes were recorded in her favour.[25] Between campaigns, she sought to educate women voters through the Women's Political Association, the Women's Parliament which the Association conducted in 1904–5, her magazine and her speaking tours of regional and country centres. She also agitated vigorously for suffrage in Victoria, which was finally granted in 1908. Her election manifestos and speeches consistently criticised capitalism and advocated such socialist measures as production for use rather than profit, redistribution of wealth, bringing public utilities under public control, appointment of women to official positions on an equal footing with men, equal pay, equal rights and the resolution of industrial disputes by conciliation and arbitration. 'Socialism', she declared, 'with all its faults and dangers, came nearest to my ideal of brotherhood'.[26] However, she also consistently refused to become a member of the Labor Party, and described herself publicly as 'a democrat with a vision of society which would enable the complete equality of women with men and decent standards for all' rather than as the socialist which her statements and her FSV membership reveal her to have been.[27] As she summarised her position, 'I am anti-party because in my experience parties place their own interests above all else'.[28] It is interesting to speculate to what extent this sentiment reflected the tensions in and around the VSP. There is a sense, too, in which these reservations echo the vestigial shyness of some London Fabians, who believed that permeating political parties was fine but declined to join or fully back them, at least until around 1912. Her attitude was not necessarily shared by all her associates, and some Labor women resigned from the WPA fearing that their president's Senate candidacy might damage the Labor cause.

NETTIE AND VANCE PALMER

Executive meetings of the FSV, held at Whitehall on 14 September and in Jones' rooms in Royal Arcade on 5 October, received reports on the progress of the living wage inquiries;[29] accepted Champion's offer of 500 forms for the collection of information on housing and living conditions;[30] resolved to enlist extra workers in order 'to continue the investigations until 500 or 1,000 cases were collected'; and invited Bishop Mercer to deliver an address at its November meeting.[31] At that point the Society's Minute Book breaks off,[32] and any remaining information about its activities is limited to passing references in letters written by its members. Nettie Higgins extended an invitation to her future husband Vance Palmer, in London in February 1909, to join her in spirit at a Society meeting in Sinclaire's church, where O'Dowd was to speak on Whitman. In April she wrote to him about a meeting where a paper on man's relation to the state by Elizabeth Lothian had spoken – in terms which epitomised the Fabian approach – 'of enlightenment gradually by education – especially, perhaps, the social education of the so-called educated classes'. The May meeting – for which Palmer's 'wraith' was summoned from London to the Lothian family home 'just beside the Exhibition Gardens, on the side nearest the Public Library' – heard and discussed readings from Wells, 'Mr Sinclaire leading mostly', following the last-minute illness of the scheduled speaker, the VSP's R.S. Ross. Ross's address had to be postponed a second time in June, when he was absent attending a conference in Broken Hill. Following its delivery shortly afterwards, no further FSV meetings seem to have taken place. 'I did like that man, better almost than anyone I've met in a year', Nettie wrote to Palmer:

> His social perspective is out in some little things, but mine's out in big ones. He has a really good imagination – *not*, not when he is making a speech, with metaphors and Yarra-bankisms crowding thick – but when he faces life as a whole and tells you what he sees and hopes in sober words. It's a logical imagination, very steady and sustained. I liked his whole atmosphere, and the young, longing look that passed over his face now and then.[33]

The author of this poised appraisal was the twenty-three-year-old Nettie Higgins – daughter of a draper turned accountant, John Higgins, and niece of Champion's erstwhile fellow Wallaby Club member, Henry Bournes Higgins. She was born at Bendigo, on

18 August 1885, and educated at Miss Rudd's Malvern Seminary, PLC, and Melbourne University, where she graduated with a BA in 1909 and an MA three years later.[34] Her early writing featured in the PLC magazine *Patchwork* and the Melbourne literary journals *Trident* and *Heart of the Rose*. In 1907 she met Vance Palmer, who was her own age and had just returned to Australia via Siberia and Japan, after a two-year stay in Britain where he had mixed extensively with the members of the London Fabian Society and involved himself in their work. Palmer was already on his way to becoming an established writer. A moving and delightful correspondence followed after Palmer's return to his home state, Queensland, and during another stay in Britain, until their marriage in 1914 began what has been called 'the most famous partnership in Australian literary history'.[35] When the FSV was established, Nettie had already become interested in socialism, perhaps with the help of O'Dowd, with whom she was in regular correspondence about literary, intellectual and political issues. As has been seen, it was to her that O'Dowd turned in his search for potential FSV members, and she became a regular attender of the Society's meetings. Palmer, for his part, was moving away from what had initially been a firm Fabian allegiance, to a position more closely approximating the VSP mainstream, and the letters which the couple exchanged shed useful light on the differences between the two camps.

The Fabians, Nettie wrote to Palmer in late 1908 or early the following year, had confused her by their references to the 'wilful ignorance and blindness' and 'imperturbable Phariseeism' of the VSP. A query to O'Dowd about his views on the class war had prompted 'a couple of hurricane paragraphs against hate as a motive force'; and Elizabeth Lothian had confessed to 'some separatist thoughts she had been having lately'. 'I can't bear to think of many little sects', Nettie added, 'when so much corporate thinking and work is needed'. Returning to the theme a month or so later, she quoted O'Dowd as saying that people who proclaimed the class war were simply acting as barbarously as the class they attacked, and that the 'revolutionists who preach class-war have the facts on their side, but the way out isn't by way of these facts'. He had gone on to say, she reported, that the chief reason for the rabid, rule-of-thumb program of the street orators was the aloofness of the educated class from the labour class, so that 'We ought to be the interpreters to them of the beneficent things in the universe; they've been so bitterly used that gentleness has no place in their minds, they've never seen sane, courteous methods in operation'. Even so, she concluded, 'He smiled and said he'd like everyone present to join the Socialist Party'. Writing after Ross's lecture, she described how he had been asked by Elizabeth Lothian why Socialists should be the only people on earth who refused to provide such valuable reforms as the old age pension, and had insisted that the Socialists should do nothing but demand Socialism. 'He seems to see no good in municipal government measures, or in the Labor Party in Parliament, at all', she said.[36]

'I have saturated myself a good deal in the Fabian atmosphere', Palmer wrote back, 'but I used to find myself wondering how much some of its members felt the things they said or merely thought them'. 'I feel more at home in the atmosphere of the Victorian Socialist Party than in the atmosphere of the Fabians', he added subsequently, and continued:

> I don't think I ever consciously dressed a part when going to one of their meetings, but if a red tie makes me more accessible to any man – well red ties are cheap. They are Pharisaical! Ignorant! Perhaps, in some ways, narrow. Yes, and yet in their meetings with all the bandying of catch-words and the singing of the Red Flag I had a sense that their emotion was real and it helped me to believe in mine. Incompatibility of ideas! The Melbourne Socialists are largely working men, with the limitations that implies in our society, but I don't think they are quite as noticeable as the limitations of Culture, as life hasn't taught anyone much if he hasn't learned to talk easily with men whose training has been different from his own.

The class war, he believed, was a fact, but class hatred was an emotion which might or might not go with it:

> The propagandists who preach to working class men find it essential to insist that the immediate interests of the capitalist and the workingman are diametrically opposed, that, taking the sum of the wealth they create, if one gets more the other must get less, and that this must continue till the capitalist system is abolished. The Fabians, who work with the more or less educated classes, recognise this, but they find it expedient to appeal to the higher social instincts. Both are intent on making Socialists and their difference is really only one of impression or using a special argument to suit a special audience. I would think preaching the class war barbarous if it really meant class hatred or the ultimate triumph of one class over another, but as the end of it is merely the abolition of the class war I can't for the life of me see anything more barbarous about it than insisting on the horror of child labour and other things incidental to the competitive system.

His last word on the matter was to deplore the 'exclusive spirit' which he had come to associate with the Fabians: 'It seems so much like trying to break down the caste of birth and money in order to set up the caste of Culture. I feel sure you would feel the same as I do if you knew the body of Victorian Socialists more intimately'.[37]

O'Dowd's condemnation of class hatred and Palmer's celebration of working-class socialists were each in its own way a product of a radically altered social environment. The Champion and Mann factors apart, the emergence of class politics in Australia now meant that it was much more difficult to bring together middle-class radicals and labour activists within a single organisation, as had been achieved with such triumphant success by Marson's South Australian Fabian Society in the early 1890s, or even by Mann, a decade and more later, through the SQC and the VSP. At the same time, the socialist cause was increasingly being denied such middle-class support as its merits might otherwise have attracted, on the grounds of its working-class associations. The upshot for the FSV was calamitous. It was unable either to restore the original Fabian character of the VSP in a way which might have enabled its relationship with the labour movement to be repaired, or clinch lasting support of its own among a number of prominent Victorians who are now best remembered as New Liberals in the Deakin mould or conservatives, but who were Fabians in the years immediately following the turn of the century.

THE LATHAM CIRCLE

The rewards of Champion's incessant and untiring networking among the New Liberals were apparent in the Fabian convictions of the young Jack Latham and the group of his personal friends and former fellow students of the University of Melbourne who comprised the Latham Circle. The Latham Circle represented the intellectual cream of Victorian society. Latham apart, its Fabian core included Frederic Eggleston, who was also a rising young barrister; Walter Murdoch, who was a university lecturer and journalist; and the budding historian and economist, Edward Shann. La Nauze notes that all of them 'in one way or another would find some place in the history of their generation'.

Latham, Eggleston, Murdoch and Shann were all members of the Boobooks dining club – a private group who dined together monthly before the reading and discussion of papers on diverse themes from literature to politics, and 'whose name reflected their nocturnal habits and the wisdom of their discussions, in the mock-serious ritual that helps to preserve the continuity of such private societies over the years'. The club was founded by Eggleston in 1902, perhaps initially as an alternative for younger men to the Wallaby Club, which in some respects it closely resembled.[38] Other Fabian Boobooks of the day included Scott, O'Dowd and Shann's older brother Frank, who was the headmaster-to-be of Trinity Grammar School. O'Dowd and Scott addressed their fellow Boobooks on several occasions, as did another member of the Fabian Society of Victoria, Sinclaire.[39] Further links between the Latham Circle and Fabians of the stamp of Scott and Champion stemmed from their mutual dedication to the strengthening of imperial ties and the organic unification of the British Empire. Latham was the secretary of the Melbourne Branch of the Imperial Federation League for much of Deakin's lengthy term as its president, and Scott, Shann and Eggleston were among its members. The recruits gained for the Round Table by Leo Curtis in the course of his lightning descent on Melbourne in 1912 included Latham, Scott, Eggleston and Murdoch, and Shann joined later, in Western Australia.[40]

Despite the tensions caused by a penchant for privacy on the part of the Round Table (which led some to see it as a clandestine organisation), its members were able to use each other to sharpen their thinking about how Australian interests might best be furthered within the imperial framework. Australian contributors played a notable part in making the group's journal, the *Round Table*, a significant source of information and opinion for an influential readership. Even so, the failure of the Round Table to achieve the objectives for which it was established had long since become plain by the time the Melbourne group finally wound up its affairs in 1984. Leonie Foster sees it as constituting 'a microcosmic reflection of the inability of Britain and other Commonwealth members, again including Australia, to devise a system of co-operation satisfactory to them all'.[41] It may well be that the Fabian socialism which Latham and such Imperial Federation League associates as Shann and Eggleston came to espouse – despite the preponderant conservatism of the IFL membership – was owed in part to the influence Champion and Scott were able to exercise in the course of contacts arising from their mutual interest in imperial issues. The connection between the Fabians and the Round Table in Victoria was maintained to the end, with Round Table membership lists shortly prior to the winding up of the group including the names of such prominent local Fabians as Frank Crean and Jim Cairns.

J.G. LATHAM

Latham was the son of a tinsmith, born at Ascot Vale on 26 August 1877; raised in a devoutly Methodist household; and educated at George Street State School in Fitzroy, Scotch College and Melbourne University. In the lean early years of his career as a barrister, when briefs were few and far between, his income was supplemented by writing for the *Argus* and lecturing in logic, contracts and personal property at the university – where he had supported himself as a student by tutoring in logic and philosophy. In 1907 he was a member of the Education Act Defence League, which was formed in opposition to the teaching of scripture in government schools; in 1909, he and Scott were co-founders of the Rationalist Society, whose more prominent members included O'Dowd and Champion; and in 1910 he was the organiser of an Australian tour for the British freethinker Joseph McCabe, whose meeting in the Melbourne Town Hall was chaired by Champion.[42] A reference to Latham in a masque presented at the forty-eighth meeting of the Boobooks (22 March 1907) reads in part:

> My Cheek with thought is lined and pale:
> My cold grey eye makes Bishops quail.[43]

The literature and modern languages journal the *Trident*, which Latham, Murdoch and O'Dowd launched in 1907, featured the series of biographical interviews with Champion which have been quoted earlier,[44] as well as writings by such other Fabians as Scott, Sinclaire and Nettie Higgins. The journal's publisher was the Lothian family, in whose home FSV meetings were held.

Champion, O'Dowd, Sinclaire and Latham were members of the Literature Club of Melbourne, and O'Dowd, Scott and Latham also belonged to the Brown Society, which Deakin's son-in-law, Herbert Brookes, founded in his home in 1907 to foster appreciation of the Manx-English poet T.E. Brown. The Brown Society also held musical recitals, which were sometimes attended by Deakin, who lived next door.[45] Frank Shann was told by his brother Edward in

May 1909 that Fabian Tracts could be borrowed from Latham – who also, by implication, could be relied upon for such support as Frank's Fabian convictions might from time to time require[46] – and, as has been seen, Latham's apology was recorded at the inaugural meeting of the FSV. Latham succeeded Edward Shann as Australian correspondent of the Empire-minded *London Standard* when Shann left for the London School of Economics in 1908. The position may well have had the effect of gradually redirecting his Fabian sympathies, by leading to service on the political committee of Deakin's Liberal Party, and the offer of an opportunity to stand for parliament the following year. As will be seen, his final break with the former FSV members probably came later, during the First World War.

EDWARD SHANN

In London Shann studied under Graham Wallas at the London School of Economics, and was taken up by the Fabians in a busy whirl of engagements where a single week's activities in May 1909 could include 'the House of Commons on Tuesday after lunch with Trevelyan, a big dinner to the Webbs on Wednesday, a series of lectures on Poor Law Reform at the Guildhall on Wednesday and Thursday'.[47] In June he was employed by the Poor Law Commission to prepare the index for Beatrice Webb's minority report, and in July he attended the Fabian Summer School in Wales, where the Webbs spoke on the National Minimum and a 'first-rate' debate on compulsory military service was chaired by Sydney Olivier. 'It is', he wrote in a letter to his brother Frank, 'from things of this kind that one draws the best London has to give, the sharp stimulus to thought that follows actual perception of the men and places that dominate political thought. If only Australia were nearer this fountain head how easy the task of moulding the soft clay of our lively national culture might become'. The Fabian leaders, he now concluded, were 'the most potent forward influence in English civilisation'.[48]

Shann was a schoolmaster's son, born in Hobart on 30 April 1884 and educated at Wesley College and Melbourne University, where his outstanding academic record included holding the James Scholarship from 1901 to 1903 and the Wyselaski Scholarship in both Constitutional History and Economics in 1904. His positions prior to leaving for London were Lecturer in Constitutional History at Melbourne, acting Professor of Philosophy at Adelaide and political secretary to the prominent MP Donald Mackinnon. Mackinnon – characterised by some as 'the next best thing to a Labor man'[49] – was a radical liberal and IFL activist, who may well have entertained Fabian sympathies in which Shann was encouraged to interest himself. Shann's fellow students at the LSE included Walter Murdoch's nephew Keith, with whom he wrote articles for the *Age*.

Trevelyan and Wallas apart, Shann sought out such leading scholars of the day as the economist Alfred Marshall and the philosopher John M'Taggart, and used references from Deakin to open the doors of politicians, bureaucrats and businessmen.[50] Advising Frank to borrow Fabian Tracts from Latham was part of a stirring plea for the older man's help in the task of persuading labourites to be 'broad-minded socialists':

> Don't desert them because a long history of social oppression has made them rather narrow and hard to remould. You are one of the men on whom the burden of softening the asperity of the Australian democrat's attitudes is laid. 'It matters not how strait the gate, how charged with punishment the scroll.' I'll be back soon, and we'll not need to be lonely in the peaceful permeation.[51]

It was Shann's strong view that responsible Australians could not do other than support the Labor Party. Deakin, he presciently advised Frank, was 'no organiser of a fighting middle party'. The conservatives, by implication, were unthinkable, and 'the class features of the Labourites' could only be accentuated if all they met with at the hands of their fellow citizens was 'denunciation and opposition'. The task, as he recommended it to Frank in classically Fabian terms, was plain:

> Permeate them with more liberal conceptions of the common weal, educate and encourage their raw emotional strivings after a national policy, and above all remember that the economic interests of the wage-earning classes are more in need of support than those of the rich.[52]

FREDERIC EGGLESTON

Shann's emphasis on gradualism and permeation would have struck a responsive chord in Eggleston, who returned to the Fabian outlook of his young manhood after deviating from it somewhat in his middle years.[53] Eggleston was the son of a lawyer, born at Brunswick on 17 October 1875, and educated at Queen's College in St Kilda and Wesley College before becoming an articled clerk in his father's firm, and joint winner of the Supreme Court Prize for the best results in his final examinations in 1897. As has been seen, he established the Boobooks with Latham in 1902, and his marriage in 1904 introduced him to the circles close to Deakin which Latham and Shann also came to frequent. In 1911 he supported the establishment of the Free Religious Fellowship, which enabled Sinclaire to remain in Melbourne after he resigned his position with the Unitarian Church.[54] His term as a municipal councillor in Caulfield from 1911 to 1920 enabled him to advocate such reforms from the Fabian agenda as the abolition of plural voting, the enfranchisement of non-voting residents and the adoption of town-planning principles along British lines.[55] He was the Australian correspondent for the *New Statesman* after the First World War, assisted in the establishment of the Workers' Education Association, and, as has been seen, was a Round Table member with Latham.[56]

Eggleston gave the most explicit account of the meaning he and his associates attached to socialism in an address to a conference held in June 1915 under the auspices of the Workers' Education Association of New South Wales, the Economic Research Society of Sydney and the Labour Council of New South Wales. Eggleston's address was delivered when the initial unity of purpose of the London Fabians had long since begun to fracture. The Webbs had denounced producer co-operation and were moving steadily down the road which would lead them – via the statutory corporation model of socialism – to the ultimate debacle of championing Stalinism in their *Soviet Communism: A New Civilisation*. Increasingly, the emphasis of their advocacy had shifted from the municipal to the state and from co-operation to central government. Dissidents within the Society were at the same time pursuing alternative visions, which differed sharply from those of the Old Gang, or leaving the Society altogether for more congenial ideological company. Guild socialists such as the Society's future presidents G.D.H. Cole and his resolute wife Margaret – and syndicalists such as Mann within the industrial movement – tugged the Fabian conscience in the direction of greater control by workers over the application of their labour and the allocation of its products and surpluses. Followers of G.K. Chesterton renounced their Fabian allegiances, so that the case for their evolving distributionist philosophy (spreading property more widely in order to prevent the concentration of economic and political power in the hands of an elite minority) could be put more freely. For their pains, the distributionists were lampooned by some as trying to resurrect the sometime liberal rallying cry of 'three acres and a cow for everyman'.[57] While they and the guild socialists ultimately split over the place of the factory system in their respective visions of the future, the motives of the two groups were essentially similar, and it may well have been that Eggleston's address arose in part from the promptings of both.

Eggleston's address also foreshadowed the ultimate revolutionising of co-operative thought by the Basque priest Don Jose Maria Arizmendiarietta. When, forty years later, Arizmendiarietta established the great industrial co-operatives at Mondragon in Spain, the historic debate between the Fabian Old Gang and its guild socialist and distributionist critics was finally resolved, substantially in favour of the latter. This also cleared the way for the rifts between the two groups to be repaired. Arizmendiarietta's achievements place him squarely among the foremost social thinkers of the twentieth century. The Mondragon co-operatives now bear conclusive witness to the fact that enterprises governed by those whose contribution to them is their labour can outperform by every measure enterprises governed by capital.[58] Workers in given industries, Eggleston argued presciently, should with the assistance of their central organisations set up co-operatives for the manufacture and supply of their products and services. Certain principles, he continued, would need to be worked out:

> In the first place, the principles of co-operative control should be definitely worked out, and not shirked. By this, I mean there should be no sentimental application to industry of political desires, but efficiency in control should alone be considered. The idea that democracy is incompatible with leadership and authority, or submission to expert control should be discarded. Secondly, the whole weight of the organised labour available for the work, and labour in other industries, with its existing organisation, should be used to secure the success of the work. Thirdly, the movement should proceed in the direction of integration or organisation of industry rather than division. The whole process should be dealt with from the buying of the goods to the distribution of the product. Similarly, the efficiency of the worker, both mentally, physically, educationally and technically, should be the care of the organisation. The whole life of the worker should be related to his work. Fourthly, the supply of the larger utilities of economic life, such as banking, insurance, building societies, and even the distribution of food, should be organised by the association of the different industries in a co-operative scheme.[59]

Eggleston's Fabian affiliations were reaffirmed towards the end of his life in a passage from his final book, *Reflections of an Australian Liberal*:

> I believe, firstly that socialism is inevitable, and must be produced in the long run by certain forces which have developed and will continue to grow. But this will be an evolutionary process in which the adjustments in human behaviour, necessary to make a socialist State effective, will be made and the norms of conduct appropriate to socialism will be adopted.[60]

His biographer Warren Osmond summarises Eggleston's political position as having been that of 'a Deakinite Liberal and even a radical Liberal', but his explicitly gradualist approach and advocacy of policies such as the establishment of co-operatives fit comfortably into the Fabian mould, and it seems clear that his description of himself as a Fabian was intended to refer as much to a lifetime perspective as to the period when it was written. 'I am really a Fabian socialist', he concluded, 'Perhaps it would be proper to describe me as a *very* Fabian socialist, because I am impressed with the difficulty in the way of realising true social values in this world of men'.[61]

WALTER MURDOCH

Eggleston's gradualism (and Shaw's apology for gradualism in *Fabian Essays*) were echoed by Eggleston's fellow Boobook, Murdoch. 'We believe', Murdoch wrote in his *Collected Essays*, 'that persuasion, tame and ineffectual as it seems to hot, impatient men, intolerably slow as it must inevitably appear to persons suffering tortures on the rack of our present way of life, is the only network which will, in the long run, succeed'.[62] For Murdoch, as for the founders of the London Society before him, the paramount objective was to eliminate poverty. Poverty – as he stressed in his school textbook *The Australian Citizen* (1912) – was one of the greatest enemies of human well-being:

> So long as the wealth of the land is unjustly distributed, so long as any man or woman through no fault of their own suffers a degrading poverty, so long as a single child is denied any of the opportunities which ought to be the common birthright of all, there is room for improvement, and a field for the actual exercise of good citizenship.[63]

The remedy was not in doubt. Following in the footsteps of mentors such as Green, Muirhead and Henry Jones, Murdoch embraced the state as the means by which reform should be brought about. 'It would be easy enough', an essay on 'Social Service' from Murdoch's early collection, *Loose Leaves*, argues, 'to show that Green would have abhorred economic socialism; equally easy to show that moral socialism was the very essence of his system'.[64] As John Docker points out, it was Murdoch's further belief that those who responded most to the precepts of the idealist philosophers comprised a kind of elite of the spirit:

> Those who wished to serve in it had an ethical duty to save society, to help humanity, to serve the nation and state – and the Empire, which would preserve the nation-state – and in doing this they made themselves whole, unified the individual self with a public end. Thus would the elite achieve 'self-realisation'.[65]

'Man', Murdoch concluded, 'can attain his supreme good only as a citizen'.[66] His sentiments evoke those of Beatrice Webb, when she defined the job of intelligent and self-respecting people as 'to build an efficient, incorruptible and non-acquisitive society',[67] or Wells with the Samurai of his *A Modern Utopia*. Further pointers to his Fabian affiliations include his appearance as a lecturer for the VSP,[68] and his use of a letter of introduction from Champion to meet such London Society luminaries as Shaw when he visited Britain in 1908.[69] Murdoch, the last of fourteen children of a Free Church of Scotland clergyman, was born in the Scottish fishing village of Rosehearty on 17 September 1874, and brought to Australia when he was ten. His education was obtained at Camberwell Grammar School, Scotch College and Ormond College at Melbourne University, where he gained his BA with first class honours in logic and philosophy in 1895, and his MA two years later. Following early positions as a school teacher, assistant lecturer in English at Melbourne University and leader writer and book reviewer for the *Argus*, he was appointed to the chair of English at the newly-created university in Western Australia where the remainder of his working life was spent.[70]

As will shortly be apparent, Latham, Eggleston, Shann and Murdoch were in varying degrees lost to the labour cause, to the point where Latham and Shann ultimately became arch-conservatives.[71] The debacle appears to have been due in part to a combination of Fabian ineptitude and labour movement passivity or hostility. The FSV lacked the intellectual vigour and sense of political purpose which otherwise might have enabled it to gain and retain the loyalties of these exceptionally able potential recruits, or harness their restless minds and abundant energies. The labour movement, it seems fair to speculate, was precluded by its hubris from recognising or availing itself of their prospective contributions to its advancement and affairs. Deakin's Liberals, in all the circumstances, offered by far the more hospitable and promising environment. Such successes as ultimately rewarded the rest of Australia's first Fabians were also mostly in fields other than politics, following similar disappointments and departures.

No comparable lack of will or vision impaired the ability of the London Society to function as a bridge for left-leaning liberals to cross into the Labour Party. Despite antipathy towards liberals on the part of some Fabians, the London Society recruited liberals and facilitated the exchange of liberal affiliations for labour affiliations. Some Fabian liberals retained their memberships of Liberal Associations and even were Liberal members of parliament, while others became Independent Labour Party members or Labour Party members and Labour MPs. The Society had three Liberal to five Labour MPs in the House of Commons following the 1906 elections; equal numbers of Liberal and Labour MPs following the January 1910 elections; and four Liberal to eight Labour MPs following the elections in December 1910.[72]

CHAPTER 6

Departures

CHARLES MARSON

The Fabians gradually dispersed, went their separate ways and, in some instances, embraced new political allegiances. Marson's departure for England prompted a warm tribute in the pages of the *Pioneer*:

> In spite of all his eccentricities and curious ritualistic notions, the Rev. C.L. Marson has done a good deal towards the awakening of the public conscience in South Australia on matters social, and his proposed departure for England will be sincerely regretted by many of the workers and by those persons with whom the 'priest of St Oswald's' has come into close association. Marson may not be an economist of a very profound type, but his sympathies are all with the down-trodden and the toiling, and there are few men in similar positions who dare publicly to denounce the vile spirit of 'commercialism' as he has done. The formation of the S.A. Fabian Society was an act of his that may yet bear fruit, and Mr Marson's lectures at the Democratic Club and elsewhere have been productive of no little good.[1]

What followed for Marson was a three-year period which has been seen by some as 'the most significant in his life'.[2] After shortlived curacies in a Durham mining community and at Christ Church in Clapham – where, once again, he was 'kicked out for socialism' – he succeeded his erstwhile socialist mentor, W.E. Moll, as curate of St Mary's in Charing Cross Road. The Anglo-Catholic flavour and Guild of St Matthew affiliations of the new pulpit were evident in the fact that the Guild's leader, Marson's fellow Fabian, Headlam, appeared there regularly 'to preach, as he was hardly allowed to do so anywhere else, the brand of sacramental, socialistic and anti-Puritan teaching which he had evolved ever since his early days in Bethnal Green'. Marson, for his own part, made the most of being able to pursue his socialist advocacy without the need 'to break new

ground or to pioneer suspect ideas and practices, whether ecclesiastical or sociological', and was able to create a comfortable home for
Clotilda and the daughter who had been born to them in Adelaide.
However, the death of the parish benefactor who was the source of
his stipend unexpectedly cut short the appointment, and his mission
had to be continued at St Mary's in Somers Town under less
congenial conditions. As a leading figure in the strike by cab drivers
in the area in 1895, he appealed for support on the grounds that
'There is no better alms than that which helps men to fight better
in the cause of justice',[3] but his own capacity for giving had again
been undermined by ill health, and he was obliged to accept the
country living of Hambridge in South Somerset.

The phase in Marson's affairs subsequent to his return to London
and prior to his departure for Hambridge was also notable for having
brought to a head his differences with Headlam over the direction
and management of the Guild of St Matthew. Marson had been
critical of Headlam as far back as 1886, when a falling-out between
them over the failure of the Guild to interest itself more in winning
over for socialism those Christians who did not share Headlam's
High Church views prompted Marson to become a co-founder of
the Christian Socialist Society. There were further difficulties in 1894,
over Headlam's criticism of Bishop Westcott, whom Marson defended
as a man who 'was called a Chartist when still an undergraduate',
and had so far been the only bishop to show much interest in social
reform. The following year, Marson's 'complete and breathtaking
analysis of "the sick state of the G.S.M"' was published in the
Church Reformer. Marson argued that the Guild was achieving less
in 1895 than it had twelve years earlier, when its membership was
only a third of the current size. The handling of members by the
Guild was 'inefficient, careless and disgraceful'; branches were
discouraged or 'stifled in their cradles' by the Guild Council; and
the Council itself was 'lazy and inefficient'. 'Have we no gospel',
Marson asked, in pointed reference to Headlam's well known
preoccupations, 'except the London School Board, the Empire
Promenade and the Ballet?'. Was there, he added, 'nothing for the
man who lives out of town and prefers all the other arts before that
of St. Vitus?'. The Guild, he concluded, was 'being unnecessarily
and gratuitously killed by mismanagement' and Headlam, while not
'wholly responsible', was 'to some extent blameworthy'.[4]

An already high level of feeling within the Guild was further inflamed when Headlam came to the aid of Oscar Wilde after he was charged with 'indecent acts' under the notorious 'Blackmailer's Charter' homosexuality provisions of section 11 of the recently adopted Criminal Law Amendment Act.[5] Headlam, who had only met Wilde twice, put up half the writer's bail, escorted him through abusive mobs to and from the Old Bailey on each day of the trial, and was waiting for him outside Pentonville Jail at the conclusion of his sentence of two years' hard labour. Marson, for once, departed from the standards expected of him as 'a man of culture, wit and charm', and behaved with what has been characterised by Sir Compton Mackenzie as 'mobster vulgarity'.[6] He was, he said, all for building a New Jerusalem, but not for 'wading through a Gomorrah first'.[7] A motion from Marson to unseat Headlam as Warden of the Guild by limiting the tenure of the position to no more than one year at a time was defeated ignominiously at the 1895 Annual General Meeting. Marson's subsequent socialist advocacy was increasingly channelled through groups such as the Christian Social Union, which had been founded in 1889, and the Church Socialist League, which met for the first time in 1906. Meanwhile, new areas of experience were opening up for him, and his life was branching out along new paths.

While the initial outcome of Marson's move to Hambridge has been seen by some as 'a bewildering gloom for the ardent reformer and episcopal suspect', he felt privileged ultimately to have discovered, as he believed, 'the greatness, the sweetness, the unexpectedness and the cleverness of God's people in the green of the world'.[8] His arrival at a point of mutual trust and affection with his new parishioners may well have been helped by his activities as a collector of the folk songs of rural England, which he saw as expressing the inner life of ordinary people 'more truly than anything else'. The pursuit acquired Fabian significance when his response to an invitation to address the London Society on rural problems took the form of a lecture and recital on 'Folk Songs of Somerset', which he provided jointly with his fellow collector and Society member, Cecil Sharp. 'Nothing', Marson believed, 'indicates more terribly the state to which the capitalist system has brought us than the contemptible, puerile and wearisome trash of our modern music hall productions'.[9] While he and Sharp exemplified a preoccupation with rural songs to the exclusion of the songs of industrial workers and other urban groups, they were also among the significant number of Fabians whose sustained interest in the links between the arts, society and politics ensured that the arts would always have their place in socialist – and ultimately Labour Party – policy analysis and development.

Marson was also at work as a writer. His first book, *Fairy Tales*, appeared in Adelaide in 1892, and subsequent titles included *The Psalms at Work, The English Jerusalem, Plato's Apology and Crito, The Following of Christ, Village Silhouettes* and – anonymously – *Angling Observations of a Coarse Fisherman*. In February 1913 his membership of the Fabian Society was resigned on the grounds of what he termed the Society's 'feminisation', but apparently without ill feeling on either side. The February 1914 issue of *Fabian News* reported the appearance of another book, *God's Co-operative Society*, incorporating the 'Huppim and Muppim and Ard' essay on religious education for which he is best remembered in church circles and dedicated, in a timely gesture of reconciliation, to 'The bravest of Captains and most skilful of Swordsmen of the Holy Ghost, Stewart Duckworth Headlam'.[10] Later the same year, his membership card in the Society's records had added to it the annotation that he was dead.

HARRY CHAMPION

Champion was bedridden for two years following a serious stroke in 1902, and in 1909 further ill health forced a sharp curtailment of his VSP and FSV involvements. Occasional brief forays into political activity – such as the Anti-Rent League and the Gas Consumers' League, which he founded around 1911,[11] and his chairing of the McCabe meeting for Latham and the Rationalist Society in 1910 – continued, but the last twenty years of his life were largely given over to the literary ventures to which his connections with the Goldstein family had introduced him. Elsie Champion largely took over the running of the Book Lovers' Library, while such energies as Champion was able to muster were divided between his magazine the *Book Lover* and the Australasian Authors' Agency, which he established in 1906 to promote the work of Australian writers. His activities as a literary entrepreneur and publisher reached their peak during the final years of the First World War, when Sydney Locke's *The Straits Impregnable* and Capel Boake's *Painted Clay* became local bestsellers under his auspices, but the brief boom ended abruptly when the cessation of hostilities in 1918 allowed the usual supplies of British books to be replenished.[12]

The *Book Lover* appeared for the last time in June 1921, and in 1922 Champion was made bankrupt for failing to pay the printer's bill for his edition of Marjorie Barnard's *The Ivory Gate*. His remaining time was spent quietly at the Goldstein home in South Yarra, where he died on 30 April 1928.[13] A generous evaluation of the Australian phase of his political career was provided by his erstwhile SDF associate and estranged friend Hyndman in 1911, when he wrote that Champion had 'largely made amends for his action in this country by his work for Socialism under the most distressing physical conditions in Melbourne, where he helped to keep alive the spirit of Social Democracy and to uphold the Red Flag against the discouraging compromises of mere Labourism'.[14] Hyndman, however, could not have been expected to be aware of the full consequences of Champion's alienation of the trade union movement in Victoria and, in any case, had himself played some part in bringing about the estrangement of the SDF from the Labour Party in Britain. *The Book of the Labour Party* was closer to the mark, with its view that Champion had 'the temper of an aristocrat and an in-born sympathy with conservative traditions, both of which prevented him from really understanding and sympathising with the minds of the masses whom he endeavoured to lead'. As Morley Roberts put the matter in a nutshell, 'He was ever a good talker and good at everything but his own affairs'.[15] All told, his was a presence, at least by the time he reached Australia, of a kind which the labour movement might reasonably have hoped to be spared.

TOM MANN

Mann took leave for Britain via Broken Hill. When the initial triumphant success of the SQC and the VSP – so great a source of hope and pride to him – gave way to discord and failure, his attention reverted to the industrial sphere, and he became an organiser for the embattled Broken Hill miners. There, in the thick of the conflict between the Combined Unions Committee and BHP, the sense of purpose which appeared to have deserted him in the face of the separatist forces around and within the VSP was rediscovered. He was able to proclaim proudly: 'I am a Dangerous Agitator and a Dangerous Man. I am an enemy to Capitalism. Knowing what

I know I hope to be increasingly dangerous as the years roll by'.[16] It was his further conclusion that 'We should absolutely drop politics as being a more mischievous cause of disintegration than any other present-day influence'. Following the miners' defeat, he was employed again briefly by the VSP as an organiser, and used his position to campaign vigorously in favour of industrial unionism and against the arbitration system, which he had come to believe militated against working-class solidarity. His departure for England on 30 June 1909 was preceded by weeks of farewell functions, where Curtin spoke for a grateful and admiring constituency which extended well beyond the ranks of the VSP. The simple tribute they paid him was that Mann had made their Socialist faith possible.[17]

Mann landed in England on 10 May 1910, to the cheers of a waiting crowd of socialists and unionists. The militant mood of the times ensured that there was an attentive audience for the industrial unionism gospel he had come to preach, and the new journal – the *Industrial Syndicalist* – he launched shortly after his arrival acquired an extensive readership. What he had to say played its part in arousing rank and file trade unionist support for a mighty surge in strike action, in circumstances where, as one perceptive observer has noted:

> Trade union leaders, almost to a man, deplored it, the government viewed it with alarm, the I.L.P. regretted this untoward disregard for the universal panacea of the ballot box, the S.D.F. asked 'Can anything be more foolish, more harmful, more unsocial than a strike'; yet disregarding everything, encouraged only by a small minority of syndicalist leaders, the great strike wave rolled on, threatening to sweep everything away before it.[18]

Syndicalism remained Mann's faith even after he became a founder member of the Communist Party of Great Britain in 1920. Following a visit to the Soviet Union in 1921, he declared that perhaps the most important of the many lessons taught by the Russian Revolution was that 'the administration or management of industry must be by councils of workers and not by parliaments'.[19] His advocacy of worker control of industry was carried further between 1924 and 1932, in his capacity as chairman of the National Minority Movement. The Amalgamated Society of Engineers made him its general secretary in 1919, as did the Amalgamated Engineering Union in 1920. He died at Grassington in Yorkshire on 13 March 1941. The Australian phase of his career amounts, as has been seen, to the creation of an organisation whose initial success and promise were dissipated, and the leadership of an industrial dispute which was lost. It is a measure of his charisma that the episode is remembered more for the larger than life quality his presence imparted to his activities than for their objective lack of success.

FREDERICK SINCLAIRE

The task that Sinclaire inherited – cleaning up after his predecessors – may well have been insurmountable. As the FSV crumbled around him, he toughened the line of his Bijou Theatre speech with a series of six midday lectures on religion and modern man which argued that conventional religion had been rendered insensitive to the need for a new social order 'with more justice and less cruelty' by its attachment to 'ancient formula and dogma' and consequent reluctance to modify and restate its doctrines 'in modern thoughts and forms'. Unsurprisingly, the *Socialist* was quick to respond to this with the accolade that 'Talking about the Unitarian Church, we wonder how many members know that Comrade F. Sinclaire's sermons there are probably the most intellectually thought-compelling and advanced delivered in Melbourne'.[20] Equally predictably, endorsement from such a source, together with the appellation 'comrade', was calculated to inflame the worst fears of those Unitarians characterised as 'conservatives of the old non-progressive school, to whom the advanced radical views of Mr Sinclaire would be anathema'.[21]

Sinclaire's welcome among his Eastern Hill flock was rapidly wearing thin. Tensions arising from his public statements on social and political issues were exacerbated by his use of church premises for political gatherings, such as those of the FSV or the Unemployment Circle which he established in 1910. At the same time, there were difficulties in maintaining attendance at the services of a church which some argued had always been 'a heart-breaking institution'.[22] Sinclaire's distress over the deteriorating situation was such that, when he took a New Zealand holiday in October 1910, the *Socialist* expressed the hope that it would be 'beneficial to his health as well as successful in scope'. The following February, it was noted in the same quarter that Sinclaire was considering becoming 'a teacher of elocution, singing, voice-production and languages',[23] and, when his resignation was submitted a few months later, it seemed briefly that he might look for a new occupation overseas.

Such was not to be the case. Faced with the loss of so major a figure in Melbourne's political, cultural and religious life, a number of Sinclaire's more enlightened fellow citizens, including Maurice Blackburn and Frederic Eggleston, met to give thought to 'whether it would be wise to make some effort to induce Mr Sinclaire to remain in Australia' and concluded that 'Mr Sinclaire would be a useful unit in our democracy, and that he would help supply the spiritual leaven necessary to leaven the materialist lump'.[24] The outcome was the establishment of a new Free Religious Fellowship, which employed Sinclaire as its minister with a salary of two pounds a week. The principles of the FRF – 'the need for a religious conception of life; the need for religion to be freed from dogma; the need for a religious organisation based on freedom; and the need for a personal effort in the making of religion'[25] – recall those of the Fellowship of the New Life three decades earlier in London. There is a sense again of *deja vu*: the Victorian Fabians were regressing to the origins of Fabian socialism rather than coming to grips with the need to assure it a future. FRF members actively involved themselves in political and social issues, while the group's magazine *Fellowship*, which appeared from 1914 until 1922, attracted around itself a select pantheon of major exponents of a national Australian culture, which included, along with Sinclaire as editor, Louis Esson, Frank Wilmot and Vance Palmer. Earlier on, Sinclaire co-edited the *Socialist* with Marie Pitt for a two-year period from March 1911 and, in 1917, the newly-formed Victorian Labour College made him its first principal and tutor in English.[26]

In many aspects the FRF resembled the Australian Church, established in the 1880s by Sinclaire's fellow Fabian, the Reverend Charles Strong. Sinclaire and Strong developed a close working relationship. Strong's writing was published in the *Fellowship* by Sinclaire, who in his turn preached and lectured for Strong.[27] The coming of war in 1914 united them in opposition both to the conflict itself and to conscription for military service. When a manifesto against conscription was signed by a number of Protestant ministers, the names of Sinclaire and Strong headed the list. Sinclaire also found himself charged with the offence of distributing a leaflet which lacked the imprimatur of the military censor. These wartime activities counted against him in the 1920s, when, having lost all hope of a uniquely Australian political, cultural and religious identity, he applied unsuccessfully for the Chair of English at

Melbourne University. He later gained a lecturing and adult education post at the University of Western Australia (supported by Murdoch), and then became Professor of English at Canterbury College, Christchurch.[28]

The later years of his life saw Sinclaire's liberal political stance tempered steadily by an increasing conservatism and when he died in 1954 he had returned full circle to the Anglican faith of his young manhood. The sum of his considerable talents – personal charm and diplomacy not least among them – suggests that, if he had preceded Champion and Mann to Australia rather than followed them, the story of Victoria's first Fabians might have developed along rather different lines, to a more fruitful ending. Instead, he and the VSP 'idealists' who promptly gathered themselves around him were attacked by the 'materialists' within the party for failing to understand or adhere to Marxism, to the point where they saw themselves as facing the prospect of expulsion,[29] and, in turn, hit back with 'the criticism that too many socialists were given to mouthing cliches which added nothing to an understanding of how socialism could be achieved in Australia'.[30] In this way, the energies which Sinclaire and his associates might otherwise have devoted to rebuilding bridges with the PLC were diverted to guarding their backs. The reverberations of the conflict linger in the correspondence between Nettie Higgins and her future husband, Vance Palmer. It was the misfortune of the first Fabians that, by the time of Sinclaire's arrival, the antagonisms within and around the VSP which his predecessors had instigated or neglected to dampen down were too great to be rectified or even contained.

ERNEST BESANT-SCOTT

Besant-Scott's marriage broke up following the conversion of his wife Mabel to Catholicism,[31] and her ultimate return to England with the only child of the marriage, Muriel. It may be that, in the eyes of her atheist husband, insult was added to injury by the fact that her instruction in her new faith was undertaken by the Catholic Archbishop of Melbourne, Dr Carr. Such was the hurt Scott experienced that for years afterwards he was unable to so much as refer to Mabel by name. In the aftermath of the separation – and perhaps as a reaction to it – his links with theosophy were severed,[32] and his Fabian activity seems to have been limited to lecturing from time to time for the Victorian Socialist Party.[33] As has been seen, he may well have exercised a significant influence over the predominantly free-thinking and Fabian-minded membership of the intellectually and academically distinguished Latham circle,[34] and he was associated with Latham, Curtin and O'Dowd in the establishment of the Rationalist Society.

In the meantime, Besant-Scott's reporting for the *Herald* of the economic vicissitudes of the 1890s and Australia's onward march to federation led him to become a keen student of history. His *Terre Napoleon: A History of French Explorations and Projects in Australia* was published in 1910, his *Laperouse* in 1912, his *The Life of Captain Matthew Flinders, R.N.* in 1914, his *The Short History of Australia* in 1916, and his *Australia During the War* and *A Short History of Melbourne University* in 1936. His 1914 appointment to the newly-created chair of history at Melbourne University was gained by a narrow margin over his fellow Fabian Shann,[35] despite the fact that he had no formal academic qualifications. His support for anti-fascism in the 1930s reflected a lifelong adherence to liberal values, and his contribution to scholarship was recognised by his knight-hood and election to the position of President of the Australian Association for the Advancement of Science shortly before his death in 1939.[36]

SOUTH AUSTRALIAN DEPARTURES

Following their establishment of the South Australian Women's League in 1895, Lucy Morice and Catherine Spence played leading roles in the inception of the all-women South Australian Co-operative Clothing Company in 1902, and, in 1905, Morice was involved in the formation of the Women's Employment Mutual Association as a new trade union by the UTLC. The same year also saw the inception of the Kindergarten Union, where she served as an executive member from 1911 to 1931, as honorary organising secretary from 1913 to 1932, and as vice-president from 1932 to 1951. In 1909, she was associated with Dr Helen Mayo in setting up the School for Mothers Institute and, as has been seen, with her sister Fabian from Victoria, Vida Goldstein, in the formation of the Women's Political Association. Her championing of the feminist cause was taken further in 1916, as vice-president of the League of

Women Voters. Asked in 1913 if she approved of the militant tactics of the English suffragettes, her answer was unequivocal:

Entirely. They have my utmost sympathy and respect; their bravery and pluck arouse all my admiration. . . . I am entirely with the militants. They know what they are about, and one pays no heed to the lying reports that are circulated. They are grand heroic women.[37]

A visit to Britain in 1903 allowed her and James to meet the Shaws and other prominent London Fabians, together with G.K. Chesterton. While her increasing preoccupation with feminism and the kindergarten movement inevitably restricted her ability to work on behalf of Fabian socialism, her Fabian loyalties were not eclipsed. Before her membership of the London Society was allowed to lapse in 1915, it had been maintained without interruption over a twenty-three year period.

James Morice, in turn, added to his initial duties as South Australian Parliamentary Librarian those of Clerk Assistant and Sergeant-at-Arms in the Legislative Assembly from 1901 to 1918, and in the Legislative Council from 1918 to 1920. He was promoted to Clerk of the Legislative Council in 1920, and in 1925 to Clerk of Parliaments, where he served until his retirement in 1936. The sense of shared purpose which characterised his long marriage was reflected in his support for Lucy Morice's Kindergarten Union work. He was treasurer of the Union from 1913 to 1920, general secretary from 1914 to 1920 and a trustee from 1922 to 1937. His death in 1943 was followed by the death of Lucy in 1951.

Following re-election to the Legislative Council in the aftermath of the fracas with Price in 1897, Charleston transferred to the Senate in 1901 as a Free Trader, only to be defeated by the Labor Party in 1903. Unsuccessful attempts to re-enter the Senate followed, as a candidate in 1906 for the Farmers' and Producers' Political Union – a forerunner of the Country Party which he had helped to establish three years earlier, and served as general secretary prior to its merging with the Liberal Union in 1910 – and a Liberal Union candidate in 1910. Despite these setbacks and differences with his former associates, Charleston's membership of the London Fabian Society was maintained until 1911. He was for many years a member of the Council of the South Australian School of Mines, and visited Britain with a committee of inquiry into technical education in 1914. He died in 1934, leaving behind him a reputation for speeches which were models of 'clearness, earnestness and comprehension'.[38]

McPherson died of cancer at the age of thirty-eight, in 1897. True to the pattern of a life wholly devoted to the well-being of his fellow workers, his last words were 'Tell the boys to pull together'.[39] His wise counsel was shortly disregarded, when the party tore itself apart over the conscription issue during the First World War. As Bede Nairn writes, by early 1916 'The roll of Australians killed and wounded in the First World War hung like a pall over Australia'. In New South Wales, for example, those ejected from the Labor Party over the conscription issue included the prime minister, W.M. Hughes, the premier, W.A. Holman, Hughes' predecessor as prime minister, J.C. Watson, and Holman's predecessor as premier, J.S.T. McGowen, together with nine of Holman's ten ministers and twenty-three of the forty-seven Members of the Legislative Assembly.[40] Thirty-one state and federal parliamentarians in South Australia were branded as disloyal by the ULP Council and Conference for supporting conscription, as were the pro-conscription members of the party executive.[41]

Guthrie's support for conscription during the bitter wartime controversies brought about his departure from the Labor Party and expulsion from the Seamen's Union. He was re-elected to the Senate as a candidate for Hughes' National Party of Australia in 1917 and 1919, and fatally injured in a tramways accident in Melbourne while still in office, in 1921. Price visited England as premier in 1908 and was able to espouse Australia's interests in meetings with the royal family and leading politicians from all the major parties, but upon his return to South Australia he fell ill, and died on 31 May 1909. The flavour of his thinking in the later stages of his career was encapsulated, perhaps, in a final statement for the London press:

> It will only require a little time for us to make ourselves a power under the Union Jack; each part of the Empire will carry its part of the burden of Empire. I believe in the destiny of white people to rule the world.

ULP members were told in his final message to them: 'The Labor Party will have its ups and downs, but the Labor cause is the cause of Humanity, and, in the end must prevail',[42] but it seems likely that he too would have sided with Hughes over conscription if he had survived to do so.

Conscription claimed its last Fabian victim in Archibald. His service as president of the ULP in 1901–2 and chairman of the Parliamentary Labor Party from 1905 until 1908, was followed in

1910 by election as Member for Hindmarsh in the House of Representatives, where he became Minister for Home Affairs in 1914, but resigned his Labor Party membership over the conscription issue two years later. He was able to hold his seat for the National Party at the 1917 elections, and served briefly as Hughes' Minister for Trade and Customs before being defeated in 1919. It was said of him that 'He slaughters the English language with pitiless ferocity every time he talks', but he was also known in the State parliament as 'a hardworking Member who always thoroughly mastered his subject', and, later, as 'one of the best-read men in Federal Parliament'.[43] His working life was concluded as a bookseller, and he died in 1926. Buttery likewise gravitated to bookselling, and the shop he opened in Pirie Street in 1892 – and later moved to Franklin Street – became Adelaide's main source of radical publications from interstate and overseas. He and his fellow Fabian Dankeld were prominent members of the Clarion Fellowship of Socialists which Tom Mann instigated in Adelaide in 1902 and, in his capacity as choirmaster for the Labor Party, he introduced an antipodean version of 'Men of Harlech', with the stirring chorus:

> Men of Labour, young or hoary,
> Would you win a name in story?
> Strike for Home, for life, for glory,
> Justice, Freedom, Right![44]

THE MFS MEMBERS

Those Victorians who, like Thomas Palmer, hoped that Strong would enter parliament and provide the Labor forces with charismatic, resolutely socialist leadership were disappointed.[45] Increasingly, the jeremiads, admonitions and exhortations which thundered from Strong's pulpit and other platforms fell on deaf ears. The exuberant, expansionist phase in the affairs of the Australian Church, which he founded and sustained for more than sixty years, was brought to an end by schism within the church itself and recession in the colonial economy. The consequent transformation of his political outlook – from implicit radicalism to an outspoken renunciation of capitalism and advocacy of socialism – resulted in the loss of many of the church's wealthier supporters at a time when there was heavy pressure from its bank for repayment of the loans raised to pay for the new headquarters in Flinders Street.[46] Nor was the situation helped by Strong's personal liability (along with Tucker) for the debts which were left behind by the village settlement scheme's abject failure. While temporary respites were experienced from time to time, the church never recovered from the strains these setbacks engendered, or again recaptured its founder's dream of an authentically national communion in the tradition of the Church of England or Scotland. Instead, it withered away quietly in numbers and influence, until the decision to wind up its affairs was taken in 1957. Such assets as remained to it were vested in a Charles Strong (Australian Church) Memorial Trust.

Strong, for his own part, continued to figure as a prominent champion of unpopular economic and social causes. His foundation of the Melbourne Peace Society in 1905 was consistent with his earlier opposition to imperialism and the Boer War, as was his subsequent opposition to the First World War, conscription and the Spanish Civil War. Conforming to the best traditions of Fabian longevity, he was ninety-eight when he died in 1942. Palmer would not have been alone in regarding him as 'one of the ablest political thinkers' he had met, or in feeling that the best thing the colony could have had happen to it would have been for its fledgling Labor Party to have gained him as a member of parliament. It was not to be. For all the good which stood to Strong's credit, he remained, in practical terms, a man whose achievements fell short of the hopes which his admirers invested in him. 'His true dignity', his biographer concludes, 'consisted not in gifts, nor in popularity, nor in success, but simply in having used his powers and boldly spoken the truth which was in him'.[47]

Palmer was courting the financial debacle and professional disgrace which, as has been seen, resulted in his exile to South Africa. Even if disaster had not overtaken him on this score, it may well have done so on another. His financial worries had begun to erode his self-control, and the strict discipline for which he was renowned was taking on overtones of savagery. A former Wesley student recalled an occasion in 1899 when, frustrated because two boys had refused to give him the name of a schoolmate who had broken bounds, Palmer publicly flogged the offenders until he was physically restrained.[48] A report of an earlier incident at University High School reveals that 'he found that a class knew nothing of the Latin set down for the day's work, and decided to cane the class':

> After a dozen or more had received punishment, a boy found courage
> to tell the flagellator that the lesson on which the class had been

examined had been set for his elder brother in the next highest class. Flogging ceased.[49]

A final reckoning might have been deferred, but it could hardly have been avoided indefinitely. The move to South Africa enabled him to put the tensions of the past behind him and embark on a new career. The early years there saw him employed as a subeditor on the *Cape Times*, editor of the weekly journal, the *Owl* and a teacher at a Marist College. His establishment of the Palmer's University Classics textbook series followed, and between 1910 and 1926 thirty titles were issued. He died in Cape Town on 29 March 1929.[50]

Meanwhile, Ross was increasingly preoccupied with his work as an elocutionist and enlarging what ultimately became a considerable public presence as an ABC broadcaster and bon vivant. In addition to the Melbourne University elocution lecturership which he held for eighteen years, he acquired overseas links which included an Associateship of the Boston School of Expression and membership of the National Speech Arts Association of America. The *Australian Encyclopedia* credits him with 'a generally distinctly valuable' influence in voice production, which 'extended over both Australia and New Zealand and covered a very lengthy period'.[51] His strong friendly society movement affiliations were marked by his appointment as principal of an elocution class which trained speakers and reciters for the Victorian Alliance around the turn of the century and as adjudicator in the elocution section of the Rechabites' Undaunted Tent, and his authorship in 1911 of *The History of Manchester Unity in Australia*. The Royal London Statistical Society admitted him as a fellow in 1900, and as a journalist he became proprietor and editor of the *Australian Financial Gazette*, co-editor of the *Australian Handbook* and a broadcaster whose radio lectures were heard over 3LO and 3AR from the inception of the Australian Broadcasting Commission until the early 1950s.

Ross was also notable for his longevity. Until almost the day of his death on 28 April 1953, at the age of ninety-six, he travelled from his Mentone home to his book-filled Albert Street attic in the city – 'a picturesque figure, with his silver hair and beard, his black sombrero, monocle and Inverness cape'. His advancing years were not allowed to blunt his insistence on high standards in the elocution and public-speaking fields to which so great a part of his energies had been devoted. Shortly before he died he confided to friends, with Shavian panache, that the funeral orations of the clergy made him shudder and that he would prefer in his own case to be the subject of a short address from a fellow member of the Bread and Cheese Club. His wish was granted.[52] A wreath from the first of the Gordon's grave pilgrimages, which he had instigated so many years previously, was bequeathed in his will to the Gordon Memorial Cottage at Ballarat.

Hamilton's Sandhurst seat was lost at the 1908 general elections. He returned to South Australia in 1910, where he served as general manager of the South Australian Fruitgrowers' Co-operative and chaired a number of wages boards prior to his winning the East Torrens seat in the South Australian Parliament for the conservative Liberal Country League in 1917, and becoming a permanent member of the LCL executive. Earlier on, he had drifted apart from his PLC colleagues, in part, perhaps, because the party's heavily trade unionist character no longer sat easily with the co-operative movement's ideology of groups and individuals working together in harmony for mutual benefit. Co-operators, on the contrary, may well have found themselves increasingly alienated by the oppressively confrontationist class war attitudes they saw as being foisted on the party by its union affiliates. In Hamilton's case, the antipathy was exacerbated following his return to South Australia, by the perceived clash of interests between the unions and the wheat, wool, grape and almond growing smallholders with whose activities he increasingly identified himself,[53] and the party's failure to embrace the Single Tax cause with sufficient fervour. By the time of his death in 1955, the last of his labour links had been behind him for almost half a century.

THE LATHAM CIRCLE

The estrangement of labour activists from middle-class radicals which ruined the Fabians was also the ruin of Deakin and the New Liberals. Wisdom and skill as an orator had earned Deakin a place in cabinet before he was twenty-four:

> His fine words were matched by able deeds. He made Victoria the leader in irrigation and factory legislation; undazzled by the great in London, he defied dictation to the colonies at the Colonial Conference. In the Convention debates he was without equal in his resolute patience ... In the confused jumble of early Commonwealth politics he forced attention to the great national purposes for which the country had

federated; unless shared by all, the full benefits of peace, prosperity and progress would be ensured to none. As a whole-hearted Australian he dreamed of a young Commonwealth that might enrich the human spirit, and as a lawyer he tried to give his dreams a legal cloak. As a Liberal with great faith in equal opportunity he wanted no class legislation.[54]

All Deakin's strengths and achievements, however, were insufficient to secure the New Liberals a lasting place on the political stage. Increasingly, they found themselves squeezed between a labour movement which was no longer willing to reciprocate their many past services and the conservatives whose cramped horizons and moral and spiritual impoverishment they deeply despised. By 1909 Deakin's followers' fears for their political futures had prompted him to become a reluctant broker for the formal unification of the liberals and conservatives in the Commonwealth Liberal Party which briefly achieved notoriety as 'The Fusion'. 'Behind me', he grieved, 'sit the whole of my opponents since Federation'.[55] The Fusion was crushed by the Labor Party at the 1909 elections. Deakin's majority in Ballarat was slashed to 443, and the associates who had been closest to him - Mauger among them - were mostly defeated. As a significant influence in the further shaping of Australian society, New Liberalism was for all practical purposes extinct. A few years later Deakin too was dead.

For many, the lustre of his public life survived the ignominy of his departure from it. He remained, in the eyes of associates such as Eggleston, 'the paradigmatic intellectual in Australian politics who managed to practise statecraft as an art and a science while infusing public life with his exalted concept of citizenship'.[56] The author of a lecture in a series delivered annually in his memory credits him with having been 'above all an innovator, creating an extraordinary range of new concepts, new policies, new laws and new institutions in areas where there was no Australian precedent'.[57] He figures for a recent historian as 'the greatest phenomenon of Australian political history, even of Australian experience'.[58] As in the cases of Curtin and Whitlam, his career and contribution are benchmarks against which subsequent leaders have measured themselves or been measured.

Denied the leader and party of their choice by the Fusion, the Latham Circle members were finally alienated from the labour movement - and in some instances from their Fabian convictions - during the First World War. The war, as David Walker writes, 'revealed the division and confusion of those who had wanted to transform their society'. At a party held to celebrate the defeat of the second conscription referendum:

> Sinclaire arrived hugging two bottles of champagne and left towards the end of the evening behaving as if he had had them both. Not long afterwards Vance Palmer was helped into Guido Baracchi's city flat where he spent the night recuperating.[59]

Round Table members took an opposite view on conscription. The feelings of the group were conveyed by articles in its journal, which characterised the rejection of the referendum at the hands of the Labor Party and its allies as a 'most deplorable humiliation for Australia', and attributed the resolutions on national defence, recruiting and imperial federation adopted by the 1918 federal Labor Party conference to the party's having been captured by 'extremists and pacifists'.[60] 'By the end of the war, many members viewed the labour movement and the Labor Party with undisguised antipathy'.[61]

The First World War was also divisive for the London Fabians – as the Boer War had been before it – but the Society there could afford a more neutral stance than that in an only recently emancipated colony, whose coming to terms with its new identity remained troublesome and problematic. While Shaw was deeply antagonistic to the conflict, and Beatrice Webb 'felt physically sick when reading the appeals of the Coalition leaders to destroy the Hun for ever',[62] their fellow executive member, Robert Ensor, has been characterised by some as 'fire-eating' and credited with wishing to have Germany 'cut into fragments'. The upshot was a tacit agreement that the Society was not the right arena for the resolution of conflicting war aims, which the protagonists could more usefully pursue through organisations of their own. At the same time, the establishment of the War Emergency Workers' National Committee became the occasion for what has been hailed as 'perhaps the most important single event in the "permeation" of the Labour Party'.[63] Sidney Webb's fellow WEWNC member and – at long last – close ally, H.M. Hyndman, has described their *modus operandi*. 'When anything important comes up', Hyndman told his wife,

> I bring out a root-and-ground revolutionary proposal, and set it well before them. That puts them in a fright; and then Webb comes in with his proposal, only a few degrees milder than mine; and they are so relieved that they pass Webb's motion unanimously.[64]

The enduring ties Webb and Henderson, the WEWNC chairman, established in the course of the Committee's work were a firm foundation for the postwar partnership to which, as has been seen, the Labour Party in its modern form is so largely attributable. No comparable 'binding' agency emerged in Australia, to compensate the labour movement for the losses inflicted on it by the war's divisive and debilitating influence.

Scott and Murdoch rose to academic eminence, while Eggleston became a well known writer, lawyer, politician and diplomat. In mid career, Eggleston was hostile to the Labor forces to which his earlier allegiance had been given, and he held ministerial office from 1924 to 1927 in the Peacock and Peacock–Allen governments, but in later life the ties of his young manhood reasserted themselves, and he was a firm supporter of the Curtin and Chifley governments. Following his defeat at the 1927 state elections, he was chairman of the Commonwealth Grants Commission 1933–41; Australian Minister to China 1941–44; and Australian Minister to the United States of America between 1944 and 1946, when a breakdown in his health, suffered during the San Francisco conference a year earlier, finally brought about his retirement from active diplomacy. In the meantime, he wrote extensively for newspapers and magazines in both Australia and Britain, as well as making notable contributions to the literature on statutory corporations and public finance and in other areas of scholarship. His *George Swinburne: A Biography* appeared in 1931, and his *State Socialism in Victoria* in 1932, his *Search for a Social Philosophy* in 1941, and his *Reflections of an Australian Liberal* in 1953. His work as a writer continued until his death on 12 November 1954.[65]

Latham, for his part, experienced a major change of heart in the course of the war and thereafter was a staunch and unbending conservative whose actions were guided, in part, by 'an apprehension of the grave menace of Bolshevism and a conviction that sedition should be prosecuted with the full weight of the law'. He was an adviser to the Hughes government in wartime Britain and at the Versailles Peace Conference, and, as Attorney-General in the Bruce–Page government, he gained an unenviable reputation for the anti-union character of his legislation and administration, which was seen by some as being paralleled by an unseemly solicitude for the employer interest. His high offices also included the Industry portfolio which Bruce added to his Attorney-Generalship in 1928; the leadership of the opposition which he assumed following Bruce's loss of his seat at the 1929 elections; and the portfolios of Attorney-General, Minister for Industry and Minister for External Affairs to which he was appointed as deputy prime minister in the Lyons government. He left the ministry for a term as Chief Justice of the High Court which lasted from 1935 until 1952 – with a brief interlude in 1940-41 when he was simultaneously Australia's first minister to Japan – and died in Richmond on 24 July 1964.[66]

Edward Shann returned to Australia from Britain in 1910, 'inspired by Fabian ideals and an intense feeling of national identity' and 'eager to participate in the building of a rational socialist society in Australia'.[67] In the event, however, his enthusiasm waned, no doubt as a consequence of the same falling out with the labour movement over war aims as was experienced by his fellow Latham circle members, and he too ultimately opted for a more conservative viewpoint. An offer of the chair of Political Science at the Imperial University in Peking was declined, and he served briefly as lecturer-in-charge of History and Economics at the University of Queensland prior to accepting appointment as foundation Professor of History and Economics at the University of Western Australia, where Murdoch was Professor of English. He was a revered teacher and trail-blazing economics researcher, who published *Cattle Chosen* in 1926, *The Boom of 1890 – and Now* in 1927, *An Economic History of Australia* in 1930, *Bond or Free?* later the same year, and *Quotas or Stable Money?* in 1933, when his distinguished contribution to the *Cambridge History of the British Empire* also appeared.

In addition, he wrote widely for both newspapers and professional journals such as the *Economic Record*, broadcast on economic topics and was co-author with Sir Douglas Copland of *The Crisis in Australian Finance* in 1931 and *The Battle of the Plans* and *The Australian Price Structure* in 1933. He became the first economic consultant to the Bank of New South Wales in 1930, a member of the Copland Committee (which prepared the Premiers' Plan) in 1931, a Commonwealth representative at the Ottawa Conference and a member of the Wallace Committee on unemployment in 1932, and a Commonwealth representative at the World Economic Conference in London and Professor of Economics at the University of Adelaide in 1933.[68] A fall from his Adelaide office window brought about his tragically premature death on the evening of 23 May 1935. The fall may well have been the result of the 'black fits' of depression which he experienced as early as 1909.[69] Murdoch, who had fallen out with him over economic issues at the depths of the slump, was among those who mourned him most deeply. He wrote, 'You don't realise how much affection you have for a man until he has gone where you have no chance of telling him'.[70]

Murdoch's own academic eminence was recognised in his appointment as Chancellor of the University of Western Australia, and his service to the community was rewarded by a CMG in 1939 and a KCMG in 1964. He is best remembered, however, as 'a famous essayist and popular educator who wrote nearly all his work for newspapers'.[71] His long-running columns included 'Books and Men' over his pen-name 'Elzevir' for the *Argus*, his essays for the 'Life and Letters' page of the *West Australian* and the 'Answers' which were syndicated for a large audience throughout Australia and New Zealand. He also broadcast for the ABC, edited collections of Australian poetry and short stories and wrote a short biography of Deakin. His championing of Douglas Credit in the 1930s said more about his sympathy for the underdog than his understanding of economics, but the causes to which his support was given in his later life also included the League of Nations, kindergarten education, anti-fascism and the defeat of the Menzies government's attempt to ban the Communist Party in 1951.[72] His death in 1964 was widely interpreted as depriving the nation of a wise and warmly humanitarian critic and counsellor.

THE FSV WOMEN

While Nettie Higgins maintained her socialist allegiance, she moved on to predominantly literary preoccupations. Living in the Dandenongs, and later in Queensland, she produced a stream of consistently excellent critical writing, ranging from newspaper and magazine columns and articles to her *Modern Australian Literature*, which won her the Lothian Prize. Other notable works included the collection of her essays published as *Talking It Over* in 1932, the biography of her uncle *Henry Bournes Higgins*, and the memoir *Fourteen Years: Extracts from a Private Journal*, which was published for her by the Meanjin Press in 1948. Her lectures and broadcasts were also widely appreciated and admired.

The rise of fascism in the 1930s rekindled her latent political energies and led to her being a participant in the International

Congress of Writers for the Defence of Culture. She was later a member of the Spanish Relief Committee, the Joint Spanish Aid Council and the Victorian branch of the International Refugee Emergency Committee, as well as the editor of a women's anti-fascism journal. In the meantime, as one observer has noted, 'By personal acquaintance or through a voluminous correspondence', she and Vance Palmer 'had become the fountainhead of wisdom, encouragement, and advice for aspiring literary artists throughout the Commonwealth'.[73] The whole thrust and purpose of her life is caught in the words used by Palmer for the work of their friend and fellow writer Frank Wilmot. Wilmot, Palmer wrote, had aimed at 'the creation of a culture that would water the dry soil of this country and give it a richer life'.[74] It was in the nature of the task that much remained to be accomplished when Nettie Higgins died suddenly on 19 October 1964.

The energies which Nettie Higgins devoted to the advancement of the writer's art were used by Elizabeth Lothian to provide 'opportunities for women to enjoy using their brains and to grow in stature intellectually'. In 1910, she was one of a number of former PLC students and university friends who formed a group called the Catalysts. The outcome of their efforts was the establishment on 8 September 1912 of the Lyceum Club for women with professional, business, cultural and intellectual interests.[75] In the same year, her long career as a much-loved classics mistress at Melbourne Church of England Girls' Grammar School commenced, and her writing of a book of patriotic poems for children, under the title of *Hearts of Oak*, may have signalled the opening of a rift with her former associates over the troublesome issue of Empire loyalties.[76] From 1917 to 1937 she was joint honorary secretary of the Provisional Committee which was formed to establish a Women's College at the university. She was a member of the Women's College Council until 1950 and, for many years, an honorary tutor for students from Women's, Ormond and Queen's.[77] Her death, on 6 May 1973, marked the passing of a notable educator.

Crowds of up to 10,000 heard Vida Goldstein speak during her 1911 tour of England, and her presence there was described by one contemporary observer as 'the biggest thing that has happened to the woman movement for some time'. At home she was instrumental in the establishment of organisations such as the National Council of Women, the Victorian Women's Public Servants' Association and the Women's Writers Club, as well as the enactment of such pioneering legislation as the 1906 Children's Court Act, which she helped to draft.[78] Her second feminist paper – the weekly *Woman Voter* – was launched in 1907 to fill the gap left behind by the demise of the *Sphere* four years earlier. Her tables on the lowest wage adequate for the support of a working man and his family in the September 1907 issue of the *Nineteenth Century and After* are credited by some with having exercised a powerful influence in the development of Mr Justice Higgins' seminal Harvester Award, and, through it, as has been seen, to the introduction of the Basic Wage.[79] If so, there was a further outcome, which may well have led to Vida's looking back on the episode with something less than total satisfaction. Higgins' concept of a wage set at the level required by the worker to maintain a family in 'frugal comfort' had the effect of entrenching lower pay for women for decades to come.

Meanwhile, not all Vida's obvious industry, ability, integrity and sincerity could prevail in the face of the entrenched party system, or stem the massive erosion of her personal popularity which resulted from her uncompromising opposition to Australia's involvement in the First World War, which she pursued as founder of the Women's Peace Army and chairperson of the Peace Alliance. The outcome of her 1917 anti-war Senate campaign was the loss of her deposit.[80] A visit to Zurich as Australian representative at the 1919 Women's Peace Conference lengthened into a three-year absence, and marked the cessation of her public involvement in most aspects of domestic politics and the women's cause.

Following her return, her attention turned increasingly to international relations and the Christian Science faith which she and her mother and sisters had first embraced around the turn of the century. Her final acts of service to the community were undertaken as a Christian Science healer and a founder, reader and president of the Melbourne Christian Science Church. She died in obscurity at the South Yarra home which she shared with her sisters on 15 August 1949.[81] The energy, inspiration and passion which this immensely talented, immensely dedicated woman poured into the emancipation of her sex epitomises all that was denied to the Labor Party – and, equally, forgone by it – as a result of the separation of its working-class and trade unionist elements from the middle-class would-be allies who made up the FSV or were closely associated with it. More, perhaps, than any other woman of her time, her presence figured as a beacon of hope for those who were victims of chauvinist incomprehension and oppression. Such were her capacities that, had the situation within the PLC been less inhospitable – and the PLC's relations with the socialist movement less strained – the Australian parliament might well have had its first woman member decades earlier than was in fact the case.

THE FSV MEN

It was left for Jones to become the only FSV member to enter parliament. Jones' innate pragmatism led him to stand down from the presidency of the VSP when its relations with the PLC soured. In April 1910 he resigned from the party to stand as a Labor candidate for the East Melbourne Legislative Council seat,[82] which he held until 1934, when a transfer to the South Western Province became necessary. In the intervening years, he was Minister without Portfolio in the Elmslie government; Minister of Public Health and in Charge of Immigration, Commissioner of Public Works and Vice-President of the Board of Lands and Works in the Prendergast government; and Minister for Mines in the two Hogan governments.[83] As Acting Treasurer during Hogan's absence overseas in 1931–32, he chaired the subcommittee of the Loan Council whose report – largely inspired by Copland and Shann – was the basis of the Premiers' Plan, and in later years he frequently referred to himself as having been the plan's author.[84] It may well be that in the selling of the plan Shann was able to draw on ties of mutual trust and friendship with Jones, stemming from when they were Fabians together in their young manhood. Comparable ties among such 'Old Gang' London Fabians as Shaw, the Webbs, Wallas and Olivier survived their many political disagreements and their waning commitment to – or, in the case of Wallas, defection from – the Society itself. The 'aged Peases' remained intimate with the 'old Oliviers', the seventy-seven-year-old Beatrice Webb recorded in her diary in 1935, on the occasion of a visit by the Peases to Passfield Corner, although 'the Peases have dropped out of any acquaintance with the aged Shaws, as we have with the aged Oliviers'.

When a premature election was forced on Hogan in 1932, Jones resigned from the Cabinet on the grounds that it had supported debt repudiation, and argued for the Premiers' Plan from United

Australia Party platforms.[85] The effect was his automatic exclusion from the Labor Party, and he was obliged to exchange the safe Labor seat which he had held since 1910 for one whose leanings were more conservative. However, Argyll's incoming UAP government reinstated him in his previous portfolio and gave him the leadership of the Council, which he had occupied on Labor's behalf since 1927. He became a UAP member in 1934, and the closing years of his parliamentary career were seen out in the company of the conservatives who had previously been his adversaries. Even so, his earlier political allegiances were never, as he saw it, wholly abandoned. To the day of his death, on 12 October 1955, he insisted – as had Ramsay MacDonald in similar circumstances before him – that he was still a socialist and always had been.[86]

O'Dowd and Jones may well have continued to see one another casually in Parliament House in Melbourne, where O'Dowd became Assistant Parliamentary Draughtsman in 1913 and then Parliamentary Draughtsman in 1931. His goals for himself had been made explicit in 1909, when his presidential lecture for the Literature Club of Melbourne on 'Poetry Militant' declared that 'In every age of human progress the poet has been the most authentic and effective creator of gods and the mythologies which give them blood and bone and power'.[87] Opinions about the extent of his success vary. Some take the view that he 'turned his intellectual ferment to a new use, made his visions a national heritage and became, for some considerable time, the leading spokesman of his age',[88] while others, no less erudite, have dismissed his work as 'a *cloaca maxima* into which has flowed all the ideological drivel of the nineteenth century – deism, pantheism, nationalism, socialism, democratism and the rest', so that 'its value as literature is nil'.[89] A fairer, more relevant summing-up, avoiding 'the condescension of posterity', may have been provided by Nettie Palmer, who knew him better than most, when she wrote shortly before his death:

It is hard to suggest what an inspiring figure Bernard O'Dowd was in those days, not only to young people trying to write but to all who had urgent hopes for a better future for mankind. O'Dowd really believed in this future or 'millenia', in spite of the scepticism suggested by his favourite punctuation mark, the note of interrogation. And for all his democratic homeliness, his generous simplicity, he had a touch of personal magic, that kindled the imagination and made it easy to believe that he was not only a poet but a sage.[90]

His collection of poems *Dawnward?* was issued in 1903, *The Silent Land* in 1906, *Dominions of the Boundary* in 1907, *The Seven Deadly Sins* in 1909, *Poems* in 1910, *The Bush* in 1912 and *Alma Venus!* in 1921.

By 1921, however, most of his poems had been written and his deep frustration was given expression in a phrase remarkable for its wry resignation: 'The Muse of Lawmaking is a jealous lass'.[91] In 1920 he had left his wife and their five children to begin a new life with his longtime fellow poet and socialist Marie Pitt, of whom Mann said, 'Keen to resent injustice and to stimulate others to strive for a worthy life, she was in close touch with the toilers, knew the work of the axeman and the miner, was familiar with the terrible effects of the miner's phthisis'.[92] O'Dowd refused Lyons' offer of a knighthood for services to literature in 1934, but kept the refusal secret, because he believed that 'To make capital out of declining the honour would be as degrading as it would be to accept it'.[93] A complete set of his poems, with an introduction by Murdoch, appeared in 1941 under the auspices of the Commonwealth Literary Fund and, during the Second World War, he worked on the staff of the official censor. His death, on 1 September 1953, was marked by his friends with a Unitarian ceremony.

The sheer longevity of Australia's first Fabians provides a notable concluding parallel with their English counterparts, as does the magnitude of their contribution to public life, and the talents forgone by the labour movement through their loss to other causes and creeds. Priests, jurists, men of letters, diplomats, legislators, educators, scholars or followers of other callings as the case may have been, their lives mostly exhibit common features, from which clear conclusions must now be drawn.

CHAPTER 7

Conclusion

The fact that most of Victoria's first Fabians – unlike their London counterparts or their precursors in South Australia – were men and women who could see no place for themselves in the labour movement of the day, or for whom no place was found, is attributable substantially to the misfortune of their having had Champion and Mann for their leaders and spokesmen. This is suggested if we construct an alternative scenario for the twenty-year period from 1890 to 1910, in which the unions are not alienated by what they saw as Champion's intervention on the side of the employers in the Maritime Strike. In this scenario, the *Worker's* call for the establishment of a Fabian Society catalyses the social forces which led to Archer's becoming a London Society member, and prompts action on the part of such other local Fabians as Strong, Ross, Palmer and Hamilton to form a Victorian Fabian Society, which is not undermined by Champion's switch of his support to the Social Democratic Federation of Victoria.

Further support for the new Society becomes available as the turn of the century approaches, from younger socialists of the stamp of Jones and O'Dowd, and organisations such as the Victorian Socialist League, the Tocsin Clubs, the Victorian Labour Federation and the Social Democratic Party of Victoria are not formed or attract smaller followings. A formidable capacity for socialist research, policy development and propaganda along London Fabian lines is developed by the Society, which the Labor Party is able to accept or reject on its merits. The impression that only working-class MPs can be trusted to represent working-class interests does not take hold, and, when prospective Fabian recruits – and possible future MPs – come forward, they are welcomed into the party and able to play their part in its affairs on an equal footing with their unionist fellow members. The Labor Party does not fall for the self-defeating fallacy that countries like Australia can be reformed by the working class in isolation from the middle class, or have to wait for a Whitlam to show it that informed consent by a majority comprised of elements from both classes is necessary in order for enduring reform to occur.

The expatriate London Fabians who arrive in Victoria from time to time are likewise made welcome, and some in due course find places in the higher councils of the party and parliament. Mann is able to apply his undivided attention to organising for the PLC, and the increases in electoral support brought about by his efforts allow scope for the adoption of a more socialist platform. A Labor government takes office at an earlier date. While a number of revolutionary socialists still reject the Labor Party on the grounds of its reformist approach, they are not able to drive a wedge between the Society and the party, or engender fears of unionists being stabbed in the back by disloyal intellectuals, and a home is found for them with the establishment of the Communist Party. The Victorian model of a co-operative relationship between the party and the Society is admired and adopted in other states, with the result that Australia retains its early reputation as a socially innovative country, and in fact leads the way for the Scandinavian social democracies which ultimately follow in its footsteps.

Pure fantasy, perhaps, but there is some pertinence in such 'counter-factual' speculation. The fact that none of these things happened – despite the South Australian experience indicating that a start could be made – is, in part, a measure of the destructive impact of Champion's overbearing ways and the inability of either him or Mann, in St John Irvine's words, to 'remain faithful to a scheme long enough to obtain a result from it'.[1] The upshot, as has been seen, was a substantial alienation of the trade unionist elements of the movement from the socialist, intellectual or merely middle-class elements who might otherwise have been loyal and useful allies. Once implanted, this estrangement was exacerbated in due course by the emergence of the Communist Party as a rival body which contested both parliamentary and union elections against Labor candidates, and, later again, by the National Civic Council and the Democratic Labor Party.

THE AUSTRALIAN FABIANS' ACHIEVEMENTS

This is not to say that the efforts of the local Fabians and their associates of other socialist persuasions that were broadly compatible with mainstream Labor opinion were wholly wasted. Nor is it to say that Fabian socialism had no future in Australia. Labor identities of the stature of Curtin and Cain cut their political teeth either directly within the Social Questions Committee and the Victorian Socialist Party in the Fabian phase of its lifecycle, or in the VSP when it was no longer an organisation in the Fabian mould, but retained vivid memories of the circumstances of its decline.[2] Having looked into the abyss and noted the unaffordable cost of separatism, they were the sooner reconciled to the parliamentary road they thereafter pursued.[3] Again, it is doubtful whether the Labor Party would have adopted the 1921 Socialist Objective in the absence of the continuous consciousness raising which the socialist agitation of the first Fabians and others was able to bring about. Although the implementation of the objective was – with the possible exception of bank nationalisation – never seriously attempted, or, perhaps, even intended, it enabled the party to go on attracting members whose horizons were not wholly limited to pragmatic considerations, and enabled the issue of ownership of the means of production, distribution and exchange on something other than a purely private and individual basis to be revisited at a later date. Further achievements credited to the VSP include the Labor Party's rejection of conscription in 1916 and its adoption of an anti-war policy two years later.[4]

In the absence of explicitly Fabian organisations on the Australian political landscape throughout the twenty and more lean years of the interwar period, Fabian thinking was spread through channels such as the Workers' Educational Association, the group around Oswald Barnett in Victoria whose activities gave rise to the ALP Slum Abolition Committee and the Victorian Housing Commission,[5] and the Australian Institute of Political Science.[6] At the same time, a new group of mainly Fabian-minded administrators – exemplified by the young H.C. Coombs – were emerging in Canberra, where their talents were deployed to full advantage after 1945 through agencies such as the Ministry of Post-War Reconstruction. The group was united, in the view of Coombs, by a community of interest 'based upon a faith in the power of government intervention to contribute positively to the sum of human welfare, to civilise the content and distribution of the product of the economic system without impairing its essential freedom or its efficiency'.[7] Audible in this is an echo of the faith of London Fabians such as

Beatrice Webb and Wells in the obligation of intelligent and self-respecting people to build an efficient, incorruptible and non-acquisitive society. Coombs outlasted twenty-three years of unbroken conservative rule, from 1949 to 1972, to join Whitlam as a Senior Advisor, head the Whitlam government's Royal Commission on Australian Government Administration, and figure as a key advocate for the advancement of Aboriginal Australians.

Whitlam epitomised the Fabian approach when the London Society had long since entered its second half-century, and the Fabian Basis had been amended through the incorporation of a self-denying ordinance which reads in part that the Society should have no collective policy beyond that implied by its commitment to democratic socialism and should put forward 'No resolution of a political character expressing an opinion or calling for action, other than in relation to the running of the Society'.[8] By the late 1940s and early 1950s there were once again thriving Fabian societies in South Australia and Victoria. Societies had been formed for the first time in Queensland, Western Australia and New South Wales, and a meeting in Melbourne in 1949 discussed the establishment of a national Fabian organisation.[9] Nothing came of this initiative, but the Victorian Fabian Society gradually moved to fill the gap by operating nationally, with members in every state and territory. The Victorian Society was an important platform for Whitlam in reforming the Labor Party and returning it to government, and key policy statements by him appeared as Fabian pamphlets. Marson's dream of labour activists and middle-class radicals working together harmoniously for social reform was at last fulfilled when Whitlam played his antipodean Sidney Webb to the Arthur Henderson of Clyde Cameron and Mick Young, in the rewriting of the party constitution and platform which preceded the 1972 elections. In the process, the estrangement of much of the party mainstream from intellectual influences, for which Champion and Mann had in part been responsible, was finally healed.

Whitlam's involvement in the ALP stemmed from a deep admiration for the party's wartime leaders, Curtin and Chifley, whom he saw as championing a more equal and democratic Australia. He was deeply affronted by the overthrow of the government's 1944 referral of powers referendum by a stubborn and deeply entrenched conservatism which he believed was contrary to much that members of the services (such as himself) had fought to achieve.[10] The vision of Labor's mission which Chifley encapsulated memorably for the New South Wales branch of the ALP at its 1949 Conference as 'our light on the hill' fired Whitlam's idealism and intellect.[11] The effect was to enlist for the Labor cause a political creativity, clarity of purpose and courage which transcended even that of Curtin.

The intensity of the sense of national identity which Whitlam brought to Labor's affairs recalls the determination of James Joyce's Stephen Daedalus 'to forge within the smithy of my soul the uncreated conscience of my race'.[12] The broad intellectual influences which shaped his outlook and actions were those of the leading London Fabian of the day, C.A.R. Crosland, and such near-Fabian American scholars as J.K. Galbraith. The consistent aim was to correct what Galbraith described as 'private affluence and public squalor'.[13] Further relevant considerations included the concept of the social wage, and the memorable aphorism of the wise American jurist Oliver Wendell Holmes Jnr: 'I like to pay taxes. In this way I buy civilisation'. It was Whitlam's conviction throughout that 'The quality of life depends less and less on the things which individuals obtain for themselves and can purchase for themselves from their personal incomes and depends more and more on the things which the community provides for all its members, from the combined resources of the community'.[14]

Eclectic by nature, Whitlam was unabashed about drawing inspiration from the experience and practices of countries comparable with Australia. His methods were quintessentially Fabian. Each new piece of work he undertook started from the principles of social justice and equality which have characterised the Society from its inception. Information was gathered methodically and meticulously analysed, in the best traditions of Sidney Webb's *Facts for Socialists*. Experts were consulted extensively, again in a way characteristic of the Society and the Webbs. The solutions which emerged were explained and justified tirelessly, through all the avenues which a skill in advocacy unmatched among his contemporaries could command.

Like the Fabian authors of *Why Are the Many Poor?* and *Facts for Socialists* before him, Whitlam cared deeply about finding a solution to the problem of poverty. Studies of poverty in Australia by scholars such as Professor Ronald Henderson of the Institute of Applied Economic and Social Research at Melbourne University and journalists such as John Stubbs – and in the United States by Michael

Harrington and Lyndon Johnson's Office of Economic Opportunity – caused him to question the adequacy of the exclusively pension-based welfare policies of the Commonwealth Department of Social Services, and to pursue alternatives, including some which were ultimately given effect through the Social Welfare Commission and the Australian Assistance Plan. His interest in national accident compensation and national superannuation was motivated primarily by a passionate conviction that no Australian should be impoverished through bad luck, disability or old age.

The Department of Urban and Regional Development stemmed in part from Whitlam's personal experience of raising a family in an outer suburb of Sydney in the absence of even such basic urban services as sewerage, but in part also from sources such as the Director of the Canadian Institute of Urban Research Humphrey Carver, whom he quoted frequently as saying that 'Building cities is by far the most difficult, complex and majestic thing that men do. In this we come nearest to what God does in creating the stars, the hills and the forests'.[15] His development of Medibank drew heavily on a Royal Commission report from Saskatchewan in Canada.

Impatient with the constraints of a moribund and stultifying federalism, he declared that:

> If we were devising anew a structure of representative government for our continent, we would have neither so few State governments nor so many local government units. We would not have a federal system of over-lapping parliaments, and a delegated but supervised system of local government. We would have a House of Representatives for international matters and national matters, an assembly for the affairs of each of our dozen largest cities and a few score regional assemblies for the areas of rural production and resource development outside those cities. Vested interests and legal complexities should not discourage or deter us from attempts to modernise and rationalise our inherited structure. Federal countries like the United States, Canada and West Germany are showing far more initiative and enterprise than Australia in adjusting yesterday's forms to today's needs.[16]

Whitlam's Fabian approach as leader of the opposition was maintained as prime minister. The Whitlam government of 1972–75 broke new ground by institutionalising Fabianism on a statutory basis, through the establishment of investigatory and recommendatory bodies such as the Schools Commission and the Hospitals and Health Services Commission. The brief of the commissions was to investigate freely and fully all aspects of the areas of government responsibility set out for them in their Acts, prepare recommendations and report publicly to the community through the national parliament as they saw fit. Commission inquiries – like the investigations of less formal Fabian bodies before them – were an effective means of bringing to public attention information and ideas which otherwise might have remained unfamiliar or inaccessible; lifting public consciousness of key issues of public policy or community aspiration; and building consensus behind initiatives which might otherwise have remained controversial. Shaw might well have applauded the implicit redefinition of the business of Fabians, from the 'Educate, Agitate, Organise' of his encapsulation to the Whitlam government's 'Investigate, Educate, Legislate'. The abolition of the commissions by the Fraser and Hawke governments has not caused their signal achievements to be forgotten, or rendered less relevant their capacity to redress the excessive incrementalism with which Australia's affairs are customarily conducted. Overall, the Whitlam agenda of 1967–75 had about it the quality which Margaret Cole ascribed to the partnership of Sidney Webb and Arthur Henderson. Like the program crafted for the Labour Party by Webb and Henderson in 1918, it embodied, in Cole's terms, 'as nearly as possible the purest milk of the Fabian word'.[17]

INTERNAL TENSIONS IN THE VSP

Tensions within the VSP have been ascribed to the existence within its ranks of two camps: on the one hand, 'a literary group, essentially middle class, which was concerned primarily with socialism's moral and cultural meaning within the Australian context', and on the other, 'a loose group of economically and politically oriented socialists who were working class, young, and to a limited degree, Marxist'. The latter, it is argued, 'aimed at instructing themselves and others in the intricacies of socialist economic and political theory as they related to Australian experience', while the former, who are seen to include O'Dowd, Champion and Marie Pitt, was concerned with the need for Australian literature 'to develop a social conscience, and thus help to shape an uplifting national destiny'.[18]

A different set of factional alignments within the VSP has been suggested by Ian Turner. On the one hand, Turner argues, there were members such as those who 'because of their emotional revulsion against capitalism or their intellectual acceptance of the Marxian prediction of social polarisation and proletarian impoverishment, have sought to establish and maintain pure revolutionary parties and unions in competition with the mass working-class organisations, in anticipation of the inevitable collapse of capitalism, the attempted restoration of authoritarian political structures, and the spread of revolutionary sentiment among the proletariat'. At the same time, he continues, there were also 'those who have seen the expansion of capitalism and the advent of bourgeois democracy as providing the possibility of a real improvement in the economic and political condition of the working-class, which is at the same time cause and consequence of the growth of the mass working-class organisations, and who have a role as an advance guard within, rather than a rival to, the mass organisations, and their future as an extension of, rather than a break with, the existing course of development'.[19]

Irrespective of which argument is accepted, relations between the two groups could not, of their nature, be other than tense, and it seems clear that the caving-in to anti-PLC separatism – and even secessionism – by Mann and his associates was more than the maintenance of an uneasy, artificial co-existence within the same organisation was worth. On balance, the Turner model seems the more appropriate and comprehensive choice for explaining the tensions among the Victorian Fabians and, particularly, the role played in them by Mann.

Victoria's first Fabians clearly fell within the category of 'those who have seen the expansion of capitalism and the advent of bourgeois democracy as providing the possibility of a real improvement in the economic and political condition of the working class'. Their perception of the future was clearly 'as an extension of, rather than a sharp break with, the existing course of social development', while their preferred role was that of 'an advance guard within, rather than a rival to' such mass organisations as the trade union movement and the Labor Party. However, far from lending themselves to categorisation as just 'a literary group, essentially middle class, which was concerned primarily with socialism's moral and cultural meaning within the Australian context', they were full-blooded Fabians in the London mould, who shared the passion for social justice which so largely motivated their London counterparts, and were a product of the same combination of social, economic and psychological factors which caused the London Fabian Society to be formed.

Many of the same reasons that prompted Archer to join the London Society within six years of its inception also ensured that there was a ready response to the local societies which Marson, Champion, Besant-Scott, Mann and Sinclaire initiated. Those who joined them recall again Hyndman's accolade of 'as promising and capable a set of men as ever threw in their lot with an advanced movement'.[20] Their subsequent careers and the notable reputations many of them gained for themselves demonstrate conclusively that it was within their capacity to have made a contribution to the labour movement equal in every respect to their London counterparts. It was miscalculation by their expatriate mentors which led to their becoming confused in the eyes of the movement with those who, in total contrast, 'sought to establish and maintain pure revolutionary parties and unions in competition with the mass working-class organisations' – as well as with those who were perceived as being innately hostile to trade union interests. Effectively – and ironically – the same galvanising energies which enabled Champion and Mann to release hitherto latent Fabian impulses within Victorian society were also a destructive force and, for the time, rendered Fabianism ineffectual in the overtly political sphere where the need for it was most acute. It was never for want of organisational talent, broad social commitment or seriousness of political purpose among Australia's first Fabians that the building of a rational socialist society failed to eventuate. Rather, the antipathy of the labour movement denied their qualities direct political application. Such contributions as their situation allowed them to make remained, in Ramsay MacDonald's memorable phrase, 'drum taps to which the step of Socialism kept time', on the march which others still to come would resume after them.[21]

Endnotes

CHAPTER 1

1. Cole, 1961, pp. 171–2.
2. Dickey, 1975, p. 231.
3. Snooks, 1988, pp. 574–5.
4. Roe, 1984, p. 58.
5. *Argus*, 22 June 1934.
6. Dalton, diary, 19 January 1938.
7. Murphy, 1975, p. 149.
8. *Worker* (Brisbane), 15 November 1890.
9. See Souter, 1981.
10. Fremantle, 1960, title page.
11. Information extracted from the records of the London Society by Patricia Pugh in preparation of her *Educate, Agitate, Organise: 100 Years of Fabian Socialism*, 1984, and made available to the author by letter 23/2/85.
12. In 1991, the Australian Fabian Society had around 1000 members, and branches in Victoria, New South Wales, Canberra, South Australia and Queensland. There was an independent Fabian Society of Western Australia.
13. Rickard, 1976, p. 307.
14. See, for example, Freudenberg, 1977; Mathews, 1985; Walter, 1980, 1986; Bowman & Grattan, 1989.
15. Whitlam wrote the Society's pamphlets *Labor and the Constitution* (1965), *Beyond Vietnam: Australia's Regional Responsibility* (1968) and *Whitlam on Urban Growth* (1969), and was the co-author of *Labor in Power: What is the Difference?* (with Bruce Grant, 1973) and *Reshaping Australian Industry: Tariffs and Socialists* (with Ken Gott and Ralph Willis, 1982). Cairns wrote *Socialism and the A.L.P.* (1963) and *Economics and Foreign Policy* (1966); Hayden *The Implications of Democratic Socialism* (1968), *National Health: the A.L.P. Program* (1972) and *Social Welfare and Economic Policy* (1974); Barnard *Australian Defence – Policy and Programmes* (1969) and Cameron *Open Government: To What Degree?* (with David Butler, 1973). Further

238

Whitlam government ministers who were Society members included R.F.X. Connor, K.S. Wriedt, J.M. Wheeldon, K.E. Enderby, D. McClelland, M.H. Cass, P.J. Keating, J.R. McClelland, L.R. Johnson, C.K. Jones, G.M. Bryant, R. Bishop and D.N. Everingham.

16. Fremantle, 1960, p. 15.
17. Whitlam, 1988, p. 2.
18. McBriar, 1962, p. 9.
19. Mackenzie & Mackenzie, 1977, p. 35.
20. Shaw, 1949, p. 65.
21. Holroyd, 1991, p. 362.
22. Weir, nd, p. 31.
23. Muggeridge & Adam, 1983, p. 193.
24. Jolliffe (ed.), 1987, p. 102.
25. ibid.
26. Mackenzie & Mackenzie (ed.), 1983, p. 193.
27. Mackenzie & Mackenzie, 1977, pp. 410–11.
28. Mackenzie & Mackenzie, 1985, p. 405.
29. Cole, 1961, p. 337.
30. Fremantle, 1960, p. 17.
31. Martin, 1949, p. 293.
32. Cole, 1961, p. xiv.
33. Trevelyan, 1931, p. 403.
34. Cole, 1961, p. 314.
35. Shaw, 1948, p. 229.
36. Cole, 1955, p. 35.
37. Shaw, 1892, p. 4.
38. Holroyd, 1988, p. 273.
39. Mackenzie & Mackenzie, 1977, pp. 112–13.
40. Briggs, 1987, p. 110.
41. For Nesbit, see ibid., chapter 4. For Besant, see Holroyd, 1988, pp. 167–71.
42. Holroyd, 1988, p. 171.
43. ibid., p. 181.
44. Mackenzie & Mackenzie, 1977, p. 95.
45. ibid., p. 64.
46. Shaw, 1892, pp. 4–5.
47. Cole, 1961, p. 337.
48. Shaw, 1931, p. viii.
49. For a full list of Webb's LCC committees, see McBriar, 1949, pp. 85–6.
50. Holroyd, 1988, p. 399.
51. McBriar, 1949, p. 96.
52. For a useful discussion of attitudes to permeation within the Society see Wolfe, 1975, pp. 309–12.
53. Shaw, 1948, p. 211.
54. Mackenzie, 1978, p. 101.

55. Elton, 1939, p. 67. For a useful discussion of the extent to which implementation of the platform was intended see McKibbin, 1974, p. 102.
56. See, for example, McBriar, 1962, & Hobsbawm, 1964, p. 258.
57. Holroyd, 1988, p. 273.
58. See McBriar, 1987.
59. Norman-Butler, 1972, p. 100.
60. Beatrice Webb, 1971, pp. 191–3.
61. Wolfe, 1975, p. 221.
62. Beatrice Webb, 1971, pp. 191–3.
63. Scarfe, 1968, p. 19.
64. Mackenzie & Mackenzie, 1982, p. 115.
65. Mackenzie, 1978, p. 104.
66. Pease, 1949, pp. 23–4. Besant returned to the fold in the 1920s, as president of the Fabian Society of India: Cole, 1961, p. 347.
67. Fremantle, 1960, p. 64.
68. For a representative account and analysis of proceedings see Britain, 1982, pp. 213–18.
69. Mackenzie, 1977, p. 85.
70. Hobsbawm, 1964, p. 259.
71. Shaw, 1948b, p. 229.
72. Pugh, 1984, p. 10.
73. Hobsbawm, 1964, p. 255.
74. Phillips also had the more important distinction of being the author of the Society's first pamphlet, *Why Are the Many Poor?*. Cole, 1961, p. 6.
75. Hobsbawm, 1964, p. 257.
76. Mackenzie, 1977, pp. 148–9.
77. Hobsbawm, 1964, p. 254.
78. Shaw, 1948, p. 229.
79. G.B. Shaw, letter to Lord Elton. Quoted in Elton, 1939, pp. 102–3. Hardie was a Society member from 1891 until his death in 1915: Pugh, 1984, p. 323.
80. Beatrice Webb, 1971, pp. 191–3.
81. Britain, 1982, p. 46.
82. Shaw, 1892, p. 27.
83. Fremantle, 1960, p. 32.
84. Shaw, 1949, p. 7.
85. La Nauze, 1979, p. 55. See also Gabay, 1992.
86. Hobsbawm, 1964, pp. 257–9.
87. ibid.
88. Middleton, 1949, p. 170.
89. ibid., p. 169.
90. Cole, 1961, p. 169.
91. The Victorian Socialist Party journal, the *Socialist*, for example, credited Sinclaire with hinting at 'a new theory of the Incarnation':

Socialist, 23 October 1908. For a fuller discussion of his views see Walker, 1976.
92. Palmer, 1960, p. 91.
93. ibid., p. 90.
94. Macintyre, 1991, p. 6.
95. ibid., p. 112.
96. Métin, 1977, p. 181.
97. Butlin, 1957, p. 11.
98. Mackenzie & Mackenzie, 1977, p. 409.
99. *Age*, 28 June 1894.
100. Rawson, 1977, p. 73.
101. Kellock, 1971, pp. 85 & 41-2.
102. Rickard, 1976, pp. 266-7.
103. Webb, 1899.
104. Hagan, 1981, p. 45.
105. Cole, 1937, p. 5.
106. Skidelsky, 1979, pp. 126 & 123.
107. Macintosh, 1978, p. 199.
108. Eggleston, 1953, p. 64.
109. *Age*, 5 August 1989.
110. Archer, letter to his brother Alfred, 12 July 1850, Archer Papers, 9/2.
111. Archer, letter to his aunt, 28 May 1854, Archer Papers, 9/2.
112. Archer, diary, 17 November 1868, Archer Papers, 9/2.
113. It was announced in the *Government Gazette* on 8 January 1878, that 218 public servants and judicial officers had been removed from their positions without warning. The action was taken by the Berry Government for tactical reasons in the course of its dispute with the Legislative Council over payment of Members of Parliament and – by extension – the Council's right to reject money Bills. Possible explanations for Archer's failure to gain reinstatement are discussed in Beever, 1971, pp. 282-92.
114. Archer, diary, 1 October 1882, Archer Papers, 9/2. The 'small means' are said to have consisted of 'carefully husbanded investments and some legal work': Beever, 1971, p. 302.
115. Britain, 1982, pp. 46 & 47.
116. Skidelsky, 1979, p. 116.
117. ibid., p. 118.
118. Hobsbawm, 1964, p. 268.
119. Skidelsky, 1979, p. 128.
120. Nind, letter to her nephew Harry, 8 January 1891, Archer Papers, 5/2/2.
121. Pelling, 1954, p. 36.
122. Austin (ed.), 1965, p. 73.
123. Freudenberg, 1977, p. 24.
124. Duncan, 1991, pp. 77 & 172.
125. Molony, 1991, p. 114.

CHAPTER 2

1. Jones, 1968, pp. 115 & 113-14.
2. ibid., pp. 99-100, 22 & 96.
3. Reckitt, 1968, p. 90.
4. Jones, 1968, p. 126.
5. Reckitt, 1968, p. 94.
6. ibid., pp. 28 & 131.
7. ibid., p. 38.
8. Kellock, 1971, p. 4.
9. Mackenzie & Mackenzie, 1977, p. 39.
10. Jones, 1968, pp. 309, 319 & 202.
11. Mackenzie & Mackenzie, 1977, p. 39; Holroyd, 1988, pp. 221 & 222.
12. Jones, 1968, p. 103.
13. Jones, 1968, pp. 308 & 309.
14. ibid., pp. 322 & 124.
15. Reckitt, 1968, pp. 148, 141 & 138.
16. Binyon, 1931, pp. 171 & 172.
17. Reckitt, 1968, p. 148.
18. Binyon, 1931, p. 172.
19. Reckitt, 1968, p. 94.
20. Rev. F.M. Etherington, unpublished biography of Marson. Quoted in Reckitt, 1968, p. 101. The manuscript has been located recently, and a typescript is being prepared at the instigation of Hugh Anderson, whose assistance with information about Marson and Clotilda Bayne I gratefully acknowledge.
21. Jones, 1968, p. 82.
22. *Quiz*, 21 February 1890, p. 2.
23. Reckitt, 1968, p. 102.
24. Etherington, in ibid., p. 103.
25. ibid., p. 103.
26. *Quiz*, 24 October 1890, p. 3.
27. *Advertiser*, 15 October 1889.
28. *Quiz*, 24 October 1890.
29. *Quiz*, 21 February 1890, p. 1.
30. Reckitt, 1968, p. 103.
31. *Quiz*, 24 October 1890.
32. Reckitt, 1968, p. 106.
33. *Quiz*, 17 July, 1891; 11 March 1892.
34. Hyndman, 1911, p. 306. He was referring to Champion, James Joynes, and R.P.B. Frost, at the time of their admission to the SDF. The *Australian Dictionary of Biography* provides information on Archibald and Charleston in volume 7, 1979, p. 89 and pp. 616-7. Guthrie is at volume 9, 1983, pp. 145-6; Mcpherson at volume 10, 1986, pp. 357-8 and Price at volume 11, 1988, pp. 287-8. For Buttery, see Statton (ed.), 1986, volume 1, p. 217.

35. Marson, 1893.
36. Shaw, 1948b, p. 229.
37. *Observer,* 25 October 1890.
38. *Advertiser,* 11 May 1891.
39. Scarfe, 1968, p. 96.
40. *South Australian Parliamentary Debates,* Legislative Council, 1891. p. 2398.
41. Métin, 1977, p. 91.
42. See Dickey, 1975; Jaensch, 1977; Scarfe, 1968.
43. Dickey, 1975, p. 235.
44. Scarfe, 1968, p. 21.
45. Burgmann, 1985, p. 1.
46. ibid., pp. 44, 32 & 92.
47. Dickey, 1975, p. 244.
48. Marson, 1893, emphasis added.
49. Scarfe, 1968, p. 1.
50. Dickey, 1975, p. 242.
51. *Advertiser,* 14 December 1897.
52. Serle (ed.), 1949, p. 143.
53. *Pioneer,* 22 August 1891.
54. ibid., 3 September 1892.
55. *Pioneer,* 5 September 1891, p. 77.
56. Shaw, 1948, p. 207.
57. *Pioneer,* 11 July 1891, pp. 47 & 51.
58. ibid., 17 September 1892, p. 190.
59. ibid., 2 November 1891.
60. Burgmann, 1985, p. 147.
61. *Weekly Herald,* 23 November 1894.
62. Burgmann, 1985, pp. 147-8.
63. *Observer,* 28 March 1891.
64. Burgmann, 1985, p. 148.
65. Jones, 1988, p. 587.
66. Mackenzie & Mackenzie, 1985, pp. 354-5.
67. Notes of visits by the Marsons to the Morices appear in Clotilda Bayne's diary for 1889-90: National Library of Australia, ms. 2733.
68. *Daily Herald,* 28 June 1913.
69. Morice L., 'Auntie Kate', typescript, quoted in Jones, 1983.
70. Woman's League, Minutes, 3 July 1896, quoted in ibid.
71. The periods for which their London memberships were retained were Walter H. Baker (1892-1902), William S. Bickford (1892-1902), David M. Charleston (1892-1911), John A. McPherson (1893-8), James P. Morice (1892-1902), Lucy Morice (1892-1915) and A.F. Pearson (1892-1902): Pugh P., letter to the author, 23/2/85.
72. *Advertiser,* 2 July 1934.
73. Cole, 1961, pp. 346 & 347. There was a nine-member society in Bombay founded by Mrs Sarah Gosling, her husband and daughter. After a

course of lectures on socialism for Europeans, four lectures 'for educated natives' were organised in the Framji Cowasji Hall on 'The history, doctrine, fallacies and adaptability of socialism to Indian life'. This Bombay Society encouraged agitation by the Anti-Usury League, believing the money-lender to be the greatest social enemy of the Indians: Pugh, 1984, p. 36.

74. *Fabian News*, December 1891, p. 3.
75. anon, 1891, p. 4.
76. *Fabian News*, January 1893, p. 44.
77. Britain, 1982, pp. 192 & 202.
78. Cole, 1961, p. 5.
79. Mackenzie & Mackenzie, 1977, pp. 93 & 24–5.
80. Shaw, 1948a, p. v.
81. McBriar, 1962, pp. 176, 182 & 177.
82. ibid., p. 180.
83. *Pioneer*, 9 July 1892, p. 154.
84. ibid., 20 February 1892, p. 73.
85. *Fabian News*, July 1894, p. 20.
86. *Advertiser*, 21 January 1921.
87. *Report of the Royal Commission on the Navigation Bill together with Appendices and Evidence*, Parliament of Australia, 1906, p. xi.
88. *Advertiser*, 21 January 1921.
89. Cook, *ADB*, 1983, pp. 145–6.
90. Hobsbawm, 1964, p. 252.
91. McBriar, 1962, pp. 170, 173 & 164.
92. anon, nd, p. 1.
93. ibid., p. 3.
94. *Pioneer*, 6 February 1892, p. 62.
95. ibid., 20 February 1892, p. 71.
96. Rayment, nd, pp. 5, 7, 9 & 11.
97. anon, nd, p. 4; original quoted in Cole, 1961, p. 337.
98. *Pioneer*, 16 April 1892, p. 105.
99. anon, nd, pp. 4 & 1.
100. Scarfe, 1968, p. 117.
101. ibid., pp. 132 & 102.
102. *Observer*, 16 May 1908.
103. Smeaton, nd, p. 13.
104. *South Australian Parliamentary Debates*, 1903, p. 30.
105. Smeaton, nd, p. 37.
106. ibid., pp. 75 & 61.
107. *Observer*, 18 September 1897.
108. Scarfe, 1968, p. 96.
109. *Pioneer*, 16 April 1892.
110. Smeaton, nd, p. 37.
111. Moss, 1985, p. 213.

112. See, for example, *South Australian Parliamentary Debates*, 1903, p. 758.
113. Childe, 1964, p. vii.
114. Childe, 1964, p. 181.
115. *Advertiser*, 14 December 1897.
116. Scarfe, 1968, p. 15.
117. *Fabian News*, May 1893, p. 12; July 1894, p. 20.
118. *Thirteenth Annual Report of the Executive Committee for the Year Ending March 31st, 1896. Adopted by the Society at the Annual General Meeting, May 22nd, 1896*, The Fabian Society, London, nd, p. 7.
119. Miller, nd, p. 370.
120. Patricia Pugh, letter to the author, 23/2/85.
121. Reckitt, 1968, p. 108. For details of the careers of Marson and other earlier Fabians subsequent to the cessation of their involvement with Australian Fabianism, see chapter 6.

CHAPTER 3

1. British investment in Australia fell from £22 million in 1889 to £1.1 million in 1894: Butlin, 1962, pp. 424, 160, 166 & 255.
2. Grant & Serle, 1957, p. 196. The level of unemployment in Victoria in 1903 was 13%: see Macarthy, 1967, p. 32.
3. Grant & Serle, 1957, pp. 195-6 & 211.
4. Macarthy, 1967, p. ix.
5. Mann, 1923, p. 195.
6. Macarthy, 1967, pp. 51-4.
7. Rickard, 1976, p. 14.
8. For a useful discussion of FPOPL and AWNL funding, and possible VEF involvement in the inception of the Kyabram movement, see ibid., pp. 177-80.
9. ibid., pp. 193 & 314.
10. La Nauze, 1979, pp. 138 & 137.
11. Ingham, 1949, p. 156.
12. Kellock, 1971, p. 86.
13. Grant & Serle, 1957, p. 196.
14. Rickard, 1976, p. 120.
15. ibid., p. 189.
16. Ingham, 1949, p. 121.
17. Burgmann, 1985, p. 106.
18. Kellock, 1971, p. 85.
19. Ingham, 1949, p. 121.
20. Turner, 1962, p. 7.
21. La Nauze, 1979, p. 373.
22. Henderson, 1973, p. 99.
23. Henderson, 1973, p. 99.
24. Britain, 1982, p. 21; Henderson, 1973, p. 157.

25. Fremantle, 1960, p. 63.
26. Whitehead, 1987, pp. 24–6.
27. Bellamy & Kaspar, 1987, pp. 107–9.
28. Hyndman, 1911, p. 307.
29. Pelling, 1953, p. 224.
30. Kellock, 1971, p. 4.
31. Champion, 1908, p. 106.
32. Mackenzie & Mackenzie, 1977, p. 21.
33. Laurence (ed.), 1965, p. 351.
34. copy in the Chubb papers.
35. Brandon, 1990, p. 1; Mackenzie & Mackenzie, 1977, p. 21.
36. Mackenzie, 1979, p. 35.
37. ibid., p. 36.
38. Mackenzie & Mackenzie, 1977, pp. 23 & 26; Mackenzie, 1979, p. 49.
39. Holroyd, 1988, p. 132. For a detailed account of the meetings, and Champion's part in them, see Mackenzie & Mackenzie, 1977, pp. 23–7, and Mackenzie, 1979.
40. Quoted in Brandon, 1990, p. 29.
41. Elton, 1939, pp. 64–5.
42. Mackenzie & Mackenzie, 1977, pp. 181 & 27.
43. Champion, 1908, p. 101.
44. Tsuzuki, 1961, p. 64.
45. Shaw, 1892, p. 7.
46. Champion, 1908, pp. 109–19.
47. *Justice*, 14 August 1886.
48. Shaw, 1892, p. 7.
49. Shaw, 1948, p. 213.
50. Pelling, 1954, p. 154. For a detailed account of the 'Tory Gold' affair and its consequences, see ibid., pp. 41–4.
51. Shaw, 1892, p. 6.
52. *Practical Socialist*, January 1886.
53. *The Times*, London, 2 May 1928.
54. Gould, 1928, p. 279.
55. *Justice*, 25 February 1889.
56. Champion, 1908, p. 116.
57. ibid., p. 128.
58. Pelling, 1953, p. 237.
59. Bentley, 1987, p. 276.
60. Champion, 1908, p. 123.
61. *Age*, 23 August 1890.
62. ibid., 16 October 1890.
63. Champion, 1891, pp. 225–7.
64. Kellock, 1971, p. 25.
65. Trades Hall Council Minutes, 14 November 1890.
66. *Age*, 22 November 1890.
67. *Justice*, 1 & 15 November 1890.

68. Margaret Parnaby believes that Besant-Scott was apprenticed to Champion, but it is hard to see how this could have been the case: Parnaby, 1975, p. 64.
69. *Australian Herald*, March 1896, pp. 105–6.
70. Shaw, 1948, pp. 211–12.
71. Wallace-Crabbe, 1988, p. 63.
72. Roe, 1986, pp. 68–9.
73. Britain, 1982, p. 192.
74. Hobsbawm, 1964, p. 257.
75. Britain, 1982, p. 192.
76. *Australasian Schoolmaster*, November 1897.
77. ibid., October 1897.
78. Blainey, Morrissey & Hulme, 1971, p. 70.
79. *Australasian Schoolmaster*, December 1901; September 1895.
80. *Table Talk*, 28 December 1894.
81. Thomson & Serle, 1972, p. 85.
82. *Table Talk*, 28 December 1894.
83. ibid.
84. See Beatrice Webb, 1891.
85. Beilharz, 1992, p. 63.
86. Claven, 1991.
87. Scates, 1981.
88. *Champion*, 27 July 1895.
89. ibid.
90. ibid., 18 April 1896.
91. Parnaby, 1975, p. 7.
92. See, for example, Boucher, 1990, pp. 423–52.
93. Badger, 1971, p. 32.
94. ibid., p. 29.
95. Macintyre, 1991, pp. 124–6.
96. Badger, 1971, p. 79.
97. ibid., pp. 99 & 104.
98. *Australian Herald*, April 1894.
99. Henderson, 1973, pp. 149 & 72.
100. Kellock, 1971, p. 35; Holroyd, 1988, p. 120; Ellis, 1939, p. 196; Whitehead, 1987, p. 29.
101. Burgmann, 1985, p. 131.
102. Fabian Society of Victoria Minutes, 22 August 1908.
103. Hobsbawm, 1964, p. 257.
104. Kelly, 1982, pp. 18, 53 & 70.
105. ibid., p. 92.
106. *Tocsin*, 18 October 1900.
107. *Australian Herald*, December 1894, my emphasis.
108. Champion may have had some justification for a proprietorial approach to the lecture series, since contemporary sources hint that it was his idea.

109. Detractors have characterised Green and Caird as teaching 'Hegelianism with a Puritan Accent'. See, for example, Davie, 1961, p. 328.
110. Anderson, 1911, pp. 217–27.
111. Boucher, 1990, pp. 438 & 426.
112. Beilharz, Considine & Watts, 1992, p. 18.
113. Parnaby, 1975, p. 18.
114. Cutler, 1956, face page.
115. Jordan, 1988, p. 129; Rickard, 1984, p. 153.
116. *Age*, 27 June 1936.
117. La Nauze, 1979, pp. 105–6.
118. Amery, 1980, p. 12.
119. For an account of Curtis' formidable charm and 'well developed technique for working people to his purposes' as his hosts in Melbourne would have experienced them, see Rowse, 1986, pp. 338–64.
120. La Nauze, 1979, pp. 478–9.
121. Kellock, 1971, pp. 49–50.
122. La Nauze, 1979, pp. 142–3.
123. ibid., p. 143.
124. ibid., p. 144.
125. *Australian Herald*, October 1894.
126. *Bulletin*, 20 September 1894.
127. *Worker*, 28 July 1894.
128. Kellock, 1971, p. 68.
129. *Worker*, 28 July 1894.
130. Burgmann, 1985, p. 119.
131. See, for example, Hobsbawm, 1964, p. 253; Wolfe, 1975, pp. 257–60, 309–12; and on liberalism Hobsbawm, 1964, pp. 260–3.
132. *Australian Herald*, December 1894.
133. anon, 1895.
134. *Champion*, 21 September 1895; 8 August 1895.
135. Kelly, 1982, pp. 510–11.
136. *Champion*, 22 June 1895.
137. Burgmann, 1985, p. 118.
138. *Champion*, 22 June 1895; 20 July 1895; 3 August 1895.
139. Holroyd, 1988, p. 267.
140. See Mackenzie & Mackenzie, 1977, p. 220.
141. *Champion*, 22 June 1895.
142. ibid., 6 July 1895; 20 July 1895; 17 August 1895.
143. ibid., 13 April 1896.
144. ibid., 27 March 1897.
145. ibid., 31 August 1895.
146. THC minutes, 13 February 1895; 3 May 1895.
147. *Argus*, 11 April 1896.
148. *Champion*, 6 July 1895.
149. ibid.

150. *Champion*, 27 July 1895.
151. ibid., 17 August 1895.
152. *Age*, 27 June 1895.
153. Cutler, 1956, pp. 2 & 90.
154. ibid., p. 94.
155. *Champion*, 24 August 1895; 28 September 1895.
156. Rickard, 1984, p. 166.
157. Hart, 1944, p. 27.
158. Deakin's name does not appear on the membership list for March 1901, and he probably resigned in 1900: ibid., p. 39.
159. *Champion*, 26 October 1895.
160. ibid., 9 November 1895; 2 November 1895.
161. ibid., 2 November 1895.
162. Britain, 1982, p. 188.
163. Burgmann, 1985, p. 118.
164. Champion's charges of bench packing appeared in the *Champion* on 7 September 1895, those of jury squaring on 14 September 1895, and those of secret compositions from 2 November to 21 December 1895.

CHAPTER 4

1. *Tocsin*, 2 July, 1903.
2. See Kellock, 1971, p. 86; Grant & Serle, 1957, p. 196.
3. Ingham, 1949, p. 177.
4. Mann, 1923, pp. 195–6.
5. Ross, 1945.
6. For example, Mann's enduring friendship with Curtin, Jones and O'Dowd; Tillett's with Jones and O'Dowd, and Hardie's with Jones.
7. Hewitt, 1974, p. 10.
8. Burgmann, 1985, p. 10.
9. ibid.
10. Victorian Socialist League, Declaration of Principles: *People and Collectivist*, 12 November 1898.
11. *Tocsin*, 4 November 1897.
12. *Age*, 1 November 1900.
13. Hewitt, 1974, pp. 295–7.
14. *Labor Call*, 23 April 1914.
15. Hewitt, 1974, p. 10.
16. Jones to O'Dowd, letter dated 13 June 1898, Merrifield Collection.
17. *Tocsin*, 9 October 1897; 7 July 1898.
18. quoted in Burgmann, 1985, p. 124.
19. ibid., p. 121.
20. The paper survived to become the official organ of the Labor Party, under the title of the *Labor Call*, in 1906. See Hewitt, p. 11.
21. *Tocsin*, 5 July 1900; 22 November 1900.

22. Hewitt, 1974, p. 12.
23. Mann, 1923, p. 12.
24. Torr, 1956, pp. 24 & 28.
25. ibid., p. 4.
26. See also Yeo, 1985.
27. Torr, 1956, p. 62.
28. Osborne, 1972, p. 9.
29. Torr, 1956, p. 62.
30. Mann, 1923, p. 54.
31. Torr, 1956, p. 179.
32. McBriar, 1962, p. 26, identifies the date as April 1886; Pugh, 1984, pp. 30-1; Cole, 1961, p. 57.
33. McBriar, 1962, pp. 197, 290-1 & 289.
34. Beatrice Webb, 1948, pp. 36, 41.
35. *Labour Elector*, 2 March 1889; 23 March 1889.
36. Osborne, 1972, pp. 26-7.
37. *Justice*, 19 August 1899.
38. Osborne, 1972, pp. 36-7.
39. ibid., pp. 39-40 & 38.
40. ibid., p. 38.
41. ibid., p. 42.
42. Mann, 1923, p. 178.
43. Burgmann, 1985, p. 128; *Tocsin*, 23 October 1902.
44. Osborne, 1972, pp. 43, 44 & 49.
45. Burgmann, 1985, p. 128.
46. Osborne, 1972, pp. 56, 57-8 & 79.
47. *Tocsin*, 26 November 1903. Mann's figures are supported by Osborne, 1972, p. 79.
48. *Tocsin*, 13 August 1903; 15 December 1904.
49. Hughes & Graham, 1968, p. 475.
50. *Tocsin*, 26 January 1905.
51. Hewitt, 1974, p. 20.
52. *Tocsin*, 18 December 1902.
53. Burgmann 1985, pp. 130-1, 133 & 132.
54. Hewitt, 1974, p. 23.
55. Lansbury, 1928, pp. 78-9.
56. Burgmann, 1985, p. 130.
57. *Tocsin*, 30 May, 1905.
58. Hewitt, 1974, pp. 28 & 29.
59. Osborne, 1972, pp. 97-8.
60. Mann, 1905, pp. 20-1.
61. Osborne, 1972, p. 269.
62. So much so, in the case of O'Dowd that he was later president of the Rationalist Society: Hewitt, 1974, p. 291.
63. Paule, 1986, p. 516.

64. Anderson, 1968, p. 14.
65. Levy, 1987, p. 175.
66. ibid., p. 181.
67. ibid., p. 179.
68. Kennedy & Palmer, 1954, p. 116.
69. Levy, 1987, p. 179.
70. La Nauze, 1979, p. 55.
71. O'Dowd to Nettie Higgins, letter, 5 September 1908, Vance & Nettie Palmer Papers, 1174/1/110.
72. Shaw, 1889, p. 200.
73. Levy, 1987, p. 177.
74. Kellock, 1971, title page.
75. *Tocsin*, 7 July 1898.
76. See Hewitt, 1974, p. 32.
77. Osborne, 1972, pp. 112-13.
78. *Tocsin*, 21 December 1905.
79. West, 1984, p. 10.
80. *Socialist*, 2 April 1906.
81. Hewitt, 1974, p. 33.
82. *Socialist*, 2 April 1906; 16 November 1905.
83. McBriar, 1987, p. 83.
84. Rickard, 1979, pp. 582-3.
85. For a useful discussion of the development of minimum wage thinking in Victoria, see Rickard, 1976, pp. 212-22.
86. *Socialist*, 2 April 1906.
87. ibid., 21 April 1906; 2 April 1906.
88. ibid., 2 April 1906.
89. Mann, 1923, p. 196.
90. Hewitt, 1974, p. 31.
91. Badger, 1971, pp. 130-7.
92. Henderson, 1973, pp. 49-68.
93. Osborne, 1972, p. 131.
94. McCarthy, 1967, pp. 68 & 83.
95. Britain, 1982, p. 191.
96. ibid., p. 129.
97. Pugh, 1984, p. 116.
98. Britain, 1982, pp. 188, 189 & 191.
99. *Socialist*, 2 April 1906. On the original Fabians and oratory, see Britain, 1982, Chapter 8.
100. *Tocsin*, 9 November 1905. In April, 1906, the headquarters was moved to Socialist Hall, at 283 Elizabeth Street. *Tocsin*, 5 May 1906.
101. *Socialist*, 2 April 1906.
102. Initially as a fortnightly, but weekly from issue number twelve: *Socialist*, 1 September 1906.
103. ibid., 2 April 1906.

104. Ross, 1977, p. 16.
105. *Socialist*, 15 September 1906.
106. ibid., 2 April 1906.
107. *Socialist*, 2 April 1906.
108. Ross, 1977, p. 29.
109. Mann, 1923, p. 198.
110. See graph, McBriar, 1962, p. 166.
111. *Socialist*, 2 April 1906.
112. Ross, 1977, pp. 17 & 27.
113. Hewitt, 1974, p. 136.
114. Ross, 1945, p. 50.
115. *Socialist*, 14 September 1907.
116. ibid., 16 June 1906.
117. Ross, 1945, p. 50.
118. Mann to Mrs Bruce, 7 July 1926; Osborne, 1972, p. 120.
119. ibid., pp. 140-1.
120. ibid., p. 139.
121. Shaw, 1892, p. 6.
122. Cole, 1961, pp. 85 & 19.
123. ibid., p. 107.
124. Mackenzie & Mackenzie (ed.), 1983, pp. 230 & 290.
125. Hewitt, 1974, pp. 39 & 40.
126. *Socialist*, 2 April 1906.
127. Cole, 1961, pp. 117-18.
128. Wells, 1934, p. 661.
129. ibid., p. 660.
130. Cole, 1961, p. 120. Wells' paper, 'The Faults of the Fabian', appears in full in Hynes, 1968, pp. 390-409.
131. Mackenzie & Mackenzie (ed.), 1984, p. 62.
132. Killigrew (ed.), 1979, p. 377.
133. Cole, 1961, p. 123.
134. Wells, 1934, p. 660.
135. Cole, 1961, p. 123.
136. MacCarthy, 1949, p. 127.
137. *Supplementary Socialist*, 4 February 1908.
138. Mizon, nd.
139. *Supplementary Socialist*, 4 February 1908.
140. *Supplementary Socialist*, 22 July 1908.
141. ibid.
142. ibid.
143. Hewitt, 1974, p. 72.
144. *Supplementary Socialist*, 22 July 1908.
145. *Socialist*, 22 June 1907.
146. Hewitt, 1974, pp. 73-4 & 75.
147. Cf. Britain, 1982, pp. 271-2.

148. *Socialist*, 9 March 1907; 15 February 1907; 6 April 1907.
149. *Labor Call*, 18 April 1907.
150. ibid., 20 June 1907; 16 May 1907; 6 June 1906.
151. *Socialist*, 8 December 1906.
152. Hewitt, 1974, pp. 57–8.
153. *Socialist*, 22 June 1907; 17 July 1908.
154. For example, a conference between the two parties, held prior to the 1908 at the suggestion of the PLC secretary, Heagney, to resolve their differences, was unsuccessful. Hewitt, 1974, pp. 76–7.
155. ibid., pp. 63–4.
156. ibid., pp. 71 & 73.
157. Osborne, 1972, p. 176.
158. For a detailed discussion of the VSP's financial position, see ibid., p. 164.
159. Hewitt, 1974, p. 8.
160. Mackenzie & Mackenzie (ed.), 1983, p. 132.
161. Cole, 1961, p. 88.

CHAPTER 5

1. *Socialist*, 11 September 1908.
2. Walker, 1976, p. 75.
3. Winston Rhodes, 1984, p. 20.
4. Scott, 1980, p. 74.
5. Undated *Argus* clipping in Sinclaire's book of newspaper clippings, quoted in ibid., p. 97.
6. *Socialist*, 23 October 1908.
7. Walker, 1976, pp. 74 & 78.
8. Britain, 1982, pp. 150, 151, 160, 298, n. 66.
9. *Argus*, 20 May 1908.
10. *Socialist*, 1 May 1908; 29 May 1908.
11. Palmer Papers, 1174/1/99.
12. *Socialist*, 5 June 1908.
13. For details of the group, see Pimlott, 1985, pp. 35–65.
14. Palmer Papers, 26 July 1908, 1174/1/109.
15. Sinclaire, Champion and Jones Letter, 14 August 1908, Merrifield Collection.
16. Fabian Society of Victoria Minutes, 22 August 1908. Minute Book in the J.P. Jones Papers.
17. Brownfoot, 1983, p. 43.
18. Henderson, 1973, p. 69.
19. Brownfoot, 1983, p. 43.
20. Henderson, 1973, p. 70.
21. Brownfoot, 1983, p. 43.
22. Henderson, 1973, p. 70.

23. Drury, 1987, p. 170.
24. Henderson, 1973, pp. 74 & 78-9.
25. Brownfoot, 1983, p. 44.
26. Henderson, 1973, pp. 88, 83 & 86.
27. Brownfoot, 1983, p. 45.
28. Henderson, 1973, pp. 82.
29. FSV Minutes, 5 October 1908.
30. A draft copy of the form is held by the La Trobe Library in its Merrifield Collection.
31. FSV Minutes, 5 October 1908, and *Socialist*, 23 October 1908.
32. The Minute Book owes its survival to the fact that members of the Jones family later pasted personal photographs into it and retained it as a family record.
33. Palmer Papers, 12 February 1909, 1174/1/32; April 1909, 1174/1/167; nd, 1174/1/170; 13 May 1909, 1174/1/174; nd, 1174/1/196.
34. Hewitt, 1974, pp. 296 & 298.
35. Heseltine, 1970, p. 13.
36. Palmer Papers, nd, 1174/1/121; April 1909, 1174/1/167; nd, 1174/1/196.
37. ibid., 26 September 1909, 1174/1/192; 4 October 1909, 1174/1/229; 26 September 1909 1174/1/192.
38. La Nauze, 1977, p. 45.
39. anon, 1980.
40. Foster, 1986, pp. 20 & 235.
41. ibid., p. 187.
42. Macintyre, 1991, p. 2.
43. anon, nd.
44. La Nauze, 1977, p. 47.
45. ibid., p. 48.
46. Shann, letter, 16/5/09.
47. ibid.
48. Shann, letters, 16/5/09, 4/6/09, 27/7/09.
49. Serle, 1986, p. 313.
50. Snooks, 1988, pp. 574-5.
51. Shann, letter, 16/5/09.
52. ibid.
53. Eggleston, 1953, pp. 53 & 57.
54. Walker, 1988, p. 616.
55. Osmond, 1985, pp. 67-71.
56. Osmond, 1981, p. 421.
57. Dale, 1982, p. 85.
58. See Mathews, 1987; Whyte & Whyte, 1988; Morrison, 1991.
59. Eggleston, nd, pp. 84-5.
60. Eggleston, 1953, p. 57.
61. Osmond, 1985, p. 48.
62. Murdoch, 1956, p. 162.

63. Murdoch, 1912, p. 236.
64. Murdoch, nd, pp. 64-7.
65. Docker, 1982, p. 81.
66. ibid., p. 82.
67. Martin, 1949, p. 293.
68. *Socialist*, 11 August 1906.
69. La Nauze, 1977, p. 51.
70. Alexander, 1986, pp. 630-1.
71. See chapter 6.
72. Alan M. McBriar, letter to the author, 18 May 1991.

CHAPTER 6

1. *Pioneer*, 16 April 1892.
2. Reckitt, 1968, p. 109.
3. C.L. Marson, letter to his father, Reckitt, 1968, pp. 110, 111 & 113.
4. Jones, 1968, pp. 149 & 150-1.
5. Hyde (ed.), 1948, p. 103.
6. Mackenzie, 1962, p. 62.
7. Jones, 1968, p. 149.
8. Reckitt, 1968, pp. 123 & 124.
9. *Fabian News*, July 1904.
10. Jones, 1968, p. 153.
11. Hewitt, 1974, pp. 109-10.
12. Henderson, 1973, pp. 152-3 & 154.
13. ibid., pp. 155-6 & 157.
14. Gould, 1928, p. 279.
15. Henderson, 1973, p. 157.
16. Mann to Jones, letter, 25 February 1909, Jones Papers.
17. *Socialist*, 9 April 1909; 17 December 1909.
18. Dangerfield, 1970, p. 272.
19. Mann, 1923, p. 323.
20. *Socialist*, 21 May 1909; 25 February 1909.
21. undated letter to the editor of *Truth*, from Sinclaire's book of newspaper clippings.
22. ibid.
23. *Socialist*, 7 October 1910; 17 February 1911.
24. *Fellowship*, November 1916.
25. Scott, 1980, p. 96.
26. Walker, 1976, p. 616.
27. Badger, 1971, p. 118.
28. Walker, 1976, p. 616.
29. The 'materialists' denied any such intention. *Socialist*, 26 June 1908.
30. Osborne, 1972, p. 182.
31. *British Australasians*, 11 July 1895.

32. Fitzpatrick, 1988, p. 544.
33. Ross, 1977, p. 19.
34. La Nauze, pp. 45-6.
35. Snooks, 1988, p. 575.
36. Fitzpatrick, 1988, p. 545.
37. *Daily Herald*, 28 June 1913.
38. Jaensch, 1979, p. 617.
39. *Australasian Typographical Journal*, January 1898, p. 2.
40. Nairn, 1990, pp. 10 & 11.
41. Dickey, 1975, p. 274.
42. Smeaton, nd, pp. 212 & 241.
43. Jaensch, 1979, p. 89.
44. Burgmann, 1985, p. 160.
45. Badger, 1971, p. 128.
46. Now occupied, ironically, by the Melbourne headquarters of Rupert Murdoch's national daily, the *Australian*.
47. Badger, 1971, p. 157.
48. De Garis, 1925, pp. 60-4.
49. Hart, 1944, p. 15.
50. Clements, 1988, p. 132.
51. *Australian Encyclopedia*, vol VII, Melbourne, p. 496.
52. *Argus*, 29 April 1953.
53. *Advertiser*, 2 September 1955.
54. Pike, 1962, pp. 144 & 158.
55. ibid. p. 573.
56. Macintyre, 1991, p. 215.
57. West, 1980, p. 1.
58. Roe, 1984, p. 18.
59. Walker, 1976, pp. 195 & 196.
60. Picken, 1918; Atkinson, 1918.
61. Foster, 1986, p. 119.
62. Fremantle, 1960, p. 210.
63. Cole, 1961, pp. 189 & 168.
64. Tsuzuki, 1961, p. 223.
65. Osmond, 1981, pp. 421-5.
66. Macintyre, 1986, pp. 3 & 4-6.
67. Snooks, 1988, pp. 575-6.
68. ibid.
69. Shann, letter, 16/5/09.
70. La Nauze, 1977, p. 66.
71. Serle, 1973, p. 124.
72. La Nauze, 1977, pp. 116-19 & 149-51.
73. Heseltine, 1970, p. 20.
74. Palmer, 1942, p. 35.
75. anon, 1973.

76. unpublished. A copy of the manuscript is held at the La Trobe Library in Melbourne.
77. anon, 1973.
78. Brownfoot, 1983, p. 44.
79. Henderson, 1973, pp. 86-8.
80. ibid., pp. 93-5.
81. Brownfoot, 1983, pp. 44-5.
82. Hewitt, 1974, p. 91.
83. Paule, 1983, p. 516.
84. Osborne, 1975, p. 35.
85. Paule, 1983, p. 516.
86. Osborne, 1975, p. 35. At a party given for MacDonald in Glasgow shortly before his death in 1937, and attended by a number of former ILP friends who in some instances had not spoken to him since 1931, 'to the great embarrassment of everyone present, MacDonald wound up the occasion with a speech insisting that he was a socialist and always had been'. Marquand, 1977, p. 788.
87. Kennedy & Palmer, 1954, p. 139.
88. Anderson, 1968, p. 14.
89. McAuley, 1959, pp. 63-4.
90. Anderson, 1968, p. 7.
91. ibid., p. 173.
92. Mann, 1923, p. 201.
93. Kennedy & Palmer, 1954, p. 173.

CHAPTER 7

1. Henderson, 1973, p. 156.
2. Hewitt, 1974, p. 288, states that Curtin's membership of the SQC and the VSP was from 1906 to 1917, but Ross, 1977, pp. 16-17, 391, suggests that it may have begun earlier. Cain joined the VSP in 1910 and was an executive member between 1916 and 1917. Hewitt, 1974, p. 288.
3. As witness Curtin's reaction to the SFA running a ticket for the VSP executive in 1912: 'The traditionalists, led by John Curtin and Frank Hyett, moved in, appointed a provisional Board of Management, and had Wilson expelled, thus precipitating the wholesale resignation of the "Internationalists" '. Turner, 1962, p. 16.
4. ibid., p. 24.
5. See Russell, 1972.
6. See Beilharz, Considine & Watts, 1992.
7. Coombs, 1983, p. 31.
8. Cole, 1961, p. 339.
9. Victoria was represented by the future Whitlam government Treasurer, Jim Cairns; NSW by Heinz Arndt, who was later Professor of Economics at the Australian National University; South Australia by

Don Dunstan, who was later a notable South Australian premier; Western Australia by Professor Fox of the Department of Philosophy at the University of Western Australia; and Tasmania - which has never had a Fabian society of its own - by Derek Van Abbe, a Victorian Society member who lectured in modern languages at the University of Tasmania from 1946 to 1948.

10. He served in the Second World War, as the navigator of an RAAF bomber.
11. Crisp, 1963, p. 414.
12. Joyce, 1948, p. 288.
13. Galbraith, 1958.
14. Whitlam, 1985, p. 3.
15. For example, see Whitlam, 1969, p. 5.
16. ibid., pp. 15-16.
17. Cole, 1961, p. 172.
18. Osborne, 1972, pp. 141-2.
19. Turner, 1962, pp. 6-7. The positions of individuals within the respective camps, however, was not immutable. Curtin and Hyett were clearly in the process of rejecting separatism, while Bennett was finding it more attractive.
20. As has been seen, he was referring to Joynes, Champion and Frost, at the time of their admission to the SDF. Hyndman, 1911, p. 306.
21. MacDonald, 1911, p. 88.

Bibliography

PRIVATE PAPERS AND ORIGINAL RECORDS

Archer W.H., Papers, University of Melbourne Archives.
Bayne C., Diary 1889-90, National Library of Australia, Ms. 2733, Canberra.
Boobooks, Minutes, University of Melbourne Archives.
Chubb P., Papers, British Library of Economic and Political Science, London.
Dalton H., Diary, British Library of Economic and Political Science, London.
Deakin A., Papers, National Library of Australia, Canberra.
Fabian Society of Victoria, Minute Book, J.P. Jones Papers, La Trobe Library, Melbourne.
Jones J.P., Papers, La Trobe Library, Melbourne.
Latham J.G., Papers, National Library of Australia, Canberra.
Mauger S., Papers, National Library of Australia, Canberra.
Merrifield S., Collection, La Trobe Library, Melbourne.
Moore W.H., Papers, University of Melbourne Archives.
O'Dowd B., Papers, La Trobe Library, Melbourne
Palmer V. & N., Papers, National Library of Australia, Canberra.
Pugh P., Archivist, Fabian Society, London. Correspondence with the author, 1986-88.
Round Table Records, University of Melbourne Archives.
Shann E.O.G., Letters in the possession of the Shann family.
Trades Hall Council, Minutes, Melbourne.
Victorian Socialist Party, Minutes, Merrifield Collection, La Trobe Library, Melbourne.

PERIODICALS

Advertiser, Adelaide
Age, Melbourne
Argus, Melbourne
Australasian Schoolmaster, Melbourne
Australian Herald, Melbourne

Australian Typographical Journal, Adelaide
Bulletin, Sydney
Champion, Melbourne
Church of England Messenger, Melbourne
Daily Herald, Adelaide
Fabian News, London
Fellowship, Melbourne
Government Gazette, Melbourne
Justice, London
Labor Call, Melbourne
Labour Elector, London
Melbourne Church of England Girls' Grammar School Magazine, Melbourne
The People and The Collectivist, Sydney
Pioneer, Adelaide
Quiz, Adelaide
Socialist, Melbourne
Supplementary Socialist, Melbourne
Tocsin, Melbourne
Trident, Melbourne
Victorian Parliamentary Debates
Worker, Melbourne

BOOKS, THESES AND ARTICLES CITED OR CONSULTED

Note: *ADB* and bracket is Nairn B. & Serle G. (ed.) *Australian Dictionary of Biography,* twelve volumes and index, Melbourne University Press.

Alexander F., 1987, 'Murdoch, Sir Walter Logie Forbes' in *ADB* (10).

Amery L., 1980, *Diaries,* volume I, *1896-1929,* ed. Barnes J. & Nicholson D., London: Hutchinson.

Anderson F., 1911, 'Liberalism and Socialism', presidential address to Section G of the Australasian Association for the Advancement of Science, *Proceedings,* Vol. XI.

Anderson H., 1968, *The Poet Militant: Bernard O'Dowd,* Melbourne: Hill of Content.

Anon, 1895, *Manifesto of the Social-Democratic Party in the German Empire as Adopted at the Erfurt Congress, 1891,* Melbourne: Melbourne Fabian Society pamphlet.

Anon, nd, *Manners and Customs of the Boobooks,* Melbourne: Boobooks.

Anon, 1980, *An Outline Chronology of the Boobooks 1902-1979,* Melbourne: document circulated for the Boobooks Membership at Meeting Number 675, 12 March, Boobooks.

Anon, nd, *Questions for Candidates for Municipal Office,* Adelaide: South Australian Fabian Society Tract No. 4.

Anon, 1891, *What Socialism Is,* Adelaide: South Australian Branch Fabian Society Tract No. 1.

Anon, 1892, *Questions for Parliamentary Candidates 1892*, Adelaide: South Australian Fabian Society Tract No. 2.

Anon, nd, *Questions for Parliamentary Candidates*, Adelaide: South Australian Fabian Tract No. 5.

Anon, nd, *Some Objections to Socialism Considered In the Light of Common Sense*, Adelaide: South Australian Fabian Society Tract No. 3.

Anon, nd, *Vote! Vote! Vote!*, Adelaide: South Australian Fabian Society leaflet.

Anon, 1973, 'Obituary: Elizabeth Lothian' in *Melbourne Church of England Girls' Grammar School Magazine*, December 1973.

Atkinson A., 1987 (ed.), *Footnote People in Australian History*, Annandale: The Fairfax Library in Association with Daniel O'Keefe Publishing.

Atkinson M., nd, (ed.), *Trade Unionism in Australia*, Sydney: Workers' Educational Association of New South Wales.

1918, in *Round Table*, December.

Austin A.G. (ed.), 1965, *The Webbs' Australian Diary*, Melbourne: Sir Isaac Pitman & Sons.

1972, *Australian Education 1788-1900: Church, State and Public Education in Colonial Australia*, Melbourne: Pitman Pacific Books.

Badger C.R., 1971, *The Reverend Charles Strong and the Australian Church*, Melbourne: Abacada Press.

Barnard L., 1969, *Australian Defence: Policy and Programmes*, Melbourne: Victorian Fabian Society Pamphlet 18.

Beever M., 1971, *W.H. Archer, Civil Servant*, MA thesis, Melbourne University.

Beilharz P., 1992, *Labour's Utopias: Bolshevism, Fabianism, Social Democracy*, London: Routledge.

Beilharz P., Considine M. & Watts R., 1992, *Arguing About the Welfare State: The Australian Experience*, Sydney: Allen & Unwin.

Bellamy J. & Kaspar B., 1987, 'Harkness, Margaret Elise (1854-1923)', in Bellamy J. & Saville J. (ed.), *Dictionary of Labour Biography*, volume VIII, London: Macmillan.

Bentley B.G., 1987, *David Lloyd George: A Political Life*, volume I, *The Architect of Change 1863-1912*, London: B.T. Batesford.

Binyon G.C., 1931, *The Christian Socialist Movement in England*, London: Society for Promoting Christian Knowledge.

Blainey G., Morrissey J. & Hulme S.E.K., 1971, *Wesley College: The First Hundred Years*, Melbourne: Robertson & Mullens.

Boucher D., 1990, 'Practical Hegelianism: Henry Jones' Lecture Tour of Australia', in *Journal of the History of Ideas*, No. 51.

Bowman M. & Grattan M., 1989, *The Reformers*, Melbourne: Dove Press.

Brandon R., 1990, *The New Women and the Old Men: Love, Sex and the Woman Question*, London: Secker & Warburg.

Briggs A. & Saville J., 1960, *Essays in Labour History*, volume I, London: Macmillan.

Briggs J., 1987, *A Woman of Passion: The Life of E. Nesbit 1858–1924*, London: Hutchinson.

Britain I., 1982, *Fabianism and Culture: A Study in British Socialism and the Arts 1884–1918*, London: Cambridge University Press.

Brownfoot J.N., 1983, 'Goldstein, Vida Jane Mary' in *ADB* (9).

Bullock A., 1960, *The Life and Times of Ernest Bevin*, volume I, *Trade Union Leader 1881–1940*, London: Heinemann.

Burgmann V., 1985, *'In Our Time': Socialism and the Rise of Labor 1885–1905*, Sydney: George Allen & Unwin.

Butlin N.G., 1957, 'The Shape of the Australian Economy 1861–1900', in the *Economic Record*, volume 33, Melbourne: Melbourne University Press.

1962, *Australian Domestic Product, Investment and Foreign Borrowing 1861–1938/39*, Cambridge: Cambridge University Press.

Cairns J.F., 1963, *Socialism and the A.L.P.*, Melbourne: Victorian Fabian Society Pamphlet 8.

Cairns J.F., 1966, *Economics and Foreign Policy*, Melbourne: Victorian Fabian Society Pamphlet 12.

Cameron C.R. & Butler D., 1973, *Open Government: To What Degree?*, Melbourne: Victorian Fabian Society Pamphlet 24.

Champion H.H., 1888, 'The New Labour Party', in *Nineteenth Century*, July 1891.

1889, 'An Eight Hour Day' in *Nineteenth Century*, September 1889.

1891, in 'The Crushing Defeat of Trade Unionism in Australia', in the *Nineteenth Century*, February 1891.

1892, 'Protection as Labour Wants It', in *Nineteenth Century*, June 1892.

1892, 'Mr Chamberlain's Programme', in *Nineteenth Century*, December 1892.

1895, *The Great Dock Strike*, Melbourne: np.

1895, *The Root of the Matter*, Melbourne: np.

1908, ' "Quorum Paus Fui": An Unconventional Autobiography', in Henderson, H.M., 1973, *The Goldstein Story*, Melbourne: Stockland Press Pty Ltd.

Childe V.G., 1964, *How Labour Governs*, Melbourne: Melbourne University Press.

Churchill R.S., 1967, *Winston S. Churchill*, Volume II, *Young Statesman 1901–1914*, London: Heinemann.

Claven J., 1991, *John Hancock and the Rise of Victorian Labor: The First Detonation of the Volcano*, Melbourne: Australian Fabian Pamphlet 52.

Clements M.A., 1988, 'Palmer, Thomas', in *ADB* (11).

Coghlan T.A., 1969, *Labour and Industry in Australia: From the First Settlement in 1788 to the Establishment of the Commonwealth in 1901*, Melbourne: Macmillan.

Cole G.D.H., 1937, *The People's Front*, London: Victor Gollancz Ltd.

Cole M., 1949, *Growing Up Into Revolution*, London: Longmans, Green & Co.
    (ed.), 1949, *The Webbs and Their Work*, London: Frederick Muller Ltd.
    1955, *Beatrice and Sidney Webb*, London: Fabian Tract 297.
    1961, *The Story of Fabian Socialism*, London: Heinemann.
Cook P., 1983, 'Guthrie, Robert Storrie', in *ADB* (9).
Coombs H.C., 1983, *Trial Balance: Issues of My Working Life*, Melbourne:
    Sun Books.
Crisp L.F., 1961, *Ben Chifley: A Biography*, Melbourne: Longman.
Cutler F.H., 1956, *A History of the Anti-Sweating Movement in Victoria
    1873-96*, BA (Hons.) Thesis, Melbourne University.
Dale A.S., 1982, *The Outline of Sanity: A Life of G.K. Chesterton*, Grand
    Rapids: Eerdmans.
Dalton H., 1953, *Call Back Yesterday: Memoirs 1887-1931*, London: Frederick
    Muller Ltd.
Dangerfield G., 1970, *The Strange Death of Liberal England*, London:
    McGibbon & Kee.
Davie G.E., 1961, *The Democratic Intellect: Scotland and Her Universities
    in the Nineteenth Century*, Edinburgh: Edinburgh University Press.
De Garis C.J., 1925, *The Victories of Failure*, Melbourne: Malvern Printing
    Company Pty Ltd.
Dickey B., 1975, 'South Australia', in Murphy D.J. (ed.), *Labor in Politics:
    The State Labor Parties in Australia 1880-1920*, St Lucia: University of
    Queensland Press.
Dinnage R., 1986, *Annie Besant*, Harmondsworth: Penguin Books Ltd.
Drury S. 1987, 'Vida Goldstein', in Atkinson A. (ed.), *Footnote People in
    Australian History*, Annandale: The Fairfax Library in Association
    with Daniel O'Keefe Publishing.
Duncan B., 1991, *The Church's Social Thinking: From Rerum Novarum to
    1931*, Melbourne: Collins Dove.
Easson M. (ed.), 1990, *The Foundation of Labor*, Sydney: Lloyd Ross Forum
    and Pluto Press.
Ebbels R.N., 1960, *The Australian Labor Movement 1850-1907*, Sydney:
    Australasian Book Society.
Eggleston F.W., 1953, *Reflections of an Australian Liberal*, Melbourne: F.W.
    Cheshire.
Ellis H., 1939, *My Life*, Boston: Houghton Mifflin Company.
Ellmann R., 1987, *Oscar Wilde*, London: Hamish Hamilton.
Elton Lord, 1939, *The Life Of James Ramsay MacDonald (1866-1919)*,
    London: Collins Publishers.
Evatt H.V., 1918, *Liberalism in Australia: An Historical Sketch of Australian
    Politics Down to the Year 1915*, Melbourne: The Law Book Company
    of Australasia Limited.
Fitzhardinge L.F., 1978, *William Morris Hughes: A Political Biography* (Two
    Volumes: *That Fiery Particle 1862-1914* and *The Little Digger 1914-52*),
    Sydney: Angus & Robertson.

Fitzpatrick B., 1969, *The British Empire in Australia 1834–1939*, Melbourne: Melbourne University Press.

Fitzpatrick K., 1988, 'Scott, Sir Ernest' in *ADB* (11).

Foster L., 1979, *The Imperial Federation League in Victoria After Federation: An Analysis of Its Structure, Personnel, Aims and Decline*, BA (Hons.) thesis, Monash University.

1986, *High Hopes: The Men and Motives of the Australian Round Table*, Melbourne: Melbourne University Press.

Fremantle A., 1960, *This Little Band of Prophets*, London: George Allen & Unwin.

Freudenberg, G., 1977, *A Certain Grandeur: Gough Whitlam in Politics*, Melbourne: Macmillan.

Gabay A., 1992, *The Mystic Life of Alfred Deakin*, Melbourne: Cambridge University Press.

Galbraith J.K., 1958, *The Affluent Society*, London: Hamish Hamilton.

Gould F.J., 1928, *Hyndman: Prophet of Socialism (1842–1921)*, London: George Allen & Unwin Ltd.

Grant J. & Serle G., 1957, *The Melbourne Scene 1803–1956*, Melbourne: Melbourne University Press.

Hagen J., 1981, *The History of the A.C.T.U.*, Melbourne: Longman Cheshire.

Harris K., 1982, *Attlee*, London: Weidenfield & Nicolson.

Hart A., 1944, *History of the Wallaby Club*, Melbourne: Anderson, Gowan Pty Ltd.

Hayden W.G., 1968, *The Implications of Democratic Socialism*, Melbourne: Victorian Fabian Society Pamphlet 16.

1972, *National Health: the A.L.P. Program*, Melbourne: Victorian Fabian Society Pamphlet 23.

1974, *Social Welfare and Economic Policy*, Melbourne: Victorian Fabian Society Pamphlet 27.

Henderson L.M., 1973, *The Goldstein Story*, Melbourne: The Stockland Press.

Heseltine H., 1970, *Vance Palmer*, St Lucia: University of Queensland Press.

Hewitt G.C., 1974, *A History of the Victorian Socialist Party 1906–1932*, MA thesis, La Trobe University.

Hobsbawm E., 1964, *Labouring Men: Studies in the History of Labour*, London: Weidenfeld & Nicolson.

Holroyd M., *Bernard Shaw*, three volumes: 1988: *The Search for Love 1856–1898*; 1989: *The Pursuit of Power 1898–1918*; 1991: *The Lure of Fantasy 1918–1950*, London: Chatto & Windus.

Hughes C.A. & Graham B.D., 1968, *A Handbook of Australian Government and Politics 1890–1964*, Canberra: Australian National University Press.

Hyde H.M. (ed.), 1948, *The Trials of Oscar Wilde*, London: William Hodge & Company.

Hyndman H.M., 1911, *The Record of an Adventurous Life*, London: Macmillan.

Hynes S., 1986, *The Edwardian Turn of Mind*, Princeton: Princeton University Press.

Ingham S.M., 1949, *Some Aspects of Victorian Liberalism, 1880-1900*, MA thesis, Melbourne University.

Jaensch D., 1977, 'South Australia' in Loveday P, Martin A.W. & Parker R.S., *The Emergence of the Australian Party System*, Sydney: Hale & Iremonger.

1979, 'Charleston, David Morley', in *ADB* (7).

1979, 'Archibald, William Oliver', in *ADB* (7).

Jones H., 1983, 'Lucy Spence Morice and Catherine Helen Spence: Partners in South Australian Social Reform', in *Journal of the Historical Society of South Australia*, no. 11.

1986, 'Morice, Louise (Lucy)', in *ADB* (10).

Jones P. d'A., 1968, *The Christian Socialist Revival 1877-1914: Religion, Class, and Social Conscience in Late-Victorian England*, Princeton: Princeton University Press.

Jordan D.J., 1988, 'Palmer, Janet Gertrude', in *ADB* (11).

Joyce J., 1948, *A Portrait of the Artist as a Young Man*, London: Jonathan Cape.

Kellock P., 1971, *H.H. Champion: The Failure of Victorian Socialism*, BA (Hons.) thesis, Monash University.

Kelly F., 1982, *The 'Woman' Question in Melbourne 1880-1914*, PhD thesis, Monash University.

Kennedy V. & Palmer N., 1954, *Bernard O'Dowd*, Melbourne: Melbourne University Press.

Killigrew M. (ed.), 1979, *Ford Maddox Ford: Memories and Impressions*, Harmondsworth: Penguin Books.

La Nauze J.A., 1974, *Walter Murdoch and Alfred Deakin on Books and Men: Letters and Comments 1900-1918*, Melbourne: Melbourne University Press

1977, *Walter Murdoch: A Biographical Memoir*, Melbourne: Melbourne University Press.

1979, *Alfred Deakin: A Biography*, Sydney: Angus & Robertson.

Lansbury, G., 1928, *My Life*, London: Constable.

Laurence D.H. (ed), 1965, *Bernard Shaw: Collected Letters 1874-1897*, London: Max Reinhart.

(ed), 1985, *Bernard Shaw: Collected Letters 1898-1910*, New York: Viking.

Levy M., 1987, 'Bernard O'Dowd', in Atkinson A. (ed.), *Footnote People in Australian History*, Annandale: The Fairfax Library in Association with Daniel O'Keefe Publishing.

Loughlin G., nd, 'Paris Nesbit, Q.C.: Lawyer, Libertine and Lunatic', in *Journal of the Historical Society of South Australia*, number 3.

Loveday P., Martin A.W. & Parker R.S., 1977, *The Emergence of the Australian Party System*, Sydney: Hale & Iremonger.

Macarthy P.G., 1967, 'Labor and the Living Wage: 1890-1910', in *Australian Journal of Politics and History*, May 1967.

Macarthy P., 1967, *The Harvester Judgement - An Australian Assessment*, PhD thesis, Australian National University.

MacCarthy D., 1949, 'The Webbs as I Saw Them', in Cole M. (ed.), *The Webbs and Their Work*, London: Frederick Muller Limited.

MacDonald J.R., 1911, *The Socialist Movement*, London: Thornton Butterworth Limited.

Macintosh J.P., 1978, 'Harold Wilson' in Macintosh J.P. (ed.), *British Prime Ministers in the Twentieth Century*, two volumes, London: Weidenfeld and Nicolson.

Macintyre S., 1987, 'Latham, Sir John Greig', in *ADB* (10).

1991, *A Colonial Liberalism: The Lost World of Three Victorian Visionaries*, Melbourne: Oxford University Press, Australia.

Mackenzie N., 1978, (ed.), *The Letters of Sidney and Beatrice Webb*, three volumes: *Apprenticeships 1873-1892*; *Partnership 1892-1912*; *Pilgrimage 1912-1947*, Cambridge: Cambridge University Press.

1979, 'Percival Chubb and the Founding of the Fabian Society', in *Victorian Studies* 23, no. 1.

Mackenzie N. & J., 1973, *The Time Traveller: The Life of H.G. Wells*, London: Simon & Schuster.

1977, *The First Fabians*, London: Weidenfeld & Nicolson. (ed.), *The Diary of Beatrice Webb*, four volumes: 1982: *Glitter Around and Darkness Within 1873-1892*; 1983: *All the Good Thing of Life 1892-1905*; 1984: *The Power to Alter Things 1905-1924*; 1985: *The Wheel of Life 1924-1943*, London: Virago Press Limited.

McAuley J., 1959, *The End of Modernity*, Sydney: Angus & Robertson.

McBriar A.M., 1949, 'Sidney Webb and the L.C.C.', in Cole M. (ed.), *The Webbs and Their Work*, London: Frederick Muller Ltd.

1962, *Fabian Socialism and English Politics 1884-1918*, Cambridge: Cambridge University Press.

1987, *An Edwardian Mixed Double - the Bosanquets versus the Webbs: A Study in British Social Policy 1890-1929*, Oxford: Clarendon Press.

McKibbin R., 1974, *The Evolution of the Labour Party 1910-1924*, Oxford: Oxford University Press.

McKinlay B., 1981, *The A.L.P.: A Short History of the Australian Labor Party*, Melbourne: Heinemann.

McMullin R., 1991, *The Light on the Hill: The Australian Labor Party 1891-1991*, Melbourne: Oxford University Press.

Manchester W., 1983, *The Last Lion: Winston Spencer Churchill*, volume I, *Visions of Glory 1874-1932*, London: Michael Joseph.

Mann T., 1905, *Socialism*, Melbourne: np.

1905, *The War of the Classes*, Melbourne: np.

1923, *Tom Mann's Memoirs*, Melbourne: The Labour Publishing Company Ltd.

Marlowe J., 1976, *Milner: Apostle of Empire*, London: Hamish Hamilton.

Marquand D., 1977, *Ramsay MacDonald*, London: Jonathan Cape.

Marson C.L., 1893, 'A Word for Fabians', in *Church Reformer*, December 1893.

Martin K., 1949, 'The Webbs in Retirement', in Cole M. (ed.), *The Webbs and Their Work*, London: Frederick Muller Ltd.

Mathews R., 1985, *David Bennett: A Memoir*, Melbourne: Australian Fabian Society Pamphlet 44.

1986 'Victoria's War Against Whitlam', in Fabian Papers, *The Whitlam Phenomenon*, Melbourne: McPhee Gribble/Penguin Books.

1987, *Employee Ownership: Mondragon's Lessons for Australia*, Melbourne: Australian Fabian Society Pamphlet 47.

Métin A., 1977, *Socialism Without Doctrine*, Chippendale: Alternative Publishing Co-operative Ltd..

Middleton J.S., 1949, 'Webb and the Labour Party', in Cole M. (ed.), *The Webbs and Their Work*, London: Frederick Muller Ltd.

Miller E.M., nd, *Australian Literature: A Bibliography to 1938*, Sydney: Angus & Robertson.

Mizon, W., nd, *A Correction*, Melbourne: np.

Molony J., 1991, *The Worker Question: A New Historical Perspective on Rerum Novarum*, Melbourne: Collins Dove.

Morrison R., 1991, *We Build the Road as We Travel*, Philadelphia: New Society Publishers.

Moss J., 1985, *Sound of Trumpets: History of the Labour Movement in South Australia*, Netley: Wakefield Press.

Murdoch W., 1912, *The Australian Citizen: An Elementary Account of Civic Rights and Duties*, Melbourne: Whitcombe & Tombs Limited.

nd, *Loose Leaves*, Melbourne: George Robertson & Company Pty Ltd.

1956, *Selected Essays*, Sydney: Angus & Robertson.

Murphy D.J. (ed.), 1975, *Labor in Politics: the State Labor Parties in Australia 1880–1920*, St Lucia: University of Queensland Press.

Nairn B., 1990, 'A Special Night at the Labor Council', in Easson M. (ed.), *The Foundation of Labor*, Sydney: Pluto Press.

Nord D.E., 1985, *The Apprenticeship of Beatrice Webb*, Boston: University of Massachusetts Press.

Norman-Butler B., 1972, *Victorian Aspirations: The Life and Labour of Charles and Mary Booth*, London: George Allen & Unwin.

O'Meagher B. (ed.), 1983, *The Socialist Objective: Labor & Socialism*, Sydney: Hale & Iremonger.

Osborne G., 1972, *Tom Mann: His Australasian Experiences 1902–1910*, PhD thesis, Australian National University.

1975, 'John Percy Jones 1875–1955: A Biographical Note', in *Labour History*, May 1975.

Osmond W.G., 1981, 'Eggleston, Sir Frederic William', in *ADB* (8).

1985, *Frederic Eggleston: An Intellectual in Australian Politics*, Sydney: Allen & Unwin.

Palmer V., 1942, *Frank Wilmot*, Melbourne: The Frank Wilmot Memorial Committee.

1954, *The Legend of the Nineties*, Melbourne: Melbourne University Press.

1960, *National Portraits*, Melbourne: Melbourne University Press.

Parnaby M., 1975, *The Socially Reforming Churchman: A Study of the Social Thought and Activity of Charles Strong in Melbourne 1880–1900*, BA (Hons.) thesis, Melbourne University.

Paule B., 1983, 'Jones, John Percy', in *ADB* (9).

Pease E., 1916, *The History of the Fabian Society*, London: Cassell.

1949, 'Webb and the Fabian Society', in Cole M. (ed.), *The Webbs and Their Work*, London: Frederick Muller Ltd.

Pelling H.M., 1953, 'H.H. Champion: Pioneer of Labour Representation', in the *Cambridge Journal*, October 1952–September 1953.

Pelling H.A., 1954, *The Origins of the Labour Party 1880–1900*, London: Macmillan & Co. Ltd.

1963, *History of British Trade Unionism*, Harmondsworth: Penguin.

1976, *A Short History of the Labour Party*, London: Macmillan.

Picken D.K., 1918, in *Round Table*, June 1918.

Pierson S., 1973, *Marxism and the Origins of British Socialism: The Struggle for a New Consciousness*, New York: Cornell University Press.

1979, *British Socialists: The Journey from Fantasy to Politics*, Harvard: Harvard University Press.

Pike D., 1962, *Australia: The Quiet Country*, Cambridge: Cambridge University Press.

Pimlott B., 1985, *Hugh Dalton*, London: Jonathan Cape.

Playford J., 1957, *Australian Labor Party Personnel in the South Australian Legislature, 1891–1957*, Adelaide, np.

Prendergast G.M., 1904, *Black and White List*, Melbourne: Tocsin Printing Company.

Pugh P., 1984, *Educate, Agitate, Organise: 100 Years of Fabian Socialism*, London: Methuen.

Radice L., 1984, *Beatrice and Sidney Webb: Fabian Socialists*, London: Macmillan.

Rawson, D.W., 1977, 'Victoria', in Loveday, P., Martin, H.W. & Parker R.S., *The Emergence of the Australian Party System*, Sydney: Hale & Iremonger.

Rayment A.W., nd, *The Rights of Labor and How to Obtain Them: An Address to the Working Men of South Australia*, Adelaide: Hutchinson, Craker & Smith.

Reckitt M.B., 1968, (ed.) *For Christ and People: Studies of Four Socialist Priests and Prophets of the Church of England Between 1870 and 1930*, London: Society for Promoting Christian Knowledge.

Rickard J., 1976, *Class and Politics: New South Wales, Victoria and the Early Commonwealth 1890–1910*, Canberra: Australian National University Press.

1984, 'The Anti-Sweating Movement in Britain and Victoria: The Politics of Empire and Social Reform', in *Historical Studies*, October 1979.

1984, *H.B. Higgins: The Rebel as Judge*, Sydney: George Allen & Unwin.

Roe J., 1986, *Beyond Belief: Theosophy in Australia 1879-1939*, Sydney: New South Wales University Press.

Roe M., 1984, *Nine Australian Progressives: Vitalism in Bourgeois Social Thought 1890-1960*, St Lucia: University of Queensland Press.

Ross L., 1945, 'The Education of John Curtin' in *Australian Highway: Journal of the Workers' Educational Association of Australia*, August 1945.

1977, *John Curtin: A Biography*, Melbourne: Macmillan.

Rowse A.L., 1986, *Memories and Glimpses*, London: Methuen.

Rowse T., 1978, *Australian Liberalism and National Character*, Melbourne: Kibble Books.

Scarfe J., 1968, *The Labour Wedge: The First Six Labour Members of the South Australian Legislative Council*, BA (Hons.) thesis, University of Adelaide.

Scarlett A., 1979, *Frank Hyett: A Political Biography*, BA (Hons.) thesis, La Trobe University.

Scates B., 1981, ' "Wobblers": Single Taxers in the Labour Movement, Melbourne, 1889-1899', in *Historical Studies*, vol. 21, no. 83.

Scott D., 1980, *The Halfway House to Infidelity: A History of the Melbourne Unitarian Church 1853-1973*, Melbourne: The Unitarian Fellowship of Australia and the Melbourne Unitarian Peace Memorial Church.

Selleck R.J.W., 1982, *Frank Tate: A Biography*, Melbourne: Melbourne University Press.

Serle G., 1973, *From Deserts the Prophets Come: The Creative Spirit in Australia 1788-1972*, Melbourne: Heinemann.

1986, 'Mackinnon, Donald', in *ADB* (10).

(ed.), 1949, *Dictionary of Australian Biography*, Sydney: np.

Shaw G.B. (ed.), 1889, *Fabian Essays in Socialism*, London: The Fabian Society.

1889, 'Transition', in Shaw G.B. (ed.), *Fabian Essays in Socialism*, London: The Fabian Society.

1892, *The Fabian Society: Its Early History*, London: Fabian Tract No. 41.

1931, 'Preface to the 1931 Reprint' in Shaw G.B. (ed.), *Fabian Essays in Socialism*, London: The Fabian Society.

1948, 'Preface', in Shaw G.B. (ed.), *Fabian Essays In Socialism 1889* (Jubilee Edition), London: The Fabian Society.

1948, 'Sixty Years of Fabian Socialism', in Shaw G.B. (ed.), *Fabian Essays in Socialism 1889* (Jubilee Edition), London: The Fabian Society.

1949, *Sixteen Self Sketches*, London: Constable.

Skidelsky R., 1979, 'The Fabian Ethic', in Holroyd M. (ed.), *The Genius of Shaw*, New York: Holt, Rinehart & Winston.

Smeaton T.H., nd, *From Stone Cutter to Premier & Minister for Education: The Story of the Life of Tom Price, a Welsh Boy who Became an Australian Statesman*, Adelaide: Hunkin, Ellis & King, Printers and Publishers.

Snooks G.D., 1988, 'Shann, Edward Owen Giblen', in *ADB* (11).

Souter G., 1981, *A Peculiar People: The Australians in Paraguay*, Sydney: Sydney University Press.

Statton J. (ed.), 1986, *Biographical Index of South Australians 1836–1885*, Adelaide: South Australian Genealogy and Heraldry Society Inc.

Sugden M.A. & Eggleston F.W., 1931, *George Swinburne: A Biography*, Sydney: Angus & Robertson Ltd.

Sydney Labour History Group, 1982, *What Rough Beast? The State and Social Order in Australian History*, Sydney: George Allen & Unwin with the Australian Society for the Study of Labour History.

Thomson K. & Serle G. (1972), *A Biographical Register of the Victorian Parliament 1859–1900*, Canberra: AGPS.

Torr D., 1956, *Tom Mann and His Times*, Volume I (1856–1890), London: Lawrence & Wishart.

Trevelyan G.M., 1931, *British History in the Nineteenth Century*, London: Longmans Green.

Tsuzuki C., 1961, *H.M. Hyndman and British Socialism*, Oxford: Oxford University Press.

Turner I., 1962, 'Socialist Political Tactics 1900–1920', in *Labour History*, May 1962.

Walker D.R., 1976, *Dream and Disillusion*, Canberra: Australian National University Press.

1988, 'Sinclaire, Frederick', in *ADB* (11).

Wallace-Crabbe C., 1988, 'O'Dowd, Bernard Patrick', in *ADB* (11).

Walter J., 1980, *The Leader; A Political Biography of Gough Whitlam*, St Lucia: University of Queensland Press.

1986, *The Ministers' Minders: Personal Advisers in National Government*, Melbourne: Oxford University Press.

Webb B., 1891, *The Co-operative Movement in Great Britain*, London: Sonnenschein.

1948, *Our Partnership*, ed. Drake B. & Cole M., London: Longmans Green.

1971, *My Apprenticeship*, Harmondsworth: Penguin Edition.

Webb S., 1899, 'Impressions of Australia', in *The People and the Collectivist*, 21 October 1899.

Webb S. & B., 1897, *Industrial Democracy*, London: Longman.

1898, *The History of Trade Unionism*, London: Longman.

1920, *A Constitution for the Socialist Commonwealth of Great Britain*, London: Longman.

Weir L. MacNeill., nd, *The Tragedy of Ramsay MacDonald: A Political Biography*, London: Secker & Warburg.

Wells H.G., 1911, *The New Machiavelli*, London: Bodley Head.

1934, *An Experiment in Autobiography*, London: Victor Gollancz.

West A., 1984, *H.G. Wells: Aspects of a Life*, London: Hutchinson.

West K., 1980, *Australian Liberalism and the Need for Change*, Melbourne: Deakin Memorial Lecture.

Whitehead A., nd, 'Champion, Henry Hyde (1859–1928)', in Bellamy J.M. & Saville J., *Dictionary of Labour Biography*, volume VIII, London: Macmillan.

Whitlam E.G., 1965, *Labor and the Constitution*, Melbourne: Victorian Fabian Society Pamphlet 11.

1968, *Beyond Vietnam: Australia's Regional Responsibility*, Melbourne: Victorian Fabian Society Pamphlet 17.

1969, *Whitlam on Urban Growth*, London: Victorian Fabian Society Pamphlet 19.

1985, *The Whitlam Government 1972–1975*, Ringwood: Penguin.

1988, Foreword to *Whitlam, Wran and the Labor Tradition: Labor History Essays*, volume 2, Sydney: Pluto Press.

Whitlam E.G. & Grant B., 1973, *Labor in Power: What Is the Difference?*, London: Victorian Fabian Society Pamphlet 22.

Whitlam E.G., Gott K.D. & Willis R., 1982, *Reshaping Australian Industry: Tariffs and Socialists*, London: Victorian Fabian Society Pamphlet 37.

Whyte W.F. & Whyte K.K., 1988, *Making Mondragon: The Growth and Dynamics of the Worker Co-operative Complex*, New York: Cornell University Press.

Winston Rhodes H., 1984, *Frederick Sinclaire: A Memoir*, Christchurch: University of Canterbury Publication No. 33.

Wolfe W., 1975, *From Radicalism to Socialism: Men and Ideas in the Formation of Fabian Socialist Doctrines 1881–1889*, Yale University Press.

Yeo S., 1985, 'A New Life: The Religion of Socialism in Britain, 1883–1896', in *History Workshop: A Journal of Socialist Historians*, autumn 1985.

Index

Aborigines, 38, 42, 232
Adelaide Single Tax Society, 53
Age, 22, 76, 119, 126, 130, 134, 140, 197
Amalgamated Miners' Association, 24-5
Amalgamated Society of Engineers, 46, 144, 208
Amery, Leo, 112-13
Anderson, Francis, 111
Andrews, George, 115
Andrews, J.A., 155
Anstey, Frank, 136, 141-2, 148, 168
Anti-Puritan League, 185
Arbitration Court, 111, 159
Archer, William, and the LFS, 3, 5, 30, 32-4; origins and career, 30-4; and the alternative scenario, 229, 237
Archibald, Reverend, 139
Archibald, William, and the SAFS, 2, 44, 59; as a bookseller, 215; as an MP, 60, 67-8, 71-2, 214-15
Argus, 22, 100, 113, 124, 134, 185, 195, 201, 223
Arizmendiarietta, Don José Maria, 199
Asquith, Cynthia, 9
Asquith, Raymond, 9
Attlee, Clement, 29
Attlee government, 1, 8, 29, 186
Australasian Authors' Agency, 206-7
Australian Assistance Plan, 234
Australian Association for the Advancement of Science, 212
Australian Church, aims, 107, 216; alleged heretical character of doctrines, 100; ancillary organisations, 107-8; and Besant-Scott, 20; and Champion, 20, 108, 125; and Ross, 99; and Strong, 3; and the Charles Strong (Australian Church) Memorial Trust, 216; and the FRF, 210; and the Goldstein family, 108, 188; and the MFS, 99; and Thomas Palmer, 100; *Australian Herald*, 108; decline and demise, 216;

foundation, 107; opens new building, 107; venue for MFS meetings, 122
Australian Co-operative Society, 108, 120-3
Australian Criminology Society, 108, 126, 134
Australian Health Society, 217
Australian Herald, 97, 108, 110, 114, 116-18
Australian Labor Party, 1-8, 23-9, 44-50, 53, 59, 65, 68-72, 71, 74, 80-1, 103-4, 108, 125-6, 133, 136-7, 141, 147, 153, 169, 179-80, 189, 192, 197, 211, 213-16, 218-20, 225-7, 229-38, 236; *see also* United Labor Party (SA), Progressive Political League (Vic), United Labor and Liberal Party (Vic), Political Labor Council (Vic).
Australian Natives' Association, 46, 155, 161
Australian Railways Union, 29, 41
Australian Socialist League, 5, 25
Australian Tramway and Motor Omnibus Employees' Association, 29
Australian Women's National League, 77
Australian Women's Sphere, 189, 255
Australian Women's Suffrage Society, 109
Austral-Theosophist, 98
Aveling, Edward, 88

Baker, Walter H., 55-6
Bannon, John, 8
Baracchi, Guido, 220
Barnard, Lance, 7, 238N
Barnard, Marjorie, 207
Barnett, Oswald, 231
Barrett, J.G., 124
Barry, Maltman, 90, 94, 96
Barton, Edmund, 99
basic wage, 111, 159, 225
Bayne, Clotilda, 41, 43, 55
Bear-Crawford, Annette, 188
Beazley, Kim, 7
Bellamy, Edward, 25, 153